7th Workshop on Cognitive Aspects of the Lexicon 2022 (CogALex VII)

Online
20 November 2022

ISBN: 978-1-7138-6314-4

Printed from e-media with permission by:

Curran Associates, Inc.
57 Morehouse Lane
Red Hook, NY 12571

CURRAN ASSOCIATES INC. proceedings.com

Some format issues inherent in the e-media version may also appear in this print version.

Printed with permission by Curran Associates, Inc. (2023)

For permission requests, please contact the Association for Computational Linguistics at the address below.

Association for Computational Linguistics
209 N. Eighth Street
Stroudsburg, Pennsylvania 18360

Phone: 1-570-476-8006
Fax: 1-570-476-0860

acl@aclweb.org

Additional copies of this publication are available from:

Curran Associates, Inc.
57 Morehouse Lane
Red Hook, NY 12571 USA
Phone: 845-758-0400
Fax: 845-758-2633
Email: curran@proceedings.com
Web: www.proceedings.com

CogALex-VII

The Workshop on Cognitive Aspects of the Lexicon

Proceedings of the Workshop

November 20, 2022

Preface

Being ubiquitous and versatile, words are important for many tasks: sharing, storing, processing and accessing information. They are vital not only for communication, the acquisition, structuring (categorization), maintenance and access of knowledge, but also for thinking: problem-solving, link discovery, detection of similarities, metaphors and analogies. This being so, one may wonder how to build tools supporting the learning of words (memorization) and the various types of usage (access/navigation). Alas, the answer is not easy, as it depends on many factors: the task or goal (production/reception), the user's background (age, expertise), the momentary cognitive state (information available at the onset of the search), the material support (book, computer), etc. Obviously, words in books, computers, and the human brain are not the same. Being aware of this, different communities (linguists, lexicographers, psychologists) have focused on different aspects: representation and organization of words in dictionaries, creation of tools supporting navigation or conceptual search (thesauri), time course of word access, etc. The situation is complex, as the respective views, methods and research goals are not quite the same, all the more as they have changed considerably over time.

For example, rather than considering the lexicon as a static entity, where discrete units (words) are organized alphabetically (database view), dictionaries are now viewed dynamically, i.e., as lexical graphs, whose entities are linked in various ways (topical relations; associations) and whose link weights may vary over time. Also, lexicographers view words as products, i.e., holistic entities, while psychologists and neuroscientists view them as processes. Words are decomposed, and their synthesis requires activation of various parts of our brain, each one of them being dedicated to a specific part (meaning, form, sound) of the final form. The normal time course starts with some input (concrete object in the real world, or, more or less clear ideas, abstract concepts) leading then, 'little by little', to an output (word form). All this is achieved in milliseconds, as normal discourse consists in the production of two to three words per second.

Computational linguists have their own ways to look at words, which also have changed quite a bit over time. Discrete count-based vector representations have successively been replaced by continuous vectors (i.e., word embeddings), and then by language-model-based contextualized representations which outperform the static models (including word-embeddings) in a broad range of tasks.

As one can see, different communities look at words from different angles, which can be an asset and a problem. It is an asset, as complementary views may help us to broaden and deepen our understanding of this fundamental cognitive resource. Yet, this diversity of perspectives can also be a problem, in particular in a dynamic field like ours that is so rapidly moving on. Hence, it becomes harder and harder for everyone, including experts, to remain fully informed about the latest changes (state of the art). This is one of the reasons why we organize this workshop. More precisely, our goal is not only to keep people informed without getting them crushed by the information glut, but also to help them to perceive clearly what is new, relevant, and hence important. Last, but not least, we would like to connect people from different communities in the hope that this may help them to gain new insights or inspiration.

This is the 7th edition of CogALex, the first one not to be associated with COLING, as CogALex-VII is part of AACL-IJCNLP 2022. We have received 14 submissions, out of which we have selected 4 for oral presentation, and 6 for posters. This amounts to a submission rate of 71% (28,5% for the papers, 42,5% for the posters). In addition, we have an invited speaker, Massimo Stella from the CogNosco Lab of the University of Exeter (UK). His talk — Multiplex networks and AI unveil the influence of the mental lexicon on picture naming and its failures by people struck with aphasia.— fits our goal perfectly well, as it demonstrates the potential of graph theory to shed some light on the structure and evolution of the mental lexicon. We would like to express our thanks to him for having accepted to be our invited speaker. Also, sincerest thanks to all the members of the Programme Committee. Their expertise was invaluable to ensure a good selection of papers despite the tight schedule. Their reviews were helpful not only for us to make the decisions, but also for the authors, helping them to strengthen their work. We hope that the work presented here will inspire you, generate fruitful discussions, and possibly lead to new ideas, insights, and collaborations.

The CogALex-VII Workshop Chairs

Organizing Committee

Michael Zock (Aix-Marseille University)
Emmanuele Chersoni (The Hong Kong Polytechnic University)
Yu-Yin Hsu (The Hong Kong Polytechnic University)
Enrico Santus (Bloomberg LP)

Program Committee

Chris Biemann (University of Hamburg)
Marc Brysbaert (Ghent University)
Nichol Castro (University at Buffalo)
Yan Cong (Feinstein Institute for Medical Research)
Simon De Deyne (University of Melbourne)
Rodolfo Delmonte (University Ca' Foscari of Venice)
Luis Espinosa Anke (Cardiff University)
Olivier Ferret (CEA List)
Jinghang Gu (The Hong Kong Polytechnic University)
Eduard Hovy (Carnegie Mellon University)
Shu-Kai Hsieh (National Taiwan University)
Philippe Langlais (University of Montréal)
Alessandro Lenci (University of Pisa)
Vito Pirrelli (ILC-CNR Pisa)
Alain Polguère (University of Lorraine)
Jakob Prange (The Hong Kong Polytechnic University)
Alessandro Raganato (University of Milan-Bicocca)
Lavinia Salicchi (The Hong Kong Polytechnic University)
Sabine Schulte im Walde (University of Stuttgart)
Didier Schwab (Grenoble Alpes University)
Cynthia Siew (National University of Singapore)
Gilles Sérasset (Grenoble Alpes University)

Table of Contents

Conference Program

November 20, 2022

17:00–17:15 (UTC +8, Taipei time) Introduction

17:15–18:15 Keynote Talk

Multiplex Networks and AI Unveil the Influence of the Mental Lexicon on Picture Naming and its Failures by People Struck with Aphasia
Massimo Stella (University of Exeter)

18:15–18:30 Short Break

18:30–19:30 Oral Presentations 1: Cognitive Modeling and Psycholinguistics

Patterns of Text Readability in Human and Predicted Eye Movements
Nora Hollenstein, Itziar Gonzalez-Dios, Lisa Beinborn and Lena Jäger

(In)Alienable Possession in Mandarin Relative Clauses
Deran Kong and Yu-Yin Hsu

19:30–20:30 Long Break

20:30–21:45 Poster Session

Do Age of Acquisition and Orthographic Transparency Have the Same Effects in Different Modalities?
Mohammad Momenian

CAT ManyNames: A New Dataset for Object Naming in Catalan
Mar Domínguez Orfila, Maite Melero Nogués and Gemma Boleda Torrent

Finetuning Latin BERT for Word Sense Disambiguation on the Thesaurus Linguae Latinae
Piroska Lendvai and Claudia Wick

Putting WordNet's Dictionary Examples in the Context of Definition Modelling: An Empirical Analysis
Fatemah Almeman and Luis Espinosa Anke

Exploring Nominal Coercion in Semantic Spaces with Static and Contextualized Word Embeddings
Chenxin LIU and Emmanuele Chersoni

A Frame-Based Model of Inherent Polysemy, Copredication and Argument Coercion
Chen Long, Laura Kallmeyer and Rainer Osswald

21:45–22:45 Oral Presentations 2: Lexical and Distributional Semantics

VISCOSE - a Kanji Dictionary Enriched with VISual, COmpositional, and SEmantic Information
Werner Winiwarter and Bartholomäus Wloka

Compositionality as an Analogical Process: Introducing ANNE
Giulia Rambelli, Emmanuele Chersoni, Philippe Blache and Alessandro Lenci

November 20, 2022 (continued)

22:45–23:00 Conclusive Remarks

Patterns of Text Readability in Human and Predicted Eye Movements

Nora Hollenstein
University of Copenhagen
nora.hollenstein@hum.ku.dk

Itziar Gonzalez-Dios
HiTZ Center - IXA (UPV/EHU)
itziar.gonzalezd@ehu.eus

Lisa Beinborn
CLTL Lab, VU Amsterdam
l.beinborn@vu.nl

Lena Jäger
University of Zurich; University of Potsdam
jaeger@cl.uzh.ch

Abstract

It has been shown that multilingual transformer models are able to predict human reading behavior when fine-tuned on small amounts of eye tracking data. As the cumulated prediction results do not provide insights into the linguistic cues that the model acquires to predict reading behavior, we conduct a deeper analysis of the predictions from the perspective of readability. We try to disentangle the three-fold relationship between human eye movements, the capability of language models to predict these eye movement patterns, and sentence-level readability measures for English. We compare a range of model configurations to multiple baselines. We show that the models exhibit difficulties with function words and that pre-training only provides limited advantages for linguistic generalization.

1 Introduction

Eye movement data of reading provides rich insights into cognitive processes of language understanding. The signal can be used to modulate the inductive bias of machine learning models towards more cognitively plausible processing which can increase model performance (Mathias et al., 2020; Hollenstein et al., 2019). It has been shown that large multilingual pre-trained language models are able to accurately predict eye tracking patterns when fine-tuned on small amounts of eye tracking data (Hollenstein et al., 2021; Takmaz, 2022; Salicchi et al., 2022).

Generally, transformer-based language models seem to be better at predicting cognitive signals of human language comprehension (e.g., self-paced reading times, eye movements, or brain activity) than language models based on other architectures (Merkx and Frank, 2021; Schrimpf et al., 2020). However, as *prediction is not explanation* (Demberg and Keller, 2019; Hale et al., 2022), we aim to dissect the predicted reading patterns and analyze them in more detail to gain clearer insights into the underlying representation of processing complexity. Eye tracking data can be very informative to evaluate sentence comprehension strategies, however, the interdependencies between the eye tracking measures need to be taken into account (Vasishth et al., 2013). We propose to use the relation between eye movements in reading and text readability in terms of linguistic complexity to better understand procedural patterns of English sentence comprehension in language models. We provide interpretable insights into the prediction errors to investigate the following two questions:
(1) What is the impact of pre-training on the performance of language models predicting human eye movements?
(2) Is the relationship between human reading patterns and English text readability preserved in the reading patterns predicted by the investigated language models?

We focus on multilingual pre-trained language models (mBERT and XLM), fine-tuned on a range of eye tracking features from reading in multiple languages (English, German, Dutch, and Russian). We build upon the approach by Hollenstein et al. (2021) and provide strong baselines and a series of model configurations to answer the first question in Section 2. Subsequently, we address the second question in Section 3, by performing an extensive readability analysis based on various aspects of English text complexity. We propose to evaluate the predicted gaze features by analyzing whether their correlation with a range of readability measures is similar to the correlation observed in human eye movement data.[1] These two contributions allow us to better interpret the ability of language models to predict human reading behaviour.

[1]Our code is available here: https://github.com/norahollenstein/readability-patterns

Proceedings of the Workshop on Cognitive Aspects of the Lexicon, pages 1–15
November 20, 2022. ©2022 Association for Computational Linguistics
https://doi.org/10.26615/978-954-452-056-4_001

Models	EN	NL	DE	RU	ALL
RANDOM BL	78.66 (0.06)	84.30 (0.11)	74.11 (4.6)	65.83 (2.55)	86.15 (0.43)
MEAN BL	89.94	90.15	84.98	85.35	92.54
MBERT					
$M_{\star}$	90.95 (0.11)	90.51 (0.31)	75.68 (3.99)	70.64 (2.38)	92.93 (0.13)
$M_{\heartsuit}$	93.73 (0.08)	91.91 (0.23)	77.41 (3.65)	77.30 (4.17)	94.68 (0.05)
$M_{\lightning}$	93.30 (0.03)	91.60 (0.36)	77.85 (2.85)	77.38 (1.85)	94.35 (0.13)
XLM-100					
$M_{\star}$	92.94 (0.05)	91.80 (0.40)	77.31 (2.75)	76.54 (1.92)	94.19 (0.10)
$M_{\heartsuit}$	**93.92** (0.07)	92.26 (0.33)	**86.38** (0.27)	**94.65** (0.88)	**94.89** (0.12)
$M_{\lightning}$	**93.92** (0.16)	**92.32** (0.36)	86.04 (0.28)	94.62 (0.84)	94.15 (1.20)

Table 1: Prediction accuracy aggregated across all eight eye tracking features (with standard deviation across three runs in parentheses). Fine-tuned models: last layer ($M_{\star}$), all layers ($M_{\heartsuit}$), all layers without pre-training ($M_{\lightning}$).

2 Multilingual Prediction of Eye Movements in Reading

Hollenstein et al. (2021) showed that language models can predict a range of eye tracking features in multiple languages. The prediction setup has been made widely available as a shared task to facilitate comparisons between models and the analysis of their inner workings (Hollenstein et al., 2022). In this work, we use a similar setup which we summarize below before we present the results of the eye tracking prediction.

2.1 Data

We use eye tracking corpora for sentences in four languages: English, Dutch, German, and Russian. Full sentences or longer naturally occurring text spans were read by multiple native speakers (see Appendix A.1 for detailed statistics) and tracked by high-precision eye trackers. The datasets report the following eye tracking features for each token of the stimulus text: (NFIX), mean fixation duration (MFD), fixation proportion (FPROP), first fixation duration (FFD), first pass duration (FPD), total reading time (TRT), number of re-fixations (NREFIX), and re-read proportion (REPROP). All features are first computed for each subject separately by aggregating over the fixations, and then averaged over all subjects.

These features arguably reflect the complete reading process at the various stages of linguistic integration, from early lexical access for word recognition (e.g., FFD) up to subsequent syntactic integration taking into account regression movements (e.g., NREFIX). For a review of which eye movement feature reflects which linguistic level, see Clifton et al. (2007).

For more detailed information about the data and the training procedure, see Hollenstein et al. (2021).

2.2 Model Configurations

The model is optimized to predict eye tracking features from reading as accurately as possible. For each token w in the input text, we predict a vector containing the eight eye tracking features listed above. We focus on the transformer-based models multilingual BERT (Devlin et al., 2019) and cross-lingual XLM-100 (Lample and Conneau, 2019). We use pre-trained checkpoints from the HuggingFace repository.[2]

We propose the following baselines to benchmark model performance. First, we compare with a random baseline (RANDOM BL), which presents model predictions made from a randomly initialized regression layer. Second, we use a mean baseline averaged across all eye tracking features (MEAN BL), which calculates the mean value for each eye tracking feature from the training data and uses it as a prediction for all words in the test data.

Since one of our goals is to evaluate the gains from fine-tuning a pre-trained LM on eye tracking data, we also compare fine-tuning all layers (we call these models $M_{\heartsuit}$), to fine-tuning only the final regression layer ($M_{\star}$). Finally, we investigate the benefits of pre-training on large language corpora

[2]xlm-mlm-100-1280 and bert-base-multilingual-cased

by comparing the fully fine-tuned pre-trained language models ($M_{\heartsuit}$) to a model trained from scratch on randomly initialized weights ($M_{\lightning}$).

2.3 Results

Since we scale all gaze features to values between 0–100, we evaluate the models using the mean absolute error (MAE). For better readability, we report the results as *prediction accuracy*, defined as 100−MAE. The results are presented in Table 1.

Baseline comparison The performance of the random baseline (RANDOM BL) is much lower than that of the mean baseline (MEAN BL), and therefore is not suitable for comparison. XLM-100 outperforms the mean baseline for all languages, but mBERT does not reach it for German (DE) and Russian (RU).

The impact of pre-training The results of the pre-trained and fine-tuned language models ($M_{\heartsuit}$) and the transformer models trained from scratch ($M_{\lightning}$) show a very similar performance. This demonstrates that the advantage of pre-training language models on large text corpora is only minimal for the task of predicting human eye movements. When fine-tuning only the regression layer ($M_{\star}$), the models yield only modest (if any) improvements over the MEAN BL. However, when all layers of a model are fine-tuned ($M_{\heartsuit}$), the differences become more notable, especially for languages where less eye tracking data is available (DE and RU).

Generally, XLM-100 yields better results than mBERT for all languages, and especially for the ones with smaller datasets (DE and RU). Our results are in line with previous work showing that XLM models perform better at zero-shot eye tracking prediction for an unseen language than mBERT (Srivastava, 2022). Similarly, Hollenstein et al. (2021) find that mBERT is outperformed by monolingual models for languages with small eye tracking training datasets.

This indicates that the architecture and training objective of a model might be more important for eye tracking prediction than pre-training on large amounts of text. Transformer architectures are promising for predicting reading times, but the extensive pre-training on text input might be superfluous, as the models learn more from the fine-tuning on psychometric features. This could mean that not much linguistic knowledge is required for eye tracking prediction. Alternately, the choice of metric (MAE) might not be the most appropriate to capture the subtleties of the task. However, as we will see in Section 3, the pre-trained models show an advantage over randomly initialized models in their correlation with text readability measures.

Evaluation of individual eye tracking features The aggregated mean baseline across all eye tracking features can be misleading because it conceals the model's prediction performance for individual features. A model that yields a superior performance on the aggregated level does not necessarily outperform the mean baseline for all features. Therefore, we zoom in on individual eye tracking features and compare the performance of the fine-tuned mBERT and XLM-100 with the mean baseline in Figure 2. The results show that mBERT fails to predict MFD, FPROP and REPROP for German and Russian, while XLM-100 outperforms the aggregate mean baseline for all languages. Some features are more strongly affected by the large degree of individual variability in human eye movements (Kidd et al., 2018). We additionally visualize the feature ranges of the predicted eye tracking features compared to the real eye tracking data in Figure 1.

3 Readability Analysis

Eye movement patterns during reading are known to be influenced by the readability of texts (Rayner et al., 2006). Singh et al. (2016) assess text readability with automatically predicted eye tracking features. Although their readability assessment model was based only on predicted reading times, it yielded results comparable to models that use extensive syntactic features to compute linguistic complexity. Wiechmann et al. (2022) find that, for English, the accuracy of eye tracking prediction is systematically linked to sentence-level text features that approximate readability.

We try to disentangle the three-fold relationship between human eye movements, the capability of language models to predict these eye movement patterns, and sentence-level readability measures for English. We analyze the correlation between model predictions and readability measures to better understand the processing patterns that the model picks up.

3.1 Measuring Readability

The readability of a text is affected by variation at all levels of linguistic processing (Beinborn et al., 2012). Feng et al. (2009) introduce a large range of

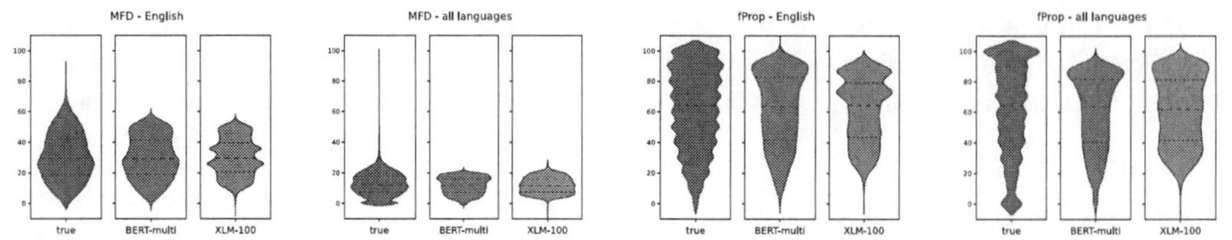

Figure 1: Feature ranges of the true eye tracking values for MFD and FPROP compared to the predicted eye tracking data (mBERT and XLM-100) for English and all four languages together.

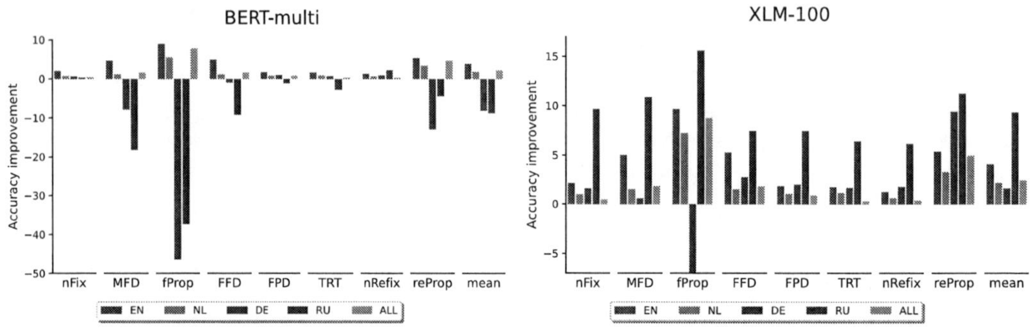

Figure 2: Improvements on prediction accuracy of the fine-tuned models mBERT and XLM-100 compared to the mean baseline across all four languages.

cognitively motivated readability measures that can be extracted using a standard natural language processing pipeline. Machine learning models trained on these measures can reliably predict the readability of texts in multiple languages (Vajjala Balakrishna, 2015). We explore a subset of 11 measures that are likely to affect eye movement patterns.

Flesch score (FLESCH): Flesch (1948) introduced the most renowned readability formula that takes the surface structure of a text into account, which is measured by the number of syllables, words and sentences. The Flesch reading ease score has been found to provide only a shallow readability estimation for English texts because it ignores deeper linguistic levels of text processing (Collins-Thompson, 2014; Bengoetxea and Gonzalez-Dios, 2021). Nahatame (2021) show that readability measures that quantify lexical and syntactic characteristics provide better approximations for predicting eye movement patterns than the Flesch score. We include it in our analysis mainly for the sake of comparison and completeness.

Word frequency (WF, ZIPF): The influence of lexical frequency on fixation duration is one of the most studied phenomena in psycholinguistic reading research. It is well established that readers tend to look longer at infrequent words (Rayner, 1977). We use the lexical frequency values provided by the `wordfreq` Python library (Speer et al., 2018) and its Zipfian variant on a logarithmic scale (Van Heuven et al., 2014).

Word length (WL): Longer words (measured in terms of number of characters) are generally fixed for longer periods. Nearly 70% of the variance in mean fixation duration can be explained by word length and word frequency (Just and Carpenter, 1980).

Sentence length (SL): We include sentence length, calculated as the number of tokens of each sentence, since the readability measures highlighted in our analysis are strongly related to the length of a sentence. Sarti et al. (2021) confirm that for all text complexity metrics, sentence length exhibits the highest correlation.

Distance to head (D2H): Sarti et al. (2021) find a strong correlation between readability measures related to dependency parsing (e.g., parse depth) and perceived complexity. Dependency features also correlate well with eye tracking patterns and can predict regressive eye movements (Lopopolo et al., 2019). In the opposite direction, Strzyz et al. (2019) show that eye tracking information can improve dependency parsing. We therefore measure

Feature	FLESCH	WL	WF	ZIPF	SL	D2H	AMB	AOA	FAM	CONC	IMAG
NFIX	-0.55	0.94	-0.54	-0.82	0.96	-0.29	-0.28	0.29	-0.46	0.45	0.43
NREFIX	-0.58	0.92	-0.55	-0.82	0.81	-0.23	-0.25	0.26	-0.35	0.33	0.32
MFD	-0.47	0.84	-0.44	-0.68	0.96	-0.26	-0.19	0.18	-0.42	0.42	0.40
FFD	-0.47	0.82	-0.43	-0.63	0.96	-0.26	-0.19	0.18	-0.42	0.42	0.41
FPD	-0.50	0.91	-0.50	-0.78	0.96	-0.28	-0.25	0.25	-0.44	0.43	0.42
TRT	-0.52	0.95	-0.54	-0.82	0.95	-0.28	-0.26	0.25	-0.44	0.44	0.42
FPROP	-0.52	0.98	-0.48	-0.72	0.99	-0.30	-0.25	0.24	-0.45	0.45	0.44
REPROP	-0.58	0.96	-0.52	-0.83	0.86	-0.23	-0.25	0.26	-0.36	0.33	0.32

Table 2: Spearman correlation coefficients of observed eye tracking features and readability measures. All correlations are significant ($p < 0.01$).

the distance to head as the number of words between the current word and its head according to the dependency tree. For example, in the sentence *She reads a mistery novel*, the distance from the word *novel* to its head *reads* is 2. We use the parser `Stanza` (Qi et al., 2020) for the dependency analysis.

Ambiguity level (AMB): The meaning of polysemous words can usually be disambiguated by processing the context. The effect of a high ambiguity level on eye movement patterns is therefore usually more pronounced for later processing measures such as NREFIX than for early gaze metrics reflecting lexical access (Foraker and Murphy, 2012; Shen and Li, 2016). We calculate the ambiguity level for each open class word (nouns, adjectives, adverbs, and verbs) as the number of possible senses (synsets) that can be found in the NLTK implementation (Bird and Loper, 2004) of WordNet (Fellbaum). The minimum ambiguity level is 1, which means that there is only one sense for a given wordform. For example, the noun *car* has an ambiguity level of five because it appears in 5 nominal synsets. For this analysis, we exclude words that do not appear in WordNet.

Age of acquisition (AOA), familiarity (FAM), concreteness (CONC), and imageability (IMAG): We include four cognitively motivated features of word complexity that are likely to affect fixation durations in reading (Juhasz and Rayner, 2006). Ratings for age of acquisition, familiarity, concreteness, and imageability (the intensity with which a word evokes a clear mental image) in the MRC Psycholinguistic Database (Wilson, 1988) are strongly associated with each other and with other readability metrics.[3] Paetzold and Specia (2016) find that word frequencies correlate with familiarity and AOA, while the depth of a word in a thesaurus hierarchy correlates with both its concreteness and its imageability. We exclude words that do not appear in the database when calculating the correlations.

3.2 Readability and Eye Movement Patterns

We calculate the Spearman correlation coefficients between the recorded eye tracking data and the readability measures for English (Table 2). The strongest correlations can be found for sentence length, word length, and lexical frequency, which confirms three widely studied effects in reading research (Sarti et al., 2021).

Predictive Power In a second step, we analyze the correlations between four of the readability measures (FLESCH, WL, ZIPF frequency, SL) and the predictions of the different models for fixation proportion and mean fixation duration for English (see Table 3).[4] The results show that for fine-tuned mBERT, while yielding lower overall prediction accuracy when aggregating across all features, the correlation of the predicted eye movement values to word frequency and length is generally more similar to the correlation of real gaze features with word frequency and length than for the XLM-100 models. When comparing fine-tuned pre-trained models ($M_{\heartsuit}$) to models trained from scratch on eye tracking data ($M_{\lightning}$), the results presented in Table 3 also show that the correlation with word length and frequency is stronger in the predictions of the

[3] https://websites.psychology.uwa.edu.au/school/mrcdatabase/uwa_mrc.htm

[4] Correlations to other gaze features show the same trends. We analyze FPROP because the models yield low prediction performance on this feature, compared to MFD, which yields high prediction results.

fine-tuned models and closer to the correlation of the real eye tracking features, showing that while pre-training might not strictly be needed for a high prediction accuracy, it does help the model to predict eye tracking features that are closer to human reading behavior in terms of text readability.

3.3 Prediction Errors

To systematically analyze the relationship between readability of the input and predictive power of the model, we focus on the prediction errors. We analyze a sample of 6,396 instances of the test set (20%) and calculate the percentage error (PE; Eq. 1) of the predictions compared to the observed scaled features.

$$PE = \frac{|Prediction - Observed|}{|Observed|} * 100 \quad (1)$$

In Table 4, we present the correlations of the readability measures with the prediction errors for eye tracking features. Imageability, familiarity, concreteness, function words, and Zipf scale frequency values show a moderate correlation to all eye tracking features, which is slightly more notable in the case of the mBERT model. Interestingly, the strongest correlation can be found to fixation proportion. This indicates that the prediction of whether a word will be fixated or not is strongly linked to its imageability and concreteness. Similar tendencies are observed for the correlations between all investigated eye tracking measures and readability measures.

4 Word-Level Analysis

As lexical aspects seem to be highly relevant, we additionally analyze the influence of the word class on prediction errors. We focus on words that cause a prediction error ≥ the third quartile value for that feature. Figure 3 shows the aggregated results for all predicted eye movement features.

4.1 Word Classes

It can be seen that the large majority of prediction errors can be attributed to function words. This tendency is consistent across all eight gaze features.[5] Function words such as determiners, pronouns, prepositions and conjunctions, usually trigger low fixation duration and high skipping probability. It has been shown that distributional models

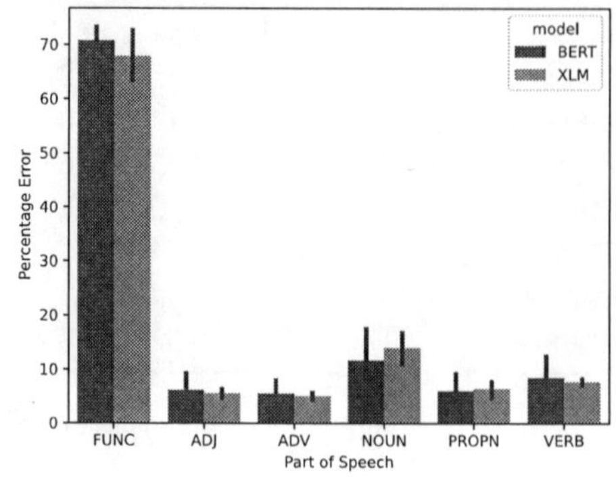

Figure 3: Percentage error per part-of-speech class, aggregated across all predicted gaze features.

are generally not well suited for representing function words (Bernardi et al., 2015) and that their representation in transformer-based models such as BERT is highly context-sensitive (Ethayarajh, 2019; Kim et al., 2019; Atanasova et al., 2020). Of the content words, nouns are most often mispredicted and responsible for around 10% of the errors. This is in line with Furtner et al. (2009), who indicated in a reading study that the noun is the most influential word class for facilitating the comprehension of other words.

4.2 A Closer Look at Function Words

We have seen that most prediction errors are caused by function words. Function or closed category words are words that are short, frequent, ambiguous, and subject to pragmatic effects in English. They are critical for language understanding.

Reading research has shown that short function words can be identified in reading without a direct fixation (Rayner et al., 1989). Similarly, Barrett and Søgaard (2015) show a negative correlation between function word frequency and fixation probability. Schmauder et al. (2000) found increased processing times in phrases immediately following a low-frequency function word. Function and content words are likely stored and accessed similarly (Diaz and McCarthy, 2009), but have different roles in text processing and constructing discourse representations. Function words show frequency effects in first fixation and first pass duration that are similar to those seen for content words. However, clear differences in reading patterns in the online processing of function and content words emerged in later processing measures (Schmauder

[5] Detailed results per feature can be found in the Appendix in Table 7.

	FPROP				MFD			
Eye tracking	FLESCH	ZIPF	WL	SL	FLESCH	ZIPF	WL	SL
Human	-0.52*	-0.72*	0.98*	0.99*	-0.47*	-0.68*	0.84*	0.96*
RANDOM BL	-0.03	-0.07	0.36	-0.16*	0.12*	-0.48	-0.20	-0.12*
MEAN BL	-0.61*	0.14*	-0.31	0.99*	-0.41*	-0.01	0.23	0.91*
$M_{\lightning}$ mBERT	-0.50*	-0.53*	0.72*	**0.99***	-0.49*	-0.52*	0.61*	**0.98***
$M_{\lightning}$ XLM-100	**-0.52***	-0.68*	0.67*	**0.99***	-0.49*	-0.65*	0.68*	0.97*
$M_{\heartsuit}$ mBERT	**-0.52***	-0.73*	**0.78***	**0.99***	**-0.48***	**-0.68***	**0.80***	0.97*
$M_{\heartsuit}$ XLM-100	-0.53*	**-0.72***	0.68*	**0.99***	-0.49*	-0.62*	0.62*	**0.98***

Table 3: Spearman correlation coefficients between real human eye tracking features or model predictions and word length, word frequency, and sentence length for **fixation proportion** (FPROP) on the left side and for **mean fixation duration** (MFD) on the right side. $M_{\lightning}$ stands for models trained from scratch and $M_{\heartsuit}$ for fine-tuned pre-trained models. Significant results are marked with * ($p < 0.01$) and results in bold are closest to human eye tracking features.

	IMAG		FAM		CONC		ZIPF		FUNCT	
Feature	BERT	XLM	BERT	XLM	BERT	XLM	BERT	XLM	BERT	XLM
NFIX	-0.18	-0.17	0.19	0.14	-0.19	-0.17	0.22	0.18	0.20	0.19
MFD	-0.18	-0.09	0.16	0.10	-0.19	-0.09	0.24	0.13	0.23	0.10
FPROP	-0.21	-0.17	0.24	0.20	-0.21	-0.17	0.34	0.26	0.29	0.22
FFD	-0.17	-0.08	0.16	0.09	-0.18	-0.09	0.23	0.12	0.22	0.10
FPD	-0.16	-0.06	0.15	0.07	-0.17	-0.06	0.19	0.07	0.18	0.06
TRT	-0.18	-0.13	0.16	0.12	-0.19	-0.14	0.21	0.16	0.19	0.16
NREFIX	-0.19	-0.14	0.22	0.16	-0.21	-0.15	0.27	0.17	0.23	0.16
REPROP	-0.14	-0.14	0.15	0.16	-0.16	-0.16	0.19	0.20	0.16	0.18

Table 4: Correlations between percentage error of the eye tracking predictions and the readability measures (imageability, familiarity, concreteness, function words and Zipf frequencies of words).

et al., 2000). These findings can be taken as evidence of the different roles the two word types have in sentence processing beyond the lexical level.

We analyze the variance in the observed eye tracking features for prepositions, determiners, and conjunctions. We calculate the standard deviation of each eye tracking feature for the six most frequent words of each category. Generally, there is a high variation in the data across all of the gaze features, and the highest deviation can be observed for mean fixation duration. To illustrate this, in Figure 4 we show the graphics of the six most common prepositions. Determiners and conjunctions are shown in Figures 5 and 6 in the Appendix (standard deviation values can also be found in Table 8 in the Appendix).

The lower fixation proportion on shorter words, together with the immense variation on the fixation duration of function words, is likely the cause for the difficulty in predicting reading times on this class accurately. The differences in skipping rate (that is, the ratio of words that are not fixated) have various origins. Skipping rate is regulated by word length (Drieghe et al., 2004), which therefore leads to differences across languages (see Fig. 1), and by proficiency, since highly proficient readers show a higher skipping rate (Eskenazi and Folk, 2015). We discuss these challenges in more detail in the next section.

5 Methodological Limitations

In this work, we make a few simplifying assumptions that are common in the field, but severely affect the interpretation of the results. We want to discuss these limitations explicitly and encourage methodological research to better address these open challenges.

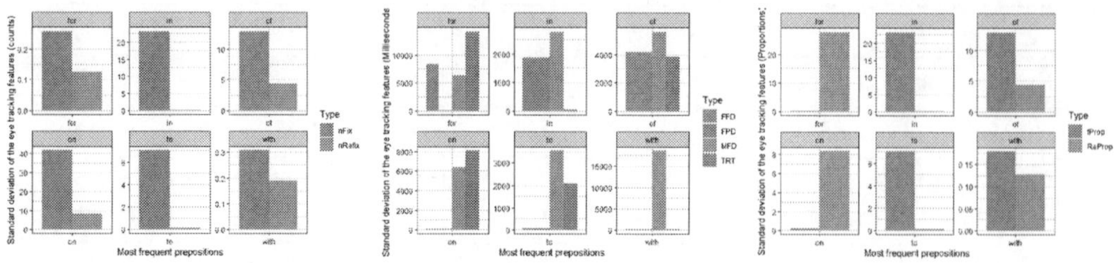

Figure 4: Standard deviations of the eye tracking features of the most frequent English prepositions. Note that the y-axis scales change in each subplot.

Token-level alignment Stimuli for eye tracking are usually pre-processed with high linguistic quality. Neural language models, on the other hand, are optimized for engineering objectives that sometimes compete with linguistic and cognitive plausibility. This discrepancy becomes obvious when inspecting the tokenization. The HuggingFace transformer-based models that we apply expect the use of subword tokenizers. Words such as close-knit! that are interpreted as a single unit in the eye tracking data are split into subword tokens (['close', '##-', '##knit']) and it remains an open challenge how to align the different units. In our implementation, we assign the same gaze features to all subtokens and choose to compute the loss only with respect to the first subtoken. It is unclear, however, if this is the best strategy as it complicates fine-grained error analyses. For example, in the eye tracking data, punctuation is not separated from the preceding token as they are usually fixated jointly. If we apply part-of-speech tagging on words with attached punctuation signs they might get assigned incorrect tags leading to skewed results. In this work, we resolved this by manually aligning tokenized text with the eye tracking stimuli for the readability analysis. However, this is laborious and limits the size of the analyzed data.

Aggregating over participants The second matter we address is the variability between readers. The negligence of individual differences is a well-known issue in cognitive science, leading to a picture of an idealized human that is largely invariant across individuals (Levinson, 2012), and the resulting insights underestimate the extent to which human sentence processing is affected by individual differences (Kidd et al., 2018). Currently, the captured individual differences are merely treated as a source of variance that is controlled for through aggregation. As in this work, most often NLP researchers aggregate across all readers due to evidence showing that this leads to more robust results regarding model performance (Klerke and Plank, 2019). However, the high variability found in some features, such as FPROP, calls for more careful data preprocessing, possibly by considering additional cognitive tests performed during data collection and performing proper outlier detection. Alternatively, single-subject and cross-subject approaches should also be considered in eye tracking prediction for more practical applications.

Cross-lingual differences Finally, eye movements depend on the stimulus and therefore contain language-specific information (Liversedge et al., 2016). Reading patterns can be related to linguistic factors of the reader's native language. Berzak et al. (2017) found evidence that similar languages have more similar reading patterns. Siegelman et al. (2022) found that readers of different languages vary considerably in their skipping rate and that this variability is explained by cross-lingual differences in word length distributions. It is unclear yet to what extent these differences affect the predictions of pre-trained language models. Therefore, more research is required on multilingual models that predict eye tracking in typologically more diverse languages.

6 Conclusion

Our results show that transformer models yield high accuracy in predicting cognitive language processing signals which confirms tendencies observed in previous work (e.g., Schrimpf et al., 2020; Michaelov et al., 2021). We go beyond aggregated performance metrics and provide a detailed analysis of the linguistic text complexity factors that underlie the prediction of eye movement patterns.

In a detailed analysis of fine-tuned language models that predict eye tracking features from reading, we found that the models learn more from the fine-tuning on psychometric features than from pre-training on textual input. However, the pre-trained models show an advantage over the randomly initialized models in their correlation to text readability measures. Although pre-training of large language models is not required to obtain high accuracy in predicting eye tracking feature from reading, it does contribute to a stronger correlation to text readability measures, making the predictions more similar to human reading behavior. The models struggle most to predict accurate eye tracking values for function words, which are exactly the class of words that exhibits large ranges in reading times and skipping rates, together with extreme variability between readers. The next step will be to extend the readability analysis to the other languages and to discern further between syntactic and semantic text difficulty and purely structural complexity.

This line of work does not only advance our understanding of language models and allows to compare their output to human language (Tuckute et al., 2022), but it also furthers research on new readability formulas supported by eye tracking data and machine learning methods (e.g., González-Garduño and Søgaard, 2018; Baazeem et al., 2021). We hope this work can serve as a stepping stone towards a more detailed evaluation setup for eye movement prediction from reading.

6.0.1 Acknowledgements

I. Gonzalez-Dios's research was partially funded by the Basque Government (Excellence Research Group, IT1570-22).
L. Beinborn's research is part of the VENI project Vl.Veni.211C.039, which is financed by the Dutch Research Council (NWO).
L. A. Jäger's research is partially funded by the German Federal Ministry of Education and Research (grant 01|S20043).

References

Pepa Atanasova, Jakob Grue Simonsen, Christina Lioma, and Isabelle Augenstein. 2020. A diagnostic study of explainability techniques for text classification. In *Proceedings of the 2020 Conference on Empirical Methods in Natural Language Processing (EMNLP)*, pages 3256–3274, Online. Association for Computational Linguistics.

Ibtehal Baazeem, Hend Al-Khalifa, and Abdulmalik Al-Salman. 2021. Cognitively driven Arabic text readability assessment using eye-tracking. *Applied Sciences*, 11(18):8607.

Maria Barrett and Anders Søgaard. 2015. Reading behavior predicts syntactic categories. In *Proceedings of the Nineteenth Conference on Computational Natural Language Learning*, pages 345–349, Beijing, China. Association for Computational Linguistics.

Lisa Beinborn, Torsten Zesch, and Iryna Gurevych. 2012. Towards fine-grained readability measures for self-directed language learning. In *Proceedings of the SLTC 2012 Workshop on NLP for CALL*, pages 11–19. Linköping University Electronic Press.

Kepa Bengoetxea and Itziar Gonzalez-Dios. 2021. Multiaztertest: A multilingual analyzer on multiple levels of language for readability assessment. *arXiv preprint arXiv:2109.04870*.

Raffaella Bernardi, Gemma Boleda, Raquel Fernández, and Denis Paperno. 2015. Distributional semantics in use. In *Proceedings of the First Workshop on Linking Computational Models of Lexical, Sentential and Discourse-level Semantics*, pages 95–101, Lisbon, Portugal. Association for Computational Linguistics.

Yevgeni Berzak, Chie Nakamura, Suzanne Flynn, and Boris Katz. 2017. Predicting native language from gaze. In *Proceedings of the 55th Annual Meeting of the Association for Computational Linguistics (Volume 1: Long Papers)*, pages 541–551, Vancouver, Canada. Association for Computational Linguistics.

Steven Bird and Edward Loper. 2004. NLTK: The natural language toolkit. In *Proceedings of the ACL Interactive Poster and Demonstration Sessions*, pages 214–217, Barcelona, Spain. Association for Computational Linguistics.

Charles Clifton, Adrian Staub, and Keith Rayner. 2007. Eye movements in reading words and sentences. In *Eye Movements:A Window on Mind and Brain*, pages 341–371. Elsevier.

Kevyn Collins-Thompson. 2014. Computational assessment of text readability: A survey of current and future research. *ITL-International Journal of Applied Linguistics*, 165(2):97–135.

Vera Demberg and Frank Keller. 2019. Cognitive models of syntax and sentence processing. In *Human Language: From Genes and Brains to Behavior*. MIT Press.

Jacob Devlin, Ming-Wei Chang, Kenton Lee, and Kristina Toutanova. 2019. BERT: Pre-training of deep bidirectional transformers for language understanding. In *Proceedings of the 2019 Conference of the North American Chapter of the Association for Computational Linguistics: Human Language Technologies, Volume 1 (Long and Short Papers)*, pages 4171–4186, Minneapolis, Minnesota. Association for Computational Linguistics.

Michele T. Diaz and Gregory McCarthy. 2009. A comparison of brain activity evoked by single content and function words: An fMRI investigation of implicit word processing. *Brain Research*, 1282:38–49.

Denis Drieghe, Marc Brysbaert, Timothy Desmet, and Constantijn De Baecke. 2004. Word skipping in reading: On the interplay of linguistic and visual factors. *European Journal of Cognitive Psychology*, 16(1-2):79–103.

Michael A. Eskenazi and Jocelyn R. Folk. 2015. Reading skill and word skipping: Implications for visual and linguistic accounts of word skipping. *Journal of Experimental Psychology: Learning, Memory, and Cognition*, 41(6):1923.

Kawin Ethayarajh. 2019. How contextual are contextualized word representations? Comparing the geometry of BERT, ELMo, and GPT-2 embeddings. In *Proceedings of the 2019 Conference on Empirical Methods in Natural Language Processing and the 9th International Joint Conference on Natural Language Processing (EMNLP-IJCNLP)*, pages 55–65, Hong Kong, China. Association for Computational Linguistics.

Christiane Fellbaum, editor. *WordNet: An Electronic Lexical Database*. MIT Press, Cambridge, MA.

Lijun Feng, Noémie Elhadad, and Matt Huenerfauth. 2009. Cognitively motivated features for readability assessment. In *Proceedings of the 12th Conference of the European Chapter of the ACL (EACL 2009)*, pages 229–237, Athens, Greece. Association for Computational Linguistics.

Rudolph Flesch. 1948. A new readability yardstick. *Journal of Applied Psychology*, 32(3):221.

Stephani Foraker and Gregory . Murphy. 2012. Polysemy in sentence comprehension: Effects of meaning dominance. *Journal of Memory and Language*, 67(4):407–425.

Marco R Furtner, John F Rauthmann, and Pierre Sachse. 2009. Nomen est omen: Investigating the dominance of nouns in word comprehension with eye movement analyses. *Advances in Cognitive Psychology*, 5:91.

Ana Valeria González-Garduño and Anders Søgaard. 2018. Learning to predict readability using eye-movement data from natives and learners. In *Proceedings of the 32nd AAAI Conference on Artificial Intelligence*, pages 5118–5124.

John T Hale, Luca Campanelli, Jixing Li, Shohini Bhattasali, Christophe Pallier, and Jonathan R Brennan. 2022. Neurocomputational models of language processing. *Annual Review of Linguistics*, 8:427–446.

Nora Hollenstein, Maria Barrett, Marius Troendle, Francesco Bigiolli, Nicolas Langer, and Ce Zhang. 2019. Advancing NLP with cognitive language processing signals. *arXiv preprint arXiv:1904.02682*.

Nora Hollenstein, Emmanuele Chersoni, Cassandra Jacobs, Yohei Oseki, Laurent Prévot, and Enrico Santus. 2022. CMCL 2022 shared task on multilingual and crosslingual prediction of human reading behavior. In *Proceedings of the Workshop on Cognitive Modeling and Computational Linguistics*, pages 121–129, Dublin, Ireland. Association for Computational Linguistics.

Nora Hollenstein, Federico Pirovano, Ce Zhang, Lena Jäger, and Lisa Beinborn. 2021. Multilingual language models predict human reading behavior. In *Proceedings of the 2021 Conference of the North American Chapter of the Association for Computational Linguistics: Human Language Technologies*, pages 106–123, Online. Association for Computational Linguistics.

Barbara J Juhasz and Keith Rayner. 2006. The role of age of acquisition and word frequency in reading: Evidence from eye fixation durations. *Visual Cognition*, 13(7-8):846–863.

Marcel A. Just and Patricia A. Carpenter. 1980. A theory of reading: From eye fixations to comprehension. *Psychological Review*, 87(4):329.

Evan Kidd, Seamus Donnelly, and Morten H Christiansen. 2018. Individual differences in language acquisition and processing. *Trends in Cognitive Science*, 22(2):154–169.

Najoung Kim, Roma Patel, Adam Poliak, Patrick Xia, Alex Wang, Tom McCoy, Ian Tenney, Alexis Ross, Tal Linzen, Benjamin Van Durme, Samuel R. Bowman, and Ellie Pavlick. 2019. Probing what different NLP tasks teach machines about function word comprehension. In *Proceedings of the Eighth Joint Conference on Lexical and Computational Semantics (*SEM 2019)*, pages 235–249, Minneapolis, Minnesota. Association for Computational Linguistics.

Sigrid Klerke and Barbara Plank. 2019. At a glance: The impact of gaze aggregation views on syntactic tagging. In *Proceedings of the Beyond Vision and LANguage: inTEgrating Real-world kNowledge (LANTERN)*, pages 51–61, Hong Kong, China. Association for Computational Linguistics.

Guillaume Lample and Alexis Conneau. 2019. Cross-lingual language model pretraining. In *Advances in Neural Information Processing Systems 32 (NeurIPS 2019)*.

Stephen C. Levinson. 2012. The original sin of cognitive science. *Topics in Cognitive Science*, 4(3):396–403.

Simon P Liversedge, Denis Drieghe, Xin Li, Guoli Yan, Xuejun Bai, and Jukka Hyönä. 2016. Universality in eye movements and reading: A trilingual investigation. *Cognition*, 147:1–20.

Alessandro Lopopolo, Stefan L. Frank, Antal van den Bosch, and Roel Willems. 2019. Dependency parsing with your eyes: Dependency structure predicts eye regressions during reading. In *Proceedings of the Workshop on Cognitive Modeling and Computational Linguistics*, pages 77–85, Minneapolis, Minnesota. Association for Computational Linguistics.

Sandeep Mathias, Diptesh Kanojia, Abhijit Mishra, and Pushpak Bhattacharyya. 2020. A survey on using gaze behaviour for natural language processing. *Proceedings of IJCAI.*

Danny Merkx and Stefan L. Frank. 2021. Human sentence processing: Recurrence or attention? In *Proceedings of the Workshop on Cognitive Modeling and Computational Linguistics*, pages 12–22, Online. Association for Computational Linguistics.

James A Michaelov, Megan D Bardolph, Seana Coulson, and Benjamin Bergen. 2021. Different kinds of cognitive plausibility: Why are transformers better than RNNs at predicting N400 amplitude? In *Proceedings of the Annual Meeting of the Cognitive Science Society*, volume 43.

Shingo Nahatame. 2021. Text readability and processing effort in second language reading: A computational and eye-tracking investigation. *Language learning*.

Gustavo Paetzold and Lucia Specia. 2016. Inferring psycholinguistic properties of words. In *Proceedings of the 2016 Conference of the North American Chapter of the Association for Computational Linguistics: Human Language Technologies*, pages 435–440, San Diego, California. Association for Computational Linguistics.

Peng Qi, Yuhao Zhang, Yuhui Zhang, Jason Bolton, and Christopher D. Manning. 2020. Stanza: A python natural language processing toolkit for many human languages. In *Proceedings of the 58th Annual Meeting of the Association for Computational Linguistics: System Demonstrations*, pages 101–108, Online. Association for Computational Linguistics.

Keith Rayner. 1977. Visual attention in reading: Eye movements reflect cognitive processes. *Memory & Cognition*, 5(4):443–448.

Keith Rayner, Kathryn H Chace, Timothy J. Slattery, and Jane Ashby. 2006. Eye movements as reflections of comprehension processes in reading. *Scientific Studies of Reading*, 10(3):241–255.

Keith Rayner, Sara C Sereno, Robin K Morris, A Rene Schmauder, and Charles Clifton Jr. 1989. Eye movements and on-line language comprehension processes. *Language and Cognitive Processes*, 4(3-4):SI21–SI49.

Lavinia Salicchi, Rong Xiang, and Yu-Yin Hsu. 2022. HkAmsters at CMCL 2022 shared task: Predicting eye-tracking data from a gradient boosting framework with linguistic features. In *Proceedings of the Workshop on Cognitive Modeling and Computational Linguistics*, pages 114–120, Dublin, Ireland. Association for Computational Linguistics.

Gabriele Sarti, Dominique Brunato, and Felice Dell'Orletta. 2021. That looks hard: Characterizing linguistic complexity in humans and language models. In *Proceedings of the Workshop on Cognitive Modeling and Computational Linguistics*, pages 48–60, Online. Association for Computational Linguistics.

A René Schmauder, Robin K Morris, and David V Poynor. 2000. Lexical processing and text integration of function and content words: Evidence from priming and eye fixations. *Memory & Cognition*, 28(7):1098–1108.

Martin Schrimpf, Idan A Blank, Greta Tuckute, Carina Kauf, Eghbal A Hosseini, Nancy G Kanwisher, Joshua B Tenenbaum, and Evelina Fedorenko. 2020. Artificial neural networks accurately predict language processing in the brain. *BioRxiv*.

Wei Shen and Xingshan Li. 2016. Processing and representation of ambiguous words in Chinese reading: Evidence from eye movements. *Frontiers in Psychology*, 7:1713.

Noam Siegelman, Sascha Schroeder, Cengiz Acartürk, Hee-Don Ahn, Svetlana Alexeeva, Simona Amenta, Raymond Bertram, Rolando Bonandrini, Marc Brysbaert, Daria Chernova, et al. 2022. Expanding horizons of cross-linguistic research on reading: The Multilingual Eye-movement Corpus (MECO). *Behavior Research Methods*, pages 1–21.

Abhinav Deep Singh, Poojan Mehta, Samar Husain, and Rajkumar Rajakrishnan. 2016. Quantifying sentence complexity based on eye-tracking measures. In *Proceedings of the Workshop on Computational Linguistics for Linguistic Complexity (CL4LC)*, pages 202–212, Osaka, Japan. The COLING 2016 Organizing Committee.

Robyn Speer, Joshua Chin, Andrew Lin, Sara Jewett, and Lance Nathan. 2018. LuminosoInsight/wordfreq: v2.2.

Harshvardhan Srivastava. 2022. Poirot at CMCL 2022 shared task: Zero shot crosslingual eye-tracking data prediction using multilingual transformer models. In *Proceedings of the Workshop on Cognitive Modeling and Computational Linguistics*, pages 102–107, Dublin, Ireland. Association for Computational Linguistics.

Michalina Strzyz, David Vilares, and Carlos Gómez-Rodríguez. 2019. Towards making a dependency parser see. In *Proceedings of the 2019 Conference on Empirical Methods in Natural Language Processing and the 9th International Joint Conference on Natural Language Processing (EMNLP-IJCNLP)*, pages 1500–1506, Hong Kong, China. Association for Computational Linguistics.

Ece Takmaz. 2022. Team DMG at CMCL 2022 shared task: Transformer adapters for the multi- and cross-lingual prediction of human reading behavior. In *Proceedings of the Workshop on Cognitive Modeling and Computational Linguistics*, pages 136–144, Dublin, Ireland. Association for Computational Linguistics.

Greta Tuckute, Aalok Sathe, Mingye Wang, Harley Yoder, Cory Shain, and Evelina Fedorenko. 2022. SentSpace: Large-scale benchmarking and evaluation of text using cognitively motivated lexical, syntactic, and semantic features. In *Proceedings of the 2022 Conference of the North American Chapter of the Association for Computational Linguistics: Human Language Technologies: System Demonstrations*, pages 99–113, Hybrid: Seattle, Washington + Online. Association for Computational Linguistics.

Sowmya Vajjala Balakrishna. 2015. *Analyzing Text Complexity and Text Simplification: Connecting Linguistics, Processing and Educational Applications*. Ph.D. thesis, Universität Tübingen.

Walter JB Van Heuven, Pawel Mandera, Emmanuel Keuleers, and Marc Brysbaert. 2014. SUBTLEX-UK: A new and improved word frequency database for British English. *Quarterly Journal of Experimental Psychology*, 67(6):1176–1190.

Shravan Vasishth, Titus von der Malsburg, and Felix Engelmann. 2013. What eye movements can tell us about sentence comprehension. *Wiley Interdisciplinary Reviews: Cognitive Science*, 4(2):125–134.

Daniel Wiechmann, Yu Qiao, Elma Kerz, and Justus Mattern. 2022. Measuring the impact of (psycho-)linguistic and readability features and their spill over effects on the prediction of eye movement patterns. In *Proceedings of the 60th Annual Meeting of the Association for Computational Linguistics (Volume 1: Long Papers)*, pages 5276–5290, Dublin, Ireland. Association for Computational Linguistics.

Michael Wilson. 1988. MRC psycholinguistic database: Machine-usable dictionary, version 2.00. *Behavior Research Methods, Instruments, & Computers*, 20(1):6–10.

A Appendix

A.1 Eye Tracking Corpora

The details of the datasets used in this work are presented in Table 5.

Language	Corpus	Subjs.	Sents.	Sent. length	Tokens	Types	Word length	Flesch
English	Dundee	10	2,379	21.7 (1–87)	51,497	9,488	4.9 (1–20)	53.3
	GECO	14	5,373	10.5 (1–69)	56,410	5,916	4.6 (1–33)	77.4
	ZuCo	30	1,053	19.5 (1–68)	20,545	5,560	5.0 (1–29)	50.6
Dutch	GECO	19	5,190	11.64 (1–60)	59,716	5,575	4.5 (1–22)	57.5
German	PoTeC	30	97	19.5 (5–51)	1,895	847	6.5 (2–33)	36.4
Russian	RSC	103	144	9.4 (5–13)	1,357	993	5.7 (1–18)	64.7

Table 5: Descriptive statistics of all eye tracking datasets. Sentence length and word length are expressed as the mean with the min-max range in parentheses. The last column shows the Flesch Reading Ease score (Flesch, 1948) which ranges from 0 to 100 (higher score indicates easier to read). Adaptations of the Flesch score were used for Dutch (NL), German (DE) and Russian (RU).

A.2 Eye Movement Features

The values of the eye tracking features vary over different ranges (see Figure 1, left-most subplots). FFD, for example, is measured in milliseconds, and average values are around 200 ms, whereas REPROP is a proportional measure, and therefore assumes floating-point values between 0 and 1. We standardize all eye tracking features independently (range: 0–100), so that the loss can be calculated uniformly over all feature dimensions.

A.3 Additional Correlation Results

In Table 6, we present additional correlations of the readability measures in relation to the eye tracking prediction errors.

	AOA		D2H		AMB	
Feature	BERT	XLM	BERT	XLM	BERT	XLM
NFIX	0.00	0.02	-0.03	-0.05	0.04	0.01
MFD	-0.09	-0.04	0.00	-0.03	0.04	0.00
FPROP	-0.18	-0.12	-0.03	-0.04	0.13	0.05
FFD	-0.09	-0.04	-0.01	-0.03	0.02	-0.01
FPD	-0.06	-0.01	0.00	-0.02	0.00	-0.04
TRT	0.02	-0.05	-0.02	-0.04	0.01	0.01
NREFIX	-0.01	0.01	0.00	-0.03	0.14	0.09
REPROP	0.05	0.01	0.01	-0.01	0.13	0.12

Table 6: Correlations between percentage error and readability measures (age of acquisition, distance to head, and ambiguity level).

A.4 Error Rate by Part-of-Speech

Table 7 shows the percentage error for each part-of-speech class and each eye tracking feature.

Feature	FUNC		ADJ		ADV		NOUN		PROPN		VERB	
	BERT	XLM	BERT	XLM	BERT	XLM	BERT	XLM	BERT	XLM	BERT	XLM
NFIX	68.54	66.10	4.69	5.44	4.63	4.82	9.38	15.76	6.38	8.26	6.38	7.88
MFD	68.86	62.16	5.32	6.32	4.57	5.94	9.63	17.39	4.69	7.50	6.94	8.19
FPROP	72.17	69.17	4.57	4.75	4.50	4.44	8.13	14.82	4.38	6.82	6.25	6.82
FFD	67.98	62.48	5.25	6.25	4.63	5.88	10.44	16.89	4.75	7.13	6.94	8.51
FPD	68.36	58.91	5.25	7.32	4.44	6.19	9.82	18.89	5.19	8.51	6.94	8.69
TRT	68.36	66.60	16.60	6.57	14.03	5.19	31.03	13.07	16.40	6.94	21.94	8.57
NREFIX	75.88	78.70	3.71	3.71	3.61	3.61	7.46	7.46	2.82	2.82	6.52	6.52
REPROP	75.88	78.70	3.71	3.71	3.61	3.61	7.46	7.46	2.82	2.82	6.52	6.52

Table 7: Percentage error for each part-of-speech class and each eye tracking feature.

A.5 Standard Deviations of Function Words

Table 8 shows the standard deviations of the predictions of the most frequent function word classes, namely prepositions (PREP), determiners (DET), and conjunctions (CONJ).

	Lemma	NFIX	FFD	FPD	TRT	MFD	FPROP	NREFIX	REPROP
PREP	at	0.20	33.87	35.96	42.79	**4562.23**	0.15	10.10	10.10
	by	0.25	43.47	44.57	51.42	**5109.68**	0.19	0.09	0.07
	for	0.26	**8365.60**	42.11	**14199.50**	**6347.25**	0.19	0.13	27.87
	from	0.25	39.08	40.07	**12828.73**	38.53	0.18	0.11	35.43
	in	23.15	**1859.10**	**1859.05**	41.57	**2782.60**	23.15	0.07	0.06
	of	12.92	**4158.18**	**4158.11**	**3839.08**	**5614.73**	12.92	4.31	4.31
	on	41.64	35.31	36.95	**8120.68**	**6406.01**	0.16	8.33	8.33
	to	7.07	35.79	37.38	**2073.26**	**3562.01**	7.07	0.08	0.07
	up	0.23	46.17	48.59	52.53	46.42	0.20	0.07	0.06
	with	0.31	43.47	47.71	62.36	**18589.94**	0.18	0.19	0.13
DET	a	12.48	**1168.31**	**1168.30**	**1168.27**	**6726.54**	17.64	0.07	0.05
	all	0.24	43.44	47.06	57.88	**11703.01**	0.18	0.12	0.08
	another	0.44	56.89	70.55	98.66	54.99	0.23	0.29	0.18
	any	0.23	40.18	42.81	50.25	39.31	0.17	0.12	0.11
	every	0.33	40.36	46.56	48.93	**36800.71**	0.15	0.25	0.14
	no	0.25	39.11	40.87	50.50	38.53	0.18	0.10	0.08
	some	0.31	46.57	49.31	60.57	**26367.42**	0.18	0.20	0.11
	that	0.26	41.07	45.10	53.25	40.90	0.18	0.15	0.11
	the	9.06	**2060.29**	919.18	**2349.22**	**5173.09**	9.06	0.11	0.08
	this	0.32	47.54	53.64	67.83	**26854.66**	0.19	0.18	0.12
CONJ	and	0.27	37.11	41.45	48.52	**5318.58**	32.99	0.11	0.08
	as	0.22	38.20	39.10	44.08	**10602.03**	0.17	0.08	0.06
	because	0.32	38.95	42.76	53.55	38.80	0.15	0.24	0.12
	but	0.31	44.79	50.00	63.22	**5564.67**	0.20	0.15	0.09
	if	0.25	47.90	49.16	56.45	47.71	0.21	0.09	0.07
	of	0.25	44.95	51.17	56.85	45.99	0.20	0.07	0.07
	or	0.22	44.45	48.68	50.86	44.59	0.18	0.08	0.07
	that	0.26	41.08	44.46	56.21	**21359.14**	0.18	0.13	0.10
	when	113.83	35.28	44.65	63.01	**18228.19**	0.17	0.21	0.14
	where	0.39	48.09	57.04	68.93	47.88	0.19	0.25	0.16

Table 8: Standard deviation of the most frequent function words.

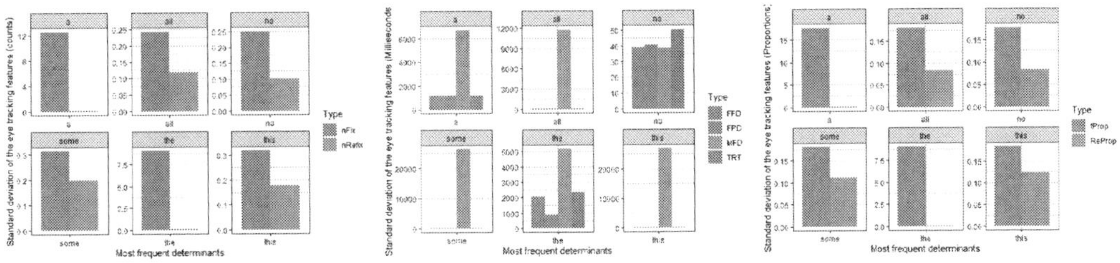

Figure 5: Standard deviations of the eye tracking features of the most frequent English **determiners**. Note that the y-axis scales change in each subplot.

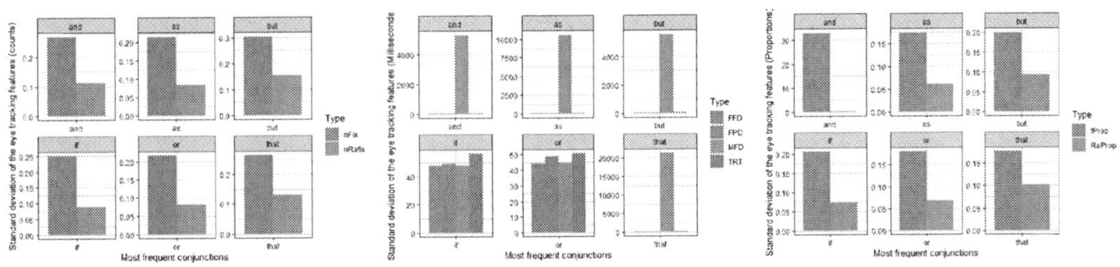

Figure 6: Standard deviations of the eye tracking features of the most frequent English **conjunctions**. Note that the y-axis scales change in each subplot.

(In)Alienable Possession in Mandarin Relative Clauses

Deran Kong and **Yu-Yin Hsu**
The Hong Kong Polytechnic University, Hung Hom, Hong Kong
yu-yin.hsu@polyu.edu.hk

Abstract

Inalienable possession differs from alienable possession in that, in the former – e.g., kinships and part-whole relations – there is an intrinsic semantic dependency between the possessor and possessum. This paper reports two studies that used acceptability-judgment tasks to investigate whether native Mandarin speakers experienced different levels of interpretational costs while resolving different types of possessive relations, i.e., inalienable possessions (kinship terms and body parts) and alienable ones, expressed within relative clauses. The results show that sentences received higher acceptability ratings when body parts were the possessum as compared to sentences with alienable possessum, indicating that the inherent semantic dependency facilitates the resolution. However, inalienable kinship terms received the lowest acceptability ratings. We argue that this was because the kinship terms, which had the [+human] feature and appeared at the beginning of the experimental sentences, tended to be interpreted as the subject in shallow processing; these features contradicted the semantic-syntactic requirements of the experimental sentences.

1 Introduction

Possessive relations are fundamental in human languages because they associate nouns to express specific relationships. Questions around the alienability between the possessor and the possessum in possessive relations has garnered considerable attention in linguistics (Vergnaud and Zubizarreta, 1992). Such alienability can be categorized in several ways. Semantically, when a possessive relation is inalienable, there is an inherent dependency between the possessor and possessum, which does not exist in the case of alienable possessions (Vergnaud and Zubizarreta, 1992). Typical examples of inalienably possessed nouns include kinship terms and body parts; for example, *Mary's brother* and *Mary's hand*, respectively. The family relation and whole-part relation are often considered intrinsic and cannot be transferred. In contrast, an alienable possession, such as *Mary's desk*, does not present such an inherent semantic dependency between the two nouns, and this type of possessive relation needs to be acquired, and can be transferred (Seiler, 1983). Several languages have distinct morphological markings of alienable and inalienable possessions (Dixon, 2000; Meyerhoff, 2002; Gebregziabher, 2012), and various syntactic structures have been proposed for them (Alexiadou, 2003). While Mandarin does not make such distinctions through morphology, some syntactic and pragmatic distinctions between these two classes of possessions exist in it (Hsu and Ting, 2006).

Normally, in Mandarin, the possessor precedes the possessed noun, and they are linearly close to each other; for example, in *laoban de gebo* ('boss's arm'), *laoban* ('boss') is the possessor, and the next noun to appear, *gebo* ('arm'), is the possessum. However, in Mandarin possessive relative clauses (PRCs), as shown in (1), the possessum and possessor are *not* adjacent. PRCs therefore provide us with a useful opportunity to examine the processing cost of resolving different types of possessions, because readers must resolve such a long-distance association to arrive at the possessive relationship between the two nouns.

(1) Fangzi/Fuqin/Gebo bei daitu
house/father/arm PASS criminal
jizhong de laoban hen shengqi.
shot DE boss very angry
'The boss whose house/father/arm was shot by the criminal was angry.'

Moreover, the possessor-possessum position is reversed in (1); i.e., the possessum appears before the possessor. It is expected that when readers encounter a kinship term or a body part, they may

Proceedings of the Workshop on Cognitive Aspects of the Lexicon, pages 16–24
November 20, 2022. ©2022 Association for Computational Linguistics
https://doi.org/10.26615/978-954-452-056-4_002

expect a possessor later in the sentence, and therefore, the inherent semantic dependency should facilitate the resolution of inalienable possessions. In contrast, an alienable possessum may not enjoy this facilitation, because the association between the possessor and the alienable possessum is not inherently salient, and this may result in a greater processing load when resolving the possessive relation becomes necessary in a later phase of sentence comprehension.

Following a review on previous studies about possessive relations and possessive structures in Mandarin (Section 2), we present two experiments (Section 3) in which an acceptability-judgment task (AJT) is used to measure the acceptability of Mandarin PRCs with three different types of possessums: alienable possessums, kinship terms, and body parts. Our results partially support the hypothesis that the inherent semantic dependency of the inalienable possessions facilitate the integration of the possessor-possessum relations, reflected by the higher acceptability of the body parts as the possessum than the alienable noun as the possessum. However, the other inalienable condition, kinship terms as the possessum, received unexpected low ratings. Section 4 briefly concludes this paper, and includes some possible explanations of its unexpected findings.

2 Alienable and Inalienable Possessions in Mandarin

While Mandarin does not require overt morphological markings on (in)alienability, contrasts between alienable and inalienable possessions are reflected at the syntactic, semantic, and discourse levels (Landau, 1999; Hsu and Ting, 2006). In this section, three examples are used to illustrate some of such differences: *de* omission, semantics in the *ba*-construction, and discourse-contextual demands.

Mandarin uses a particle, *de*, to link two nouns to form certain semantic associations, and possessive relation is one of them (Li and Thompson, 1989; Hsu, 2009; Li, 2012). Example (2) is an alienable possessive phrase, and (3) is an inalienable one. When two nouns express a family relation and the possessor is a pronoun, the particle *de* can be omitted, e.g., (2). However, omitting the particle *de* may be ungrammatical if the relation is alienable and when the phrase is presented in isolation, as shown in (3). While kinship relations seem to consistently allow the *de* omission and to enjoy a special status in possessive phrases in the literature, the above-mentioned contrast between (2) and (3) does not always hold. For example, when the inalienable possession is evaluated within context, as shown in example (4), the omission vs. non-omission of *de* does not influence its acceptability.

(2) wo (de) baba
I DE father
'my father'

(3) wo *(de) zhuozi
I DE desk
'my desk'

(4) Wo (de) xuexiao zhengzai juxing
I DE school currently hold
yanjiang bisai.
speech contest
'My school is holding a speech contest.'

The term alienability implies a property or entity that can be conveyed from one individual to another. Putting alienable and inalienable possessions in the *ba*-construction, which often involves a meaning related to disposal, highlights these differences around transferring possession, as well as how such differences of (in)alienability affect sentence acceptability. In (5), the *wallet* originally belonged to *Zhangsan*, establishing an alienable possessive relation, and after a giving event, the possession of the *wallet* is transferred to *Lisi*. In contrast, inalienable possessive phrases exhibit more resistance to transferring possession via the *ba*-construction. For example, sentence (6) is grammatical, only in specific circumstances whereby *Zhangsan*'s sending of his brother to *Lisi* makes sense. Importantly, in this case, the kinship is not actually transferred; that is, the brother is still *Zhangsan*'s. Body parts, on the other hand, cannot be accepted under normal conditions, leading to the unacceptability of (7). [1]

(5) Zhangsan ba qianbao songgeile Lisi.
Zhangsan BA wallet give-ASP Lisi
'Zhangsan has given (his) wallet to Lisi (as a gift).'

[1] "?" indicates that a sentence sounds odd, and "*" indicates that a sentence is ungrammatical.

(6) Zhangsan ba didi songgeile Lisi.
Zhangsan BA brother give-ASP Lisi
'Zhangsan has given (his) brother to Lisi.'

(7) *Zhangsan ba gebo songgeile Lisi.
Zhangsan BA arm give-ASP Lisi
'Zhangsan has given (his) arm to Lisi.'

The effect of (in)alienability on sentence acceptability can also be observed at the discourse level. The semantic distinction between inalienable and alienable possessive nouns is that the former implies a specific possessor in the interlocutors' common ground, whereas the latter does not necessarily trigger such a possessive association, and can stand alone. For example, (8) is acceptable even though it is not specified whose plant it is. In contrast, (9) and (10) are less acceptable if the possessors are not indicated in the discourse.[2]

(8) Zhiwu bei taiyang shaisile。
plant PASS sun burn-die-ASP
'The plant was killed by the sun.'

(9) ?Sunnv bei taiyang
granddaughter PASS sun
shaishangle。
burn-hurt-ASP
'(Someone's) granddaughter was sunburnt.'

(10) ?Gebo bei taiyang shaishangle。
arm PASS sun burn-hurt-ASP
'(Someone's) arm was sun-burnt.'

To summarize, inalienable and alienable possessions trigger different syntactic, semantic, and discourse requirements and these can affect the acceptability of sentences. Nouns related to kinship terms and body parts often trigger a possessive dependency and increase contextual demands, whereas typical nouns allowing alienable possessions behave differently. The following section presents two AJT experiments using Mandarin PRCs to test the effects of (in)alienability on sentences' acceptability.

[2]An anonymous reviewer pointed out that if sentence (9) is used in a conversation, it sounds acceptable because a rational/cooperative listener will assume the speaker to be the possessor. We agree with this observation, and with the same reviewer's observation that in future research, it would therefore be worthwhile to design dialogues with multiple agents expressing sentences like (8) to (10), and use them to investigate people's understandings of them. Here, we originally intended to argue that sentences like (9) and (10) are less acceptable when no possessor can be associated with the subject.

3 Experiments

3.1 Experiment 1

3.1.1 Participants and Procedure

Our participants in Experiment 1 were Mainland Chinese college students studying in Hong Kong, all of whom were native speakers of Mandarin. Their average self-rated Mandarin proficiency on a scale of 1 to 7 (with 1 = 'not fluent at all', and 7 = 'extremely fluent') was 6.75. Attention filters were included in the experiment to ensure that the participants understood the task and finished it conscientiously. Of the initial pool of 114 participants, 17 failed the attention filters, leaving 97 participants' data for analysis.

The participants rated the acceptability of the sentences on a 5-point Likert scale, ranging from 1 as 'totally unacceptable' to 5 as 'totally acceptable'. The data were collected using an online questionnaire platform.

3.1.2 Materials

Mandarin PRCs were adopted as the basis for our investigation of the cost of the possessor-possessum integration among three different possessive conditions. In the PRCs used in Experiment 1, the possessum was at the beginning of the realtive clause, and the possessor – immediately following the relativizer particle *de* – was the head noun of the relative clause, locating at the end of the relative clause. The possessor also served as the matrix subject of the experimental sentence. Because the possessor and the possessum were not adjacent, the participants reading these sentences needed to form long-distance associations. Example (11) consists of one set of the experimental conditions, in which Condition A is the alienable condition, and Conditions B and C are inalienable ones, for kinship terms and body parts, respectively. In addition, a short context sentence was provided before each of the PRC target sentences, to help them read more naturally. In all, Twenty-four sets were constructed and were distributed into four lists [3]; each participant only read one condition from each set.

[3]Because filler items from other studies were included, there were four lists instead of three.

(11) (Context) In this extremely hot weather,

a. Zhiwu bei taiyang shaisi de
plant PASS sun burn-die DE
A-Yong gandao shifen shangxin.
A-Yong feel very sad
'A-Yong, whose plant was killed by the sun, felt very sad.'

b. Sunnv bei taiyang
granddaughter PASS sun
shaishang de A-Yong gandao
burn-hurt DE A-Yong feel
shifen shangxin.
very sad
'A-Yong, whose granddaughter was sunburnt, felt very sad.'

c. Gebo bei taiyang shaishang de
arm PASS sun burn-hurt DE
A-Yong gandao shifen shangxin.
A-Yong feel very sad
'A-Yong, whose arms were sunburnt, felt very sad.'

It has been argued that sentences with higher complexity are likely be harder to process, and consequently, readers tend to rate their acceptability as lower (Chomsky and Miller, 1968; Fanselow and Frisch, 2006). Our items were designed to be completely uniform in their structural complexity. Yet, as compared to inalienable possessions, alienable ones may be more costly to integrate, as doing so calls for the possessor to acquire the possessor-possessum relations (Alexiadou, 2003). Therefore, we predicted that the inalienable conditions (Conditions B and C) would receive higher AJT ratings than the alienable one (Condition A).

3.1.3 Results

The mean rating and standard deviation (SD) for each condition are listed in Table 1. Condition C, in which the body parts were the possessed nouns, received the highest mean acceptability rating. Condition A, the alienable condition, was rated as less acceptably on average than Condition C was. But surprisingly, the other inalienable condition, Condition B, received the lowest acceptability rating. The results of the three conditions are visualized in Figure 1, in which the box represents 50% of the central data, and the line inside it representing the median. The whiskers are the range of the data excluding outliers, which are indicated by the small black dots. The three large black dots are the average ratings of each condition. The colored dots are the average ratings by item. The lines connecting the colored dots indicate that items are from the same sentence set.

Condition	Mean	SD
A(alienable nouns)	4.07	1.22
B(kinship terms)	3.36	1.44
C(body parts)	4.43	0.87

Table 1: Average ratings and standard deviations for each condition.

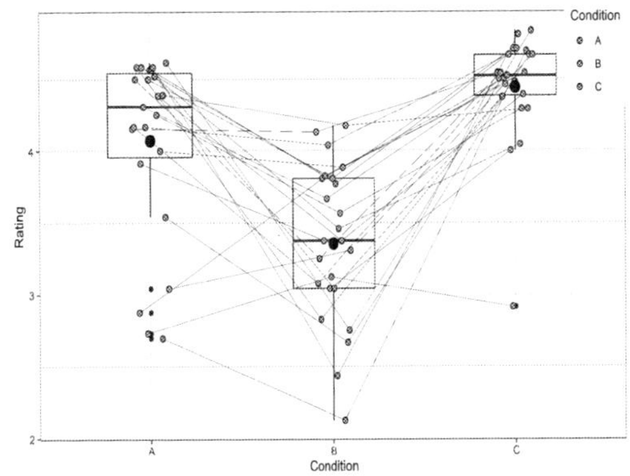

Figure 1: Ratings for different conditions, Experiment 1.

To test whether the differences among the conditions were significant, a cumulative link mixed model was fit using the clmm() function in the ordinal package in R. The outcome variable was RATING, and the predictor was CONDITION, which had three levels: Condition A, Condition B, and Condition C. The random variables were PARTICIPANT and ITEM, including varying intercepts. A pairwise post hoc analysis showed that the differences among the conditions were significant (Table 2).

To summarize, the inalienable condition in which body parts were the possessed nouns being rated highest, and was significantly higher than the alienable condition.

However, the kinship-terms condition's rating

Contrast	Estimate	SE	*z*.ratio	*p*.value
A - B	-1.397	0.125	-11.166	<.0001
A - C	0.837	0.133	6.297	<.0001
B - C	2.235	0.136	16.395	<.0001

Table 2: Contrasts among conditions; Model: Rating C̃ondition + (1|Participant) + (1|Item)

was significantly lower than that of the other two conditions. We wonder whether this was because some kinship terms used in the materials, such as, *zhier* ('brother's son'), and *waisun* ('daughter's son'), are not as frequently encountered in day-to-day Madnarin speech as the other kinship terms. Specifically, the occurrence of the kinship terms in the BCC corpus (`http://bcc.blcu.edu.cn/`; Mean: 34086, Range: 2555-144007) was also markedly lower than those of the alienable nouns (Mean: 584435, Range: 3067-172563), and body parts (Mean: 45939, Range: 10875-232015). Hence, we balanced both the frequencies of words across the three conditions, and then conducted another round of AJT, as reported below.

3.2 Experiment 2

3.2.1 Participants and Procedure

Sixty-six college students from Mainland China who had not participated in Experiment 1 were recruited for Experiment 2. All self-reported Mandarin as their native language. The procedure of this AJT experiment was the same for Experiment 1, except that, after the participants finished the experiment *per se*, we interviewed some of them who had given low ratings to most of the Condition B items (kinship terms).

3.2.2 Materials

Experiment 2's materials were similar to those of Experiment 1, except in the following two respects. First, some of the critical words (i.e., the possessum) were changed to maintain a balance counts of strokes across conditions (Range and Mean for each condition: A: 9-22, 14.63; B: 5-26, 14.54; C: 8-28 16.67) and the frequencies of words (Range and Mean for each condition: A: 3067-172563, 51034; B: 4331-144007, 38814; C: 10152-232015, 61621; frequency is according to the BCC corpus). Second, to lower processing demand, the predicate of each experimental sentence was shortened, from 16 characters (as in Experiment 1), to 14 characters (the separate context sentences were unaffected). For example, *gandao* ('feel') in (11) was dropped, and the sentence remained grammatical.

3.2.3 Results

The results of Experiment 2 closely replicated the findings in Experiment 1. That is, body parts as the possessed nouns (Condition C) received the highest rating (Mean = 4.15, SD = 1.03), the alienable possession (Condition A) was rated lower (Mean = 3.85, SD = 1.13); and the kinship terms as the possessum (Condition B) once more received the lowest rating (Mean = 3.16, SD = 1.27). The clmm() model and pairwise comparisons again showed the differences among conditions were significant (*ps* $< .0001$).

Importantly, the group variance of the kinship-terms condition was also the largest, which is another repetition of the findings of Experiment 1. To ensure that this unexpected result did not arise because a few items received extremely low ratings while others were acceptable, we looked for systematic differences among the average ratings for each item.[4] However, this item-by-item analysis revealed no such differences. Indeed, among the 24 kinship terms we tested, 21 received average ratings lower than 3.5, as against overall average ratings for the alienable-nouns and body-parts conditions of 3.85 and 4.15, respectively. Specifically, the majority of kinship terms used as the possessum were rated as 'probably unacceptable' or 'not sure'.

We also conducted individual-level analysis, which revealed that not all participants assigned low ratings to Condition B. That is, a subset of them consistently rejected Condition B, while another tended to find its items acceptable. Therefore, we decided to reexamine the results in terms of the participants' *tendency* to accept items in each condition. In Experiment 2, all participants read eight sentences from each condition, and we deemed them to have rejected a given condition if they rated at least six out of the eight as '1-totally unacceptable' or '2-probably unacceptable'. Conversely, if a participant rated six out of the eight sentences in a condition as '4-probably acceptable' or '5-totally acceptable', they were counted as accepting that condition. Other cases were classified as 'not sure'. Table 3 summarizes the numbers and percentages of participants who rejected, accepted, or were unsure about each condition. No participants consistently rejected Condition A or Condition C, and indeed, the majority of them consistently accepted these two conditions. But twelve participants consistently rejected Condition B. For that reason, we conducted a post-experiment interviews with these 12 participants. Data from the interviews will be presented and dis-

[4]This was done at the suggestion of an anonymous reviewer. We appreciate this advice.

Condition	Rejecting	Accepting	Not Sure
A	0 (0.00)	34 (51.52)	32 (48.48)
B	12 (18.18)	20 (30.30)	34 (51.52)
C	0 (0.00)	50 (75.76)	16 (24.24)

Table 3: Numbers and percentages (in parentheses) of participants rejecting and accepting each condition.

cussed in the next section.

4 Discussion and Concluding Remarks

Our study sought to explore whether different types of possessive relations affect the integration of long-distance dependency in Mandarin relative clauses. This study supports the (in)alienablity effect in some respects. The fact that our participants gave their highest acceptability ratings to PRCs with body parts as their possessed nouns suggests that inherent part-whole association facilitates the resolution of the possessor-possessum relations inside of relative clauses. In other words, when readers encounter a term for a body part, they expect to find a possessor in the sentence to fulfill the semantic dependency. Thus, Condition C of body parts being rated more acceptable than the inalienable Condition A was consistent with our prediction, and supports the idea that inherent semantic association facilitates the resolution of long-distance dependency.

When we consider subtypes of alienable possessive relationships, however, we found some unexpected results. Given the operation of (in)alienability effects in the resolution of long-distance dependency, it would be reasonable to predict that kinship terms as the possessed nouns should also receive ratings higher than those in the alienable condition, just as we found with nouns in the condition of body parts. However, our results contradicted this prediction: Condition B received the lowest ratings. This may be related to an essential characteristic of Condition B: that both the possessor and possessum are humans, unlike in the other two conditions in which the possessum is inanimate. The same [+human] feature may interfere with the resolution of 'who did what to whom' in a relative clause that contains multiple animate references (Mak et al., 2002; Gordon et al., 2001, 2002). Moreover, kinship terms in our experimental items appear at the beginning of the clause, which tends to be regarded as the subject in shallow processing (Christianson et al., 2001; Qian et al., 2018; Ferreira et al., 2002). Coupled with the [+human] feature, the clause's initial position gives the kinship term great salience, but as the sentence unfolds, it turns out that it is possessed by the head noun and is not the subject of the sentence. This contradiction requires a proper reanalysis of thematic roles, resulting in a demand of additional processing demand, and therefore lower ratings of acceptability ratings.

Interview comments made by those Experiment 2 participants who rated Condition B as having low acceptability supported these views. As Table 3 shows, twelve participants consistently rated PRCs with kinship terms as the possessum as unacceptable. When we asked them why, one participant commented that she rated sentences like (12) low because their meanings did not correspond to her expectations: since it was the *qinqi* ('relative') who was hit, it should be that *qinqi* rather than the other person (*Laofeng*) should be sympathized with. Another participant reported that she found such sentences illogical because they mixed important information from the insignificant nouns. These comments support our conjecture that the two human nouns in Condition B require readers to decide whether the main event is expressed by the possessum or the possessor, complicating the comprehension process for the sentence as a whole. It is important to note that these concerns could not arise in the other two conditions because the possessed nouns were inanimate, and thus did not fit the descriptions of the predicate.

(12) Qinqi bei meiti dashang de
relative PASS press hit-hurt DE
Laofeng shiren tongqing.
Laofeng evoke sympathy
'Laofeng, whose relatives were hit and hurt by the press, evoked sympathy.'

Some participants seemed to adopt the 'good-enough' processing strategy (Qian et al., 2018) when they rated the sentences;[5] therefore, the additional processing efforts required by items in Condition B rendered them unable to comprehend such sentences. One participant reported that

[5]One anonymous reviewer suggested that we conduct a follow-up study in which the level of processing (shallow or deep) is manipulated by including a secondary task. We appreciated this suggestion very much, and plan to conduct an eye-tracking experiment in which the participants answer comprehension questions, designed to trigger different levels of processing, after reading the sentences.

PRCs with kinship terms as the possessum were too challenging for him to process, so he just rated them as 'unacceptable' and admitted that if he had spent more time reading such sentences, he would have understood them. We did not ask our participants to answer comprehension questions in this AJT paradigm, but it is possible that their processing was shallow (Sanford and Graesser, 2006). It would be intriguing to examine if, when a deep comprehension processing is forced, participants' ratings for the PRCs with kinship terms as the possessums would be higher. Further studies could explore this possible phenomenon by modifying our tasks, e.g., by including comprehension questions or asking the participants to 'think aloud' while making the judgements.

Notably, our findings that the body-parts condition was rated the highest, then the alienable possessions, and then the kinships, are consistent with the frequency results of a corpus study on the Mandarin passive construction with retained objects (PCRO) (Yue and Wu, 2019). PCROs with body parts, alienable possessions, and kinship terms as the retained objects are illustrated in (13-15):

(13) Ta bei daduanle biliang.
he PASS hit-broken-ASP nose
'His nose was broken (by someone).'

(14) Ta bei ren touzoule
He PASS someone steel-away-ASP
qianbao.
wallet
'His wallet was stolen by someone.'

(15) Ta bei ren qiangle laogong.
she PASS people rob-ASP husband
'Her husband was taken away from her by someone else.'

In a PCRO, the subject and the retained object formed a possessive relationship, and like the PRC structure in our study, the possessor and possessum are not adjacent to each other. The results of corpus analyses (Yue and Wu, 2019) show that body parts are the most common retained objects, accounting for 41.7% of all 422 instances, whereas typical nouns as the alienable possessums made up 29.8% of the data. Although kinship terms are allowed in possessive phrases, there were only nine instances found in the corpus, making up 1.9% of the PCROs found in the corpus. Yue and Wu (2019) argued from a cognitive perspective that the possessive relationship needs to have inferential accessibility, and that retained objects should be included in the semantic framework of the subject. The animacy and the cognitive prominence of the kinship terms both make it difficult for them to be the objects of PCROs. This idea echoes our suggestions that the [+human] feature and the clause-initial position of kinship terms seem to increase PRCs' processing loads.

This leaves one to wonder if the (in)alienability effect would come into force for kinship terms if the [+human] feature were controlled in the alienable and inalienable conditions. Lin (2007) developed a self-paced reading experiment using human nouns as the possessums for both the inalienable condition (16a) and the alienable condition (16b), and showed that the reading time for the head nouns of the inalienable condition (16a) was significantly faster than that for the alienable condition (16b). This finding supports the facilitation by inherent inalienable semantics.

(16) a. Fuqin bei jingcha zhuazou
father PASS police take
de zongcai xiande shifen
DE boss appear very
huangzhang.
nervous
'The boss whose father was taken by the police appeared very nervous.'

b. Yuangong bei jingcha zhuazou
employee PASS police take
de zongcai xiande shifen
DE boss appear very
huangzhang.
nervous
'The boss whose father was taken by the police appeared very nervous.'

It is important to bear in mind that our findings were based on two AJT experiments. Although people's explicit judgments can reflect the processing difficulties of sentences to some extent (Chomsky and Miller, 1968; Fanselow and Frisch, 2006), it would be worthwhile in the future to use online methods, such as the self-paced reading paradigm and eye-tracking technology, to measure readers' reaction times and eye-gaze patterns when processing PRCs. We also assumed that readers would search for a possessor when they found the inalienable possessum at the beginning of the sentence.

That means a gap would be detected as long as readers encountered the first noun in the two inalienable conditions. Several following-up questions could usefully be asked about this presumably detected gap. For instance, do readers start searching for potential fillers for this gap as soon as they detected it? Would this gap results in a temporary slowdown in reading times, due to the unit being unresolved and needing to be held in mind? Does early preparation for a filler-gap dependency facilitate the processing of the latter part of the sentence? Because answering them will require fine-grained and region-specific data, we leave these questions to our future research.

To conclude, our results demonstrate the following effects of (in)alienability on sentence acceptability. First, semantically inherent whole-part relationships facilitate the resolution of the long-distance dependency between the possessor and possessum in PRCs. Second, the fact that the kinship terms, despite also forming alienable possessions, received the lowest acceptability ratings in both our AJT experiments suggests that the [+human] feature and/or the salient syntactic position led to considerable confusions when the readers only adopted shallow processing. Previous research has found that when the possessed nouns are human nouns for both the inalienable and alienable conditions, the former has a processing advantage (Lin, 2007). Thus, future studies could explore more types of possessive relationships in different syntactic structures, as well as using different experimental paradigms to test the (in)alienability effects on sentence comprehension and processing.

Acknowledgements

We would like to thank the three anonymous reviewers for their insightful comments. We would also like to thank Bingxian Chen and Chenxin Liu for their technical support. This research was made possible by the department general research fund (G-UALS) from the Department of Chinese and Bilingual Studies at the Hong Kong Polytechnic University.

References

Artemis Alexiadou. 2003. Some notes on the structure of alienable and inalienable possessors. In Martine Coene and Yves D' hulst, editors, *From NP to DP: Volume 2: The Expression of Possession in Noun Phrases*, chapter 6, pages 167–188. John Benjamins, Amsterdam.

Noam Chomsky and George A. Miller. 1968. Introduction to the formal analysis of natural languages. *Journal of Symbolic Logic*, 33(2):299–300.

Kiel Christianson, Andrew Hollingworth, John F Halliwell, and Fernanda Ferreira. 2001. Thematic roles assigned along the garden path linger. *Cognitive psychology*, 42(4):368–407.

Robert MW Dixon. 2000. Categories of the noun phrase in jarawara. *Journal of Linguistics*, 36(3):487–510.

Gisbert Fanselow and Stefan Frisch. 2006. Effects of processing difficulty on judgments of acceptability. *Gradience in grammar: Generative perspectives*, pages 291–316.

Fernanda Ferreira, Karl GD Bailey, and Vittoria Ferraro. 2002. Good-enough representations in language comprehension. *Current directions in psychological science*, 11(1):11–15.

Keffyalew Gebregziabher. 2012. The alienable-inalienable asymmetry: Evidence from tigrinya. In *Selected Proceedings of the 42nd Annual Conference on African Linguistics*, pages 161–182.

Peter C Gordon, Randall Hendrick, and Marcus Johnson. 2001. Memory interference during language processing. *Journal of experimental psychology: learning, memory, and cognition*, 27(6):1411.

Peter C Gordon, Randall Hendrick, and William H Levine. 2002. Memory-load interference in syntactic processing. *Psychological science*, 13(5):425–430.

Yu-Yin Hsu. 2009. Possessor extraction in mandarin chinese. In *University of Pennsylvania Working Papers in Linguistics*, volume 15.

Yu-Yin Hsu and Jen Ting. 2006. On the possessive multiple nominative construction in mandarin chinese. In *14th Annual Conference of the International Association of Chinese Linguistics*.

Idan Landau. 1999. Possessor raising and the structure of vp. *Lingua*, 107(1-2):1–37.

Charles N Li and Sandra A Thompson. 1989. *Mandarin Chinese: A functional reference grammar*, volume 3. Univ of California Press.

Y-H Audrey Li. 2012. de in mandarin e in taiwanese. *Studies in Chinese Linguistics*, 33(1):17–40.

Chien-Jer Charles Lin. 2007. Processing (in)alienable possessions at the syntax-semantics interface. In *Interfaces in linguistics: New research perspectives*. Citeseer, Oxford University Press.

Willem M Mak, Wietske Vonk, and Herbert Schriefers. 2002. The influence of animacy on relative clause processing. *Journal of memory and language*, 47(1):50–68.

Miriam Meyerhoff. 2002. Formal and cultural constraints on optional objects in bislama. *Language Variation and Change*, 14(3):323–346.

Zhiying Qian, Susan Garnsey, and Kiel Christianson. 2018. A comparison of online and offline measures of good-enough processing in garden-path sentences. *Language, Cognition and Neuroscience*, 33(2):227–254.

Anthony J Sanford and Arthur C Graesser. 2006. Shallow processing and underspecification. *Discourse Processes*, 42(2):99–108.

Hansjakob Seiler. 1983. Possessivity, subject and object. *Studies in Language. International Journal sponsored by the Foundation "Foundations of Language"*, 7(1):89–117.

Jean-Roger Vergnaud and Maria Luisa Zubizarreta. 1992. The definite determiner and the inalienable constructions in french and in english. *Linguistic inquiry*, 23(4):595–652.

Hui Yue and Heng Wu. 2019. Types of possessive relationship and cognitive analysis on the licensing of prco. *Chinese Teaching in the World*, 33:58–69.

Do age of acquisition and orthographic transparency have the same effects in different modalities?

Mohammad Momenian
Department of Chinese and Bilingual Studies, Faculty of Humanities
The Hong Kong Polytechnic University
Yuk Choi Road 11, Hung Hom, Kowloon, Hong Kong
mohammad.momenian@polyu.edu.hk

Abstract

This paper is intended to study the effects of age of acquisition (AoA) and orthographic transparency on word retrieval in Persian, which is an understudied language. A naming task (both pictures and words) and a recall task (both pictures and words) were used to explore how lexical retrieval and verbal memory are affected by AoA and transparency. Seventy two native speakers of Persian were recruited to participate in two experiments. The results showed that early acquired words are processed faster than late acquired words only when pictures were used as stimuli. Transparency of the words was not an influential factor. However, in the recall experiment a three-way interaction was observed: early acquired pictures and words were processed faster than late acquired stimuli except the words in the transparent condition. The findings speak to the fact that language-specific properties of languages are very important.

1 Introduction

The majority of research on word retrieval and recall are done only on few languages of the word such as English (Cycowicz et al.,1997; Snodgrass & Vanderwart,1980), Dutch (Shao & Stiegert, 2016), French (Alario & Ferrand,1999; Bonin et al.,2003), Spanish (Cuetos et al.,1999; Manoiloff et al.,2010) and Italian (Dell'Acqua et al., 2000; Navarrete et al., 2019). There are only few reports available in other languages of the world such as Persian.

Age of acquisition (AoA) is known to have a strong effect on word retrieval. Words which are learned earlier are usually processed faster than late acquired words (Alario et al.,2004). This finding has been replicated across several languages in

Fixed effects	Estimate	Std. Error	t value
(Intercept)	915.32	31.44	29.11
Condition	265.35	-37.34	-7.10
AoA	169.14	17.16	9.86
Condition*AoA	-147.16	15.59	-9.44

Random effects	Variance	Standard Deviation
Items	2833	53.22
Subjects	10540	102.66
Residual	31399	177.20

Table 1: Summary of significant effects in the reaction time experiment

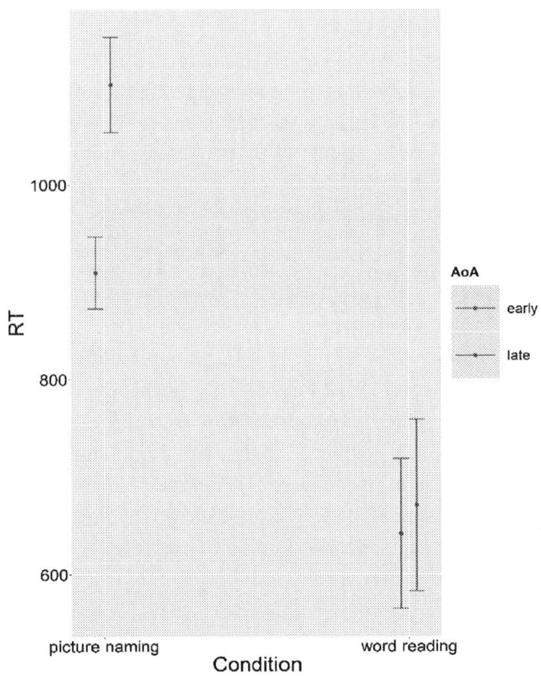

Figure 1: Interaction between Condition and AoA

Proceedings of the Workshop on Cognitive Aspects of the Lexicon, pages 25–30
November 20, 2022. ©2022 Association for Computational Linguistics
https://doi.org/10.26615/978-954-452-056-4_003

picture naming. However, when it comes to word recall, the findings are mixed. For example, Cortese et al. (2010, 2015) showed that later acquired stimuli were recalled better than early acquired ones. Raman et al., (2018) found no effects of AoA.

Where AoA effect interacts with orthographic transparency is another question. Orthographic transparency refers to the level of consistency in grapheme to morpheme correspondence. For instance, the word car is orthographically transparent, while the word night is not. Arbitrary Mapping Hypothesis (AMH) (Ellis & Lambon Ralph, 2000) posits that AoA effect is only observable in words where print to sound correspondence is inconsistent (opaque). They believe that AoA effects is diminished in the transparent orthographies. Findings from highly transparent orthographies in other languages such as Turkish failed to replicate the predictions of AMH (Raman, 2006).

The aim of this paper is to see if previous findings could be replicated in Persian which is an understudied language. Persian orthography is both opaque and transparent thus allowing researchers to test AoA effects within one single language. This report is intended to see if AoA interacts with transparency similarly across both naming and recall tasks.

If predictions of ARH are correct, it is hypothesized that in both modalities (words vs. picture) of naming and recall tasks AoA should only show an effect in the opaque condition. In the transparent condition, AoA effect should disappear based on ARH predictions.

2 Methods

2. 1 Participants

Number of participants in this study included 72 native speakers of Farsi. Thirty six people participated in the naming experiment (mean age: 23.27, gender: 22 male) and 36 in the recall experiment (mean age: 21.56, gender: 17 male). They were all undergraduate university students. The participants had normal or corrected to normal visual acuity, and reported no history of neurological or psychiatric disorders. They received course credit and gave informed consent before their participation.

2. 2 Materials

Sixty words and their pictures were selected from Farsi Snodgrass and Vanderwart naming battery (Bakhtiar, Nilipour, & Weekes, 2013). These words and pictures were divided, on the basis of a 3.8 cut-off point, into two categories: early acquired and late acquired words. Each category of words was then divided into 15 opaque and 15 transparent ones. The stimuli included both tools and animals. Orthographic transparency was defined based on how well the letters in a word were matched with the sounds in the same words. For instance, the word 'car' in English is transparent, but 'psychology' is not as transparent because not all the letters have a phonological representation in the production stage of the word.

2.3 Procedure

Recall experiment: in this experiment the participants were required to recall the words and pictures that were just presented to them. Half of the participants recalled the words and the other half recalled the pictures. It should be noted that a distractor task was performed by the participants for about two minutes after the presentation of the words or pictures was finished in order to create a delay in the recall process. After this, the participants were required to write down as many names as possible they could remember. There was no time limit on finishing the task.

Reaction time experiment: This experiment follows the same procedure adopted in the recall one. Using DMDX software, half of the participants named the pictures. In the same session, the other half of the participants read words for the same pictures. Ten words or pictures were used as practice items so that the participants would get familiar with the type of the task. Each word was shown to the participants for 1500ms and each picture was presented for 2000ms. If participants could not answer in the time provided, the software moved on to the next item automatically. Participants were instructed not to cough or make any unnecessary noises during this task particularly at the beginning of each picture. Any response which did not match with the correct most dominant name of the picture was considered incorrect.

3 Results

Linear Mixed Effect (LME) Modeling is gaining popularity in psycholinguistic research. LME modeling offers several advantages over the classic statistical analyses. LME modeling takes into account item and subject random effects which leads to higher generalizability of findings to the larger population and stimuli (Baayen, Davidson, & Bates, 2008). In this study, lme4 package (https://cran.r-project.org/web/packages/lme4/) was used in R software (R Development Core Team, 2012) in order to analyze the data in both experiments.

3. 1 Reaction time experiment

Our dependent variable was transformed reaction time (RT) using common log trans-formation. The model tested included all fixed variables such as AoA (early vs. late), transparency (transparent vs. opaque), and condition (picture vs. print) and their interactions along with the random effects for subjects and items. Random intercepts were not included because the variables had less than 5 levels which could result in singularity. To test the collinearity among the variables, a variance inflation factor (VIF) was used. Variables with a VIF above 5 should be removed from the analysis based on the recommendation by Craney and Surles (2002). In order to find which variables and interaction had significant effects, conditional F-tests were adopted because doing Lilehood Ratio Tests (LRT) on the fixed effects is anti-conservative and could result in misleading findings (Pinheiro & Bates,2000). Kenward-Roger approximations were used to calculate denominator degrees of freedom which have shown more acceptable type 1 error rates in comparison with LRT and Wald tests (Kuznetsova, Brockhoff, &Christensen,2017).

The results of the analysis for this section are presented in Table 1. Since the interaction between Condition and AoA is significant, it doesn't make sense to look into main effects. See Figure 1 for the interaction patterns.

3. 2 Recall experiment

Since the response variable in this experiment was a binomial variable, a generalized linear mixed effect model (GLMER) was used. First, a full model was created including AoA, transparency, and condition as main effects, AoA*transparency*condition as the interaction effect, and random effects of subjects and items. Conditional F-tests were used to find the significant effects just like the reaction time experiment.

The results of the analysis for the recall experiment are presented in Table 2. For the interactions, see Figure 2.

4 Discussion and Conclusion

Regardless of the interaction patterns, the significant effect of AoA in this report is in line with many previous picture naming studies in other languages (Alario et al., 2004) and Persian (Nilipour, Bakhtiar, Momenian, & Weekes, 2017). Words and pictures which were learned earlier were processed faster and recalled more accurately than the late acquired stimuli regardless of the modality. However, the existence of interactions in both the reaction time and recall analyses reveals that AoA effect is more complicated than a simple main effect.

The results of the reaction time experiment are not consistent with previous studies. First, there was no interaction between AoA and transparency predicted by AMH (Morrison & Ellis, 2000). Second, AoA had a significant effect only in the picture naming modality, while the effect disappeared in the word reading modality. It is believed that AoA is a fundamental property of lexical retrieval and is independent of the modality. In other words, no matter whether the stimuli are presented as print or picture, the effect should be there. This is a counterintuitive finding which needs further investigation in the future studies.

The results from the recall experiment are partially consistent with AHM. Although, transparency and AoA did not have any interaction in the picture recall, the interaction observed in the word recall is consistent with AHM predictions. Based on AHM predictions, the AoA effect disappeared in the transparent

Fixed effects	Estimate	Std. Error	z value
(Intercept)	-1.11	0.10	-10.2
AoA	-0.62	0.17	-3.66
Condition*AoA *Transparency	1.02	0.40	2.49

Random effects	Variance	Standard Deviation
Items	0.27	0.52
Subjects	0.15	0.39

Table 2: Summary of significant effects in the recall experiment

condition. What is still counterintuitive is that why this effect is only observed in word recall and not in picture recall. If AoA effect is independent of modality, a similar effect should have been witnessed in both modalities.

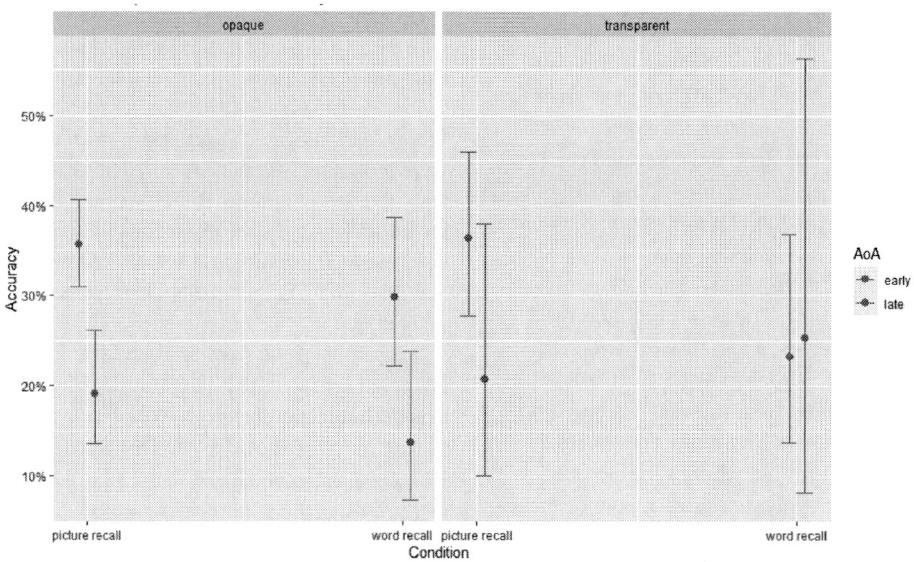

Figure 2: The interactions in the recall experiment

We did not control for other variables such as imageability, visual complexity, familiarity, and frequency. It's possible that the effects observed in this study could be attributed to lack of control over these variables. The number of items was not too many limiting the power of the study and hence generalizability of the findings. Moreover, the participants in the reaction time and recall experiments were different which could be another limitation due to lack of control over inter-individual variability. For these reasons, we believe our findings should be interpreted with caution. However, the counterintuitive findings could pave the way for future studies in other languages. We need more studies with null or counterintuitive effects indeed.

The data and codes for this manuscript are available at the following DOI 10.17605/OSF.IO/RTPH6.

References

Alario, F. X., & Ferrand, L. 1999. A set of 400 pictures standardized for French: Norms for name agreement, image agreement, familiarity, visual complexity, image variability, and age of acquisition. *Behavior Research Methods, Instruments, & Computers : A Journal of the Psychonomic Society,31*(3), 531–552.

Alario, F. X., Ferrand, L., Laganaro, M., New, B., Frauenfelder, U. H., & Segui, J. 2004. Predictors of picture naming speed. *Behavior Research Methods, 36*(1), 140-155.

Bakhtiar, M., Nilipour, R., & Weekes, B. S. 2013. Predictors of timed picture naming in Persian. *Behavior Research Methods, 45*(3), 834-841.

Baayen, R. H., Davidson, D. J., & Bates, D. M. 2008. Mixed-effects modeling with crossed random effects for subjects and items. *Journal of memory and language, 59*(4), 390-412.

Bonin, P., Meot, A., Lagarrigue, A., & Roux, S. 2015. Written object naming, spelling to dictation, and immediate copying: Different tasks, different pathways? *Quarterly Journal of Experimental Psychology ,68*(7), 1268–1294.

Cortese, M. J., Khanna, M. M., & Hacker, S. 2010. Recognition memory for 2,578 monosyllabic words. *Memory, 18*(6), 595-609.

Cortese, M. J., McCarty, D. P., & Schock, J. 2015. A mega recognition memory study of 2897 disyllabic words. *The Quarterly Journal of Experimental Psychology, 68*(8), 1489-1501.

Craney, T. A., & Surles, J. G. 2002. Model-Dependent Variance Inflation Factor Cutoff Values. *Quality Engineering, 14*(3), 391-403.

Cuetos, F., Ellis, A. W., & Alvarez, B. 1999. Naming times for the Snodgrass and Vanderwart pictures in Spanish. *Behavior Research Methods, Instruments, & Computers: A Journal of the Psychonomic Society, 31*(4), 650–658.

Cycowicz,Y.M., Friedman,D., Rothstein,M.,& Snodgrass,J.G. 1997. Picture naming by young children: Norms for name agreement, familiarity, and visual complexity. *Journal of Experimental Child Psychology, 65*(2), 171–237.

Dell'Acqua, R., Lotto, L., & Job, R. 2000. Naming times and standardized norms for the Italian PD/DPSS set of 266 pictures: Direct comparisons with American, English, French, and Spanish published databases. *Behavior Research Methods, Instruments, & Computers: A Journal of the Psychonomic Society,32*(4), 588–615.

Ellis, A. W., & Lambon Ralph, M. A. 2000. Age of acquisition effects in adult lexical processing reflect loss of plasticity in maturing systems: Insights from connectionist networks. *Journal of Experimental Psychology: Learning, Memory, and Cognition,26*(5),1103/1123.

Kuznetsova, A., Brockhoff, P. B., & Christensen, R. H. B. 2017. lmerTest Package: Tests in Linear Mixed Effects Models. *Journal of Statistical Software, 82* (13), 26.

Manoiloff, L., Artstein, M., Canavoso, M. B., Fernandez, L., & Segui, J. 2010. Expanded norms for 400 experimental pictures in an Argentinean Spanish-speaking population. *Behavior Research Methods,42*(2), 452–460.

Morrison, C. M., & Ellis, A. W. 2000. Real age of acquisition effects in word naming and lexical decision. *Br J Psychol, 91 (Pt 2)*, 167-180.

Navarrete, E., Arcara, G., Mondini, S., & Penolazzi, B. (2019). Italian norms and naming latencies for 357 high quality color images. *PLoSOne,14*(2), e0209524.

Nilipour, R., Bakhtiar, M., Momenian, M., & Weekes, B. S. 2017. Object and action picture naming in brain-damaged Persian speakers with aphasia. *Aphasiology, 31*(4), 388-405.

Pinheiro, J., & Bates, D. 2000. *Mixed-Effects Models in S and S-PLUS*.USA: Springer.

Raman, I. (2006). On the age-of-acquisition effects in word naming and orthographic transparency: Mapping specific or universal? *Visual cognition, 13*(7-8), 1044-1053.

Raman, I., Raman, E., İkier, S., Kilecioğlu, E., Uzun Eroğlu, D., & Zeyveli, Ş. 2018. Differential effects of age of acquisition and frequency on memory: evidence from free recall of pictures and words in Turkish. *Writing Systems Research, 10*(1), 1-14.

Snodgrass, J. G., & Vanderwart, M. 1980. A standardized set of 260pictures: Norms for name agreement, image agreement, familiarity, and visual complexity. *Journal of Experimental Psychology: Human Learning and Memory,6*(2), 174.

Response to reviewers' comments:

I included figures in the manuscript which clearly show the RTs and accuracy for each condition.

I updated the analysis pipeline adding a few points which were missing in the previous manuscript.

The codes and data have been made available online at the following DOI 10.17605/OSF.IO/RTPH6.

I added extensive information to the introduction and discussion making the paper fitter for CogAlex objectives and audience.

CAT ManyNames: a New Dataset for Object Naming in Catalan

Mar Domínguez Orfila
Universitat Pompeu Fabra
Barcelona Supercomputing Center
mar.dominguez01@estudiant.upf.edu

Maite Melero Nogués
Barcelona Supercomputing Center
maite.melero@bsc.es

Gemma Boleda Torrent
Universitat Pompeu Fabra
gemma.boleda@upf.edu

Abstract

Object Naming is an important task within the field of Language and Vision that consists of generating a correct and appropriate name for an object given an image. The ManyNames dataset uses real-world human annotated images with multiple labels, instead of just one. In this work, we describe the adaptation of this dataset (originally in English) to Catalan, by (i) machine-translating the English labels and (ii) collecting human annotations for a subset of the original corpus and comparing both resources. Analyses reveal divergences in the lexical variation of the two sets showing potential problems of directly translated resources, particularly when there is no resource to a proper context, which in this case is conveyed by the image. The analysis also points to the impact of cultural factors in the naming task, which should be accounted for in future cross-lingual naming tasks.

1 Introduction

Most NLP resources are only available for a small percentage of languages (Joshi et al., 2020), being the rest of the languages spoken in the world left behind. This affects also Catalan, which can be considered a moderately under-resourced language (Armengol-Estapé et al., 2021). In the Language and Vision area, although significantly large datasets of annotated images have been created for a variety of tasks for English, to date no resources of this kind exist for Catalan. In this work we present CAT ManyNames[1], the Catalan version of the ManyNames dataset, which is the first available resource for the task of Object Naming in Catalan. The dataset has been translated from the English version and its test set has been human annotated to assess the quality of the translation. We also provide analyses of the sources of variation between the human annotated dataset and its translated counterpart.

2 Background

2.1 Object Naming: an Interdisciplinary Task

Naming an object accounts for picking out a nominal to refer to it (Silberer et al., 2020a), and is a linguistic phenomenon that can show lexical variation. On the one hand, objects can belong to different semantic categories at the same time (i.e., a baby boy belongs to the categories PERSON, CHILD, BOY, HUMAN, etc.), which, according to Brown (Brown, 1958) could all be valid alternatives for naming that object. On the other hand, the three different levels within semantic categorization[2] identified by Rosch et al. (Rosch et al., 1976) can all be valid alternatives for naming the same object as well. Although the basic-level categories are considered to be the most natural terms for speakers when referring to objects (Hajibayova, 2013; Jolicoeur et al., 1984; Rosch et al., 1976), these are not universal categories since they are restricted by perceptive, cognitive and environmental factors that can result in lexical variation (Berlin, 2014; Graf et al., 2016; Malt, 1995; Wierzbicka, 1996).

While the task of Object Naming has been studied in both Language and Vision and Psycholinguistics, and it is related to Object Recognition tasks in Computer Vision, each field has a different approach to the task:

Within the field of Language and Vision, datasets typically collect free and natural referential utterances[3] produced by annotators for a given real-world image. Some relevant datasets are RefCOCO

[1] Available at https://huggingface.co/datasets/projecte-aina/cat_manynames

[2] The superordinate level (i.e., animal), the basic level (i.e., dog), and the subordinate level (i.e., Chihuahua)

[3] In semantics, a referring expression is a piece of language (typically a noun phrase) used with a particular referent in mind that refers to something or someone, or a clearly delimited collection of things or people (Hurford et al., 2007).

Proceedings of the Workshop on Cognitive Aspects of the Lexicon, pages 31–36
November 20, 2022. ©2022 Association for Computational Linguistics
https://doi.org/10.26615/978-954-452-056-4_004

(and its newer variant RefCOCO+) (Yu et al., 2016), Flickr30k Entities (Plummer et al., 2015), and VisualGenome (Krishna et al., 2017). Although naming occurs within those datasets, it is not normally marked up and linked to its corresponding image regions.

The task of picture naming constitutes an important experimental paradigm on research in Cognitive Science and Psycholinguistics, and has been traditionally used to assess language impairments and difficulties recalling general knowledge from semantic memory (Snodgrass and Vanderwart, 1980). Subjects reach a high agreement in this task, but it must be taken into account that participants are normally shown line drawing pictures that depict a prototypical category rather than real-world images that show objects in a context.

In Computer Vision, the task of Object Recognition identifies and classifies objects into several different categories (Russakovsky et al., 2015). Nevertheless, current recognition benchmarks use labels and images from ImageNet (Deng et al., 2009) that assume a single ground-truth label, ignoring linguistic variation.

As we can see, the task of Object Naming is addressed differently in Cognitive Science, Language and Vision and Computer Vision, but it would highly benefit from bringing together the particularities of each field so as to generate and provide quality resources.

2.2 The ManyNames Dataset

The ManyNames dataset (Silberer et al., 2020a) provides up to 36 crowd-sourced names for 25K object instances extracted from VisualGenome (Krishna et al., 2017). Unlike other Language and Vision datasets, it focuses on Object Naming rather than collecting complete utterances. Data collection was inspired by the picture naming norms developed in Psycholinguistics (Snodgrass and Vanderwart, 1980) but using real-world images of objects in a visual context, making it suitable for analysis and modeling of object naming, as well as for research in Language and Vision.

Images were selected from seven domains[4] (ANIMALS_PLANTS, BUILDINGS, CLOTHING, FOOD, HOME, PEOPLE, VEHICLES) by defining 52 synsets from VisualGenome in order to collect instances from different taxonomic levels. Instances were sampled depending on the size of the number of names obtained per synset in order to balance the collection. The annotations were collected by setting a crowdsourcing elicitation task on Amazon Mechanical Turk (AMT). The procedure required several annotation rounds, in which problematic cases such as unclear bounding boxes or occluded objects were discarded. Because of noise in the data, a second version of ManyNames (MN v2) was released (Silberer et al., 2020b), which is a verified dataset that contains consistent response sets with adequate responses that refer to the same object only. The resulting dataset contained substantial variation (2.2 names per object on average in MN v2). ANIMALS_PLANTS obtained the highest agreement, whereas PEOPLE reached a particularly low agreement. The analysis performed on the Bottom-Up model (Anderson et al., 2018) using the ManyNames dataset (Silberer et al., 2020b) showed that single-label data underestimated model effectiveness against multi-label data, obtaining a lower accuracy. This demonstrates that, compared to single-label resources for Object Naming, the ManyNames dataset provides a more accurate picture of human naming preferences by taking into account linguistic variation.

[4]All domains are based on McRae's feature norms (McRae et al., 2005) except PEOPLE, which was considered to be salient due to its prominence for humans.

3 A New Dataset for Object Naming in Catalan

The main motivations for using the ManyNames dataset as source data are (i) its consideration of linguistic variation in Object Naming, which is widely ignored up to now in Computer Vision, and (ii) the better accuracy that has shown to perform against single-label datasets in Language and Vision modelling. In order to obtain a Catalan version of ManyNames, we decided to automatically translate all the annotations in the original English dataset to Catalan using a state-of-the-art Machine Translation (MT) tool. To assess the quality of the resulting resource, we collected real human annotations for a subset of the dataset, consisting of around 1K images. Although the size of the manually annotated subset may seem small, it can be considered standard for a test set with the purpose of evaluating the quality of automatic annotations. Table 1 shows an overview of the columns contained in the CAT ManyNames dataset.

Column	Type	Description
responses	dict	Correct responses and their counts
topname	str	The most frequent name of the object
domain	str	The ManyNames domain of the object
incorrect[5]	dict	Incorrect responses and their counts
singletons[6]	dict	All responses which were given only once
total_responses	int	Sum count of correct responses
split	str	Use of the images in training, test and validation
vg_object_id	int	The VisualGenome id of the object
vg_image_id	int	The VisualGenome id of the image
topname_agreement[7]	int	Top name responses divided by total responses
jaccard_similarity[8]	int	Jaccard similarity index of the responses column
raw_responses[9]	dict	Uncorrected responses in the human annotated test set

Table 1: Description of the columns in the CAT ManyNames

3.1 Translated Annotations

Two different neural MT systems were considered before carrying out the translation of the ManyNames dataset: SoftCatalà and Google Translate.

Softcatalà is an open-source initiative [10] that, among other free NLP tools, offers automatic translation services between Catalan and several languages based on neural network technology (Mas, 2021). The popular Google Translate engine, which provides translation services between more than 100 language pairs (Caswell and Liang, 2020), was also considered.

Given the lack of linguistic context in the annotations to be translated (which were, in most cases, a single word), sense disambiguation was a major linguistic issue that needed to be solved before carrying out the automatic translation. Since no current MT system is yet able to take advantage of images as context [11], ad-hoc linguistic contexts were automatically inserted in each input string in order to compensate for this. The linguistic patterns were added using regular expressions depending on the domain. For example, in the domain HOME, the following pattern was used: "I bought a/an [word] for my home." .

Once the linguistic contexts were added, the resulting sentences from the training split of the data were translated with both SoftCatalà and Google translate. In order to evaluate which system performed a better translation, a random sample of 500 sentences out of the total translated sentences was collected and its quality was manually evaluated. 403 sentences out of 500 had an identical translation in both systems, but in 74 cases Google Translate got a more accurate translation than SoftCatalà (which only surpassed Google Translate in 23 examples), probably due to having been trained with larger amounts of data. As a result, Google Translate was considered as a better option for performing the automatic translation of the dataset. The linguistic patterns added in order to disambiguate were removed after the translation of the whole dataset, and repeated words, as well as their counts, were merged.

3.2 Manual Annotation of the Test Set

In order to gather as many manual annotations as possible for the test set, an annotation campaign was launched for a subset of 1,072 images. For this, we used 22 different Google Forms[12], each containing 50 images[13]. Participants were asked to fill one of the Google forms (picked at random) and name the object, animal or person inside the bounding box with the first name that came to their mind. Demographic information about participants was collected during the survey, such as age, gender and region of origin. Statistics show that they were quite balanced in terms of age and gender, but in terms of geographical variation, the Central Catalan dialect was largely over-represented. At the end of the campaign, a total of 220 native Catalan speakers had participated, gathering a total of 10,072 annotations, corresponding to 10 annota-

[10] Visit the following link for further information: https://github.com/Softcatala/nmt-softcatala

[11] Please note that in order to carry out the automatic translation, images were not considered

[12] Among the main reasons to use Google forms are its simplicity of use and the possibility to fill in surveys from a mobile device.

[13] Except the last one, which contained 22 images.

tions per image[14].

Post-processing steps for the human annotations included spellchecking the responses. After this step, possible erroneous responses were filtered out by comparing the corrected responses to the *incorrect* translated column of the ManyNames dataset and were also manually revised. In the process, possible offensive and/or inadequate content were also eliminated. Counts were added once the filtering process was finished. The resulting manually annotated subset has been published with an open license[15].

4 Analysis and Discussion

The purpose of the analysis was, on the one hand, to assess the quality of the automatic translation in the subset that had been human annotated by comparing both the translation and the human annotations, and on the other, to explore possible differences in lexical choices based on cultural biases. To this end, the accuracy of the top name, the degree of variation per image, the average number of different responses per image and the agreement on the top name were computed for both test sets.

The most immediate measure to evaluate the quality of the translated test set was to compute the accuracy of the translation of the most frequent response per image (aka the top name) by comparing it with the corresponding top name in the human annotated set. This accuracy only reached 67,91%, which is a clear indication of how different both resources are.

Another interesting metric to be computed was the degree of lexical variation in the two sets. Despite the difference in the number of annotations (36 for the translated vs 10 for the human annotated), the average number of types in the translated test set was 2.1 responses per image, whereas in the human annotated test set, it was 3.1[16], showing greater lexical variation in the human annotated test set. To account for this clear divergence, we could hypothesize that often two different names get conflated into one in the translation process. However, the ratio of the translated dataset (2.1) is very close to the 2.2 names per object on average in the original ManyNames dataset.

A related metric that was also applied is agreement on the top name per image, which is computed by dividing the number of responses for the top name by the number of total responses. Since more variation is observed in the human annotated set, we expect a higher agreement in the translated set. Indeed, the median is higher in the translated data (0.93) than in the human annotated data (0.7).

A qualitative analysis was performed by sorting both test sets by domain and top name and manually inspecting them to spot divergent cases of translation between English and Catalan. Several findings account for the observed richer lexical variation in Catalan: it was found that Catalan speakers tended to choose a subordinate name (*portaveu, esportista, tennista, etc.*) rather than a taxonomic name (*dona, noi, noia, etc.*) in the PEOPLE domain, the exception being images that involved specific terminology of an activity or a sport not specific to the Catalan culture, i.e. baseball or skateboarding. In those cases, Catalan speakers tended to choose the basic level (*jugador, noi*) rather than the subordinate level (*batedor, patinador*). Certain domains, such as CLOTHING showed Catalan to be more specific than English (which had repercussions in the translation). For example, *jacket* can be translated as *americana* or *jaqueta*, depending on the formality of the event. In addition, Catalan speakers may opt for the use of a diminutive (*trenet* vs *tren*), but this is a lexical option that English speakers do not have.

Our analyses show major divergences between the automatically translated dataset and the manually annotated subset, both in terms of degree of internal lexical variation and accuracy of the translated top names. Manual inspection of the results further confirms that these divergences can be attributed to linguistic and even cultural differences. Automatic translation of language resources from well-resourced languages to less-resourced ones is a common practice in NLP and related fields. Our results show that linguistic and cultural differences may affect the quality of automatically translated resources, such as the one presented here.

5 Conclusions

In this paper, we have presented a new dataset for the task of Object Naming in Catalan, namely CAT ManyNames. The new resource is the result of

[14] Time constraints prevented us from gathering more annotations per image, but for the purposes of the present exercise, 10 annotations looks like an acceptable number

[15] Available at https://huggingface.co/datasets/projecte-aina/cat_manynames

[16] As for the types by domain, the human annotated test set has more types in all domains except in FOOD and CLOTHING, where both test sets have the same number of types.

the machine translation of the English ManyNames dataset, with some pre- and post-processing steps. It also includes a subset of 1,072 images which has been entirely human annotated with 10 annotations per image. The comparison between the translated and the human annotated subsets reveals cultural-based divergences in lexical choices that can affect the quality of the machine-translated resource. Our results shows potential weaknesses in resources built up by translating annotations, particularly in the Language and Vision field, where context is provided by the image and thus is not available to the machine translation system. Since current literature on Object Naming within the Language and Vision field is scarce, these findings could serve as a starting point for research on cross-lingual Object Naming, and on the impact of automatic translation in the annotatation of multilingual resources.

6 Acknowledgements

This research was supported by the Generalitat de Catalunya through the AINA project. We thank our colleagues in the Text Mining Unit at the Barcelona Supercomputing Center, who provided insight and expertise that greatly assisted the research. We would also like to thank the anonymous reviewers for their insightful comments.

References

Peter Anderson, Xiaodong He, Chris Buehler, Damien Teney, Mark Johnson, Stephen Gould, and Lei Zhang. 2018. Bottom-up and top-down attention for image captioning and visual question answering. In *Proceedings of the IEEE conference on computer vision and pattern recognition*, pages 6077–6086.

Jordi Armengol-Estapé, Casimiro Pio Carrino, Carlos Rodriguez-Penagos, Ona de Gibert Bonet, Carme Armentano-Oller, Aitor Gonzalez-Agirre, Maite Melero, and Marta Villegas. 2021. Are multilingual models the best choice for moderately under-resourced languages? A comprehensive assessment for Catalan. In *Findings of the Association for Computational Linguistics: ACL-IJCNLP 2021*, pages 4933–4946, Online. Association for Computational Linguistics.

Brent Berlin. 2014. *Ethnobiological classification: Principles of categorization of plants and animals in traditional societies*, volume 185. Princeton University Press.

Roger Brown. 1958. How shall a thing be called? *Psychological review*, 65(1):14.

Isaac Caswell and Bowen Liang. 2020. Recent advances in google translate.

Jia Deng, Wei Dong, Richard Socher, Li-Jia Li, Kai Li, and Li Fei-Fei. 2009. Imagenet: A large-scale hierarchical image database. In *2009 IEEE Conference on Computer Vision and Pattern Recognition*, pages 248–255.

Caroline Graf, Judith Degen, Robert XD Hawkins, and Noah D Goodman. 2016. Animal, dog, or dalmatian? level of abstraction in nominal referring expressions. In *CogSci*.

Lala Hajibayova. 2013. Basic-level categories: A review. *Journal of Information Science*, 39(5):676–687.

James R Hurford, Brendan Heasley, and Michael B Smith. 2007. *Semantics: a coursebook*. Cambridge university press.

Pierre Jolicoeur, Mark A Gluck, and Stephen M Kosslyn. 1984. Pictures and names: Making the connection. *Cognitive psychology*, 16(2):243–275.

Pratik Joshi, Sebastin Santy, Amar Budhiraja, Kalika Bali, and Monojit Choudhury. 2020. The state and fate of linguistic diversity and inclusion in the NLP world. In *Proceedings of the 58th Annual Meeting of the Association for Computational Linguistics*, pages 6282–6293, Online. Association for Computational Linguistics.

Ranjay Krishna, Yuke Zhu, Oliver Groth, Justin Johnson, Kenji Hata, Joshua Kravitz, Stephanie Chen, Yannis Kalantidis, Li-Jia Li, David A Shamma, et al. 2017. Visual genome: Connecting language and vision using crowdsourced dense image annotations. *International journal of computer vision*, 123(1):32–73.

Barbara C Malt. 1995. Category coherence in cross-cultural perspective. *Cognitive psychology*, 29(2):85–148.

Jordi Mas. 2021. Resum de l'any 2020 a softcatalà.

Ken McRae, George S Cree, Mark S Seidenberg, and Chris McNorgan. 2005. Semantic feature production norms for a large set of living and nonliving things. *Behavior research methods*, 37(4):547–559.

Bryan A Plummer, Liwei Wang, Chris M Cervantes, Juan C Caicedo, Julia Hockenmaier, and Svetlana Lazebnik. 2015. Flickr30k entities: Collecting region-to-phrase correspondences for richer image-to-sentence models. In *Proceedings of the IEEE international conference on computer vision*, pages 2641–2649.

Eleanor Rosch, Carol Simpson, and R Scott Miller. 1976. Structural bases of typicality effects. *Journal of Experimental Psychology: Human perception and performance*, 2(4):491.

Olga Russakovsky, Jia Deng, Hao Su, Jonathan Krause, Sanjeev Satheesh, Sean Ma, Zhiheng Huang, Andrej Karpathy, Aditya Khosla, Michael Bernstein, et al. 2015. Imagenet large scale visual recognition challenge. *International journal of computer vision*, 115(3):211–252.

Carina Silberer, Sina Zarrieß, and Gemma Boleda. 2020a. Object naming in language and vision: A survey and a new dataset. In *Calzolari N, Béchet F, Blache P, Choukri K, Cieri C, Declerck T, Goggi S, Isahara H, Maegaard B, Mariani J, Mazo H, Moreno A, Odijk J, Piperidis S, editors. Proceedings of the 12th Language Resources and Evaluation Conference; 2020 May 13-15; Marseilles, France. Stroudsburg (PA): ACL; 2020. p. 5792-801.* ACL (Association for Computational Linguistics).

Carina Silberer, Sina Zarrieß, Matthijs Westera, and Gemma Boleda. 2020b. Humans meet models on object naming: A new dataset and analysis. In *Proceedings of the 28th International Conference on Computational Linguistics*, pages 1893–1905.

Joan G Snodgrass and Mary Vanderwart. 1980. A standardized set of 260 pictures: norms for name agreement, image agreement, familiarity, and visual complexity. *Journal of experimental psychology: Human learning and memory*, 6(2):174.

Anna Wierzbicka. 1996. *Semantics: Primes and universals: Primes and universals*. Oxford University Press, UK.

Licheng Yu, Patrick Poirson, Shan Yang, Alexander C Berg, and Tamara L Berg. 2016. Modeling context in referring expressions. In *European Conference on Computer Vision*, pages 69–85. Springer.

Finetuning Latin BERT for Word Sense Disambiguation on the *Thesaurus Linguae Latinae*

Piroska Lendvai
Department for Digital Humanities Research & Development
Bavarian Academy of Sciences and Humanities
Munich, Germany
piroska.lendvai@badw.de

Claudia Wick
Thesaurus Linguae Latinae
Bavarian Academy of Sciences and Humanities
Munich, Germany
claudia.wick@thesaurus.badw.de

Abstract

The *Thesaurus Linguae Latinae* (TLL) is a comprehensive monolingual dictionary that records contextualized meanings and usages of Latin words in antique sources at an unprecedented scale. We created a new dataset based on a subset of sense representations in the TLL, with which we finetuned the Latin-BERT neural language model (Bamman and Burns, 2020) on a supervised Word Sense Disambiguation task. We observe that the contextualized BERT representations finetuned on TLL data score better than static embeddings used in a bidirectional LSTM classifier on the same dataset, and that our per-lemma BERT models achieve higher and more robust performance than reported by Bamman and Burns (2020) based on data from a bilingual Latin dictionary. We discuss the differences in sense organizational principles between these two lexical resources, and report about our dataset construction and improved evaluation methodology.

1 Introduction

In the field of Natural Language Processing (NLP), there is a growing amount of languages for which contextualized representation models are created. For Latin, a pretrained BERT model (cf. Devlin et al., 2018) was published by Bamman and Burns (2020), which they finetuned for four classical NLP tasks, among others for Word Sense Disambiguation (WSD). WSD, an area of computational semantics, has been approached in NLP by several machine learning setups (for an overview cf. Navigli, 2009 and Bevilacqua et al., 2021), and recent works (e.g. Scarlini et al., 2020) have also targeted the use of neural models and architectures in combination with lexical knowledge bases and encyclopaedic resources.

WSD is typically cast as supervised classification, where the learning task consists of predicting the appropriate sense label for one or more focus tokens in their context unit, e.g. within a sentence. Based on the application end task, sense labels can be defined in a variety of ways, e.g. aiming to distinguish coarse or fine granularity of senses, binary or multiple sense distinctions, etc. Creating labeled data for a supervised WSD application is nontrivial. Large, sense-annotated benchmark datasets are scarce, especially in languages other than English. A promising resource to be utilized for Latin WSD could be the Latin Wordnet[1]; for its evaluation and references cf. Franzini et al. (2019). Seeking proxy resources and methods to leverage WSD resources is important, since it is expensive to manually produce a sense labeled corpus from scratch that captures contextual information for several senses of a word. Therefore, our study aims to contribute insights into methods that use dictionaries for automatically assigning sense labels.

Bamman and Burns (2020) (henceforth: B&B) constructed WSD data for BERT, a transformer-based language model, by taking the textual examples (i.e., quotes from antique sources) inventorized for a particular headword (aka 'lemma') in the bilingual *Latin Dictionary* of Lewis and Short (1879): to each quote snippet in the first two sense groups of each lemma, they assigned its sense category (i.e., I or II) as gold standard label.

Inspired by this sense inventory creation (i.e., bi-

[1] https://latinwordnet.exeter.ac.uk

Proceedings of the Workshop on Cognitive Aspects of the Lexicon, pages 37–41
November 20, 2022. ©2022 Association for Computational Linguistics
https://doi.org/10.26615/978-954-452-056-4_005

nary class labeling) method of B&B, we requested data for the same lemmas that B&B presented, from a currently proprietary resource: the *Thesaurus Linguae Latinae*[2] (TLL)[3]. The TLL is a comprehensive monolingual Latin dictionary that aims to record all meanings of all ancient Latin words, citing all (or a representative sample) of its seen attestations. The TLL is vast: it is estimated to comprise cca. 53k-56k entries as of now[4], so it likely holds a major part of the quotes that occur in L&S and thus in the B&B WSD dataset.

The prospect of comparing WSD performance across datasets constructed from two dictionaries – one bilingual, another monolingual – was intriguing in several scholarly respects, a.o. for gaining quantitative insights into dictionary structuring practices, or even for attempting to validate sense structuring in an empirical way. After inspecting the data, we realized that a direct comparison of machine learning performance based on data constructed from the TLL resp. from L&S would be methodologically flawed:

1. We made pilot analyses of the quotes across the B&B and TLL sense labeled data, and noted that sense categorization in TLL and L&S draws on very different semantic principles: for one and the same lemma, the subset of quotes labeled with sense I in B&B can be distributed across both sense class I and II in TLL, and/or vice versa.

2. Working with the methodology of B&B of constructing sense-balanced data would not allow unleashing the full potential of the TLL data size. As we chose not to discard quotes (i.e., did not match the amount of quotes in the smaller sense label set), our TLL dataset became orders of magnitude larger and sense-label-wise possibly more aggregative, thus likely coarser-grained.

Our aims in the current contribution were thus:

- Investigating methods and challenges for experimentally validating sense representations and their WSD distinction
- Giving account of joint work between the Humanities and the NLP communities that deliver complementary expertise
- Reusing a pretrained contextual representation model for Latin, released by Bamman and Burns (2020)
- Reproducing the WSD experiment of Bamman and Burns (2020) via the benchmark data, code, and baseline classifier they released[5]
- Repeating the WSD experiment by finetuning Latin BERT on new WSD data that we constructed from the TLL
- Observing sense organization principles and scale across the two datasets
- Improving experimental methodology by providing a detailed evaluation in terms of F-macro scoring in a per-lemma-WSD-setup.

The paper is structured as follows: first, a short exploratory analysis is given for the B&B resp. the TLL data in terms of the original resources and their construction principles. Afterwards we report on the finetuning experiments and we summarize the study with a conclusion section.

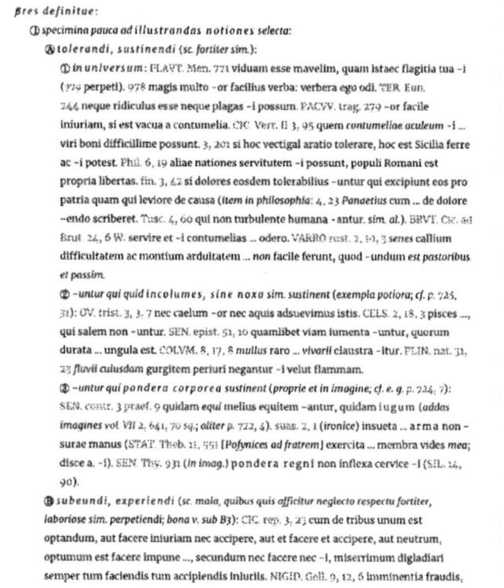

β res definitae:

① specimina pauca ad illustrandas notiones selecta:

Ⓐ tolerandi, sustinendi (sc. fortiter sim.):

① in universum: PLAVT. Men. 771 viduam esse mavelim, quam istaec flagitia tua -i (774 perpeti). 978 magis multo -or facilius verba: verbera ego odi. TER. Eun. 244 neque ridiculus esse neque plagas -i possum. PACVV. trag. 279 -or facile iniuriam, si est vacua a contumelia. CIC. Verr. II 3, 95 quem *contumeliae aculeum* -i ... viri boni difficillime possunt. 3, 201 si hoc vectigal aratio tolerare, hoc est Sicilia ferre ac -i potest. Phil. 6, 19 aliae nationes servitutem -i possunt, populi Romani est propria libertas. fin. 3, 42 si dolores eosdem tolerabilius -untur qui excipiunt eos pro patria quam qui leviore de causa (*item in philosophia*: 4, 23 *Panaetius* cum ... de dolore -endo scriberet. Tusc. 4, 60 qui non turbulente humana -antur. *sim. al.*). BRVT. Cic. ad Brut. 24, 6 W. servire et -i contumelias ... odero. VARRO rust. 2, 10, 3 *senes* callium difficultatem ac montium arduitatem ... *non* facile ferunt, quod -undum *est pastoribus et passim.*

② *-untur qui quid incolumes, sine noxa sim. sustinent (exempla potiora; cf. p. 725, 31)*: OV. trist. 3, 3, 7 nec caelum -or nec aquis adsuevimus istis. CELS. 2, 18, 3 pisces ..., qui salem non -untur. SEN. epist. 51, 10 quamlibet viam iumenta -untur, quorum durata ... ungula est. COLVM. 8, 17, 8 *mullus* raro ... *vivarii* claustra -itur. PLIN. nat. 31, 23 *fluvii cuiusdam* gurgitem periuri negantur -i velut flammam.

③ *-untur qui pondera corporea sustinent (proprie et in imagine; cf. e. g. p. 724, 7)*: SEN. contr. 3 praef. 9 quidam *equi* melius equitem -antur, quidam iugum (*addas imagines* vol. VII 2, 641, 70 sq.; *aliter* p. 722, 4). suas. 2, 1 (*ironice*) insueta ... arma non -surae manus (STAT. Theb. 11, 551 [*Polynices ad fratrem*] exercita ... membra vides *mea*; disce a. -i). SEN. Thy. 931 (*in imag.*) pondera regni non inflexa cervice -i (SIL. 14, 90).

Ⓑ *subeundi, experiendi (sc. mala, quibus quis afficitur neglecto respectu fortiter, laboriose sim. perpetiendi; bona v. sub B3)*: CIC. rep. 3, 23 cum de tribus unum est optandum, aut facere iniuriam nec accipere, aut et facere et accipere, aut neutrum, optumum est facere impune ..., secundum nec facere nec -i, miserrimum digladiari semper tum faciendis tum accipiendis iniuriis. NIGID. Gell. 9, 12, 6 imminentia fraudis,

Figure 1: Excerpt from the nested structure of the TLL article for the lemma *patior*, meant for human reading.

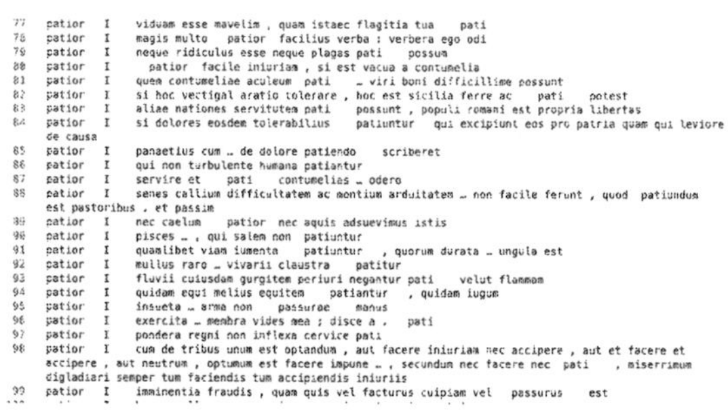

```
77  patior  I  viduam esse mavelim , quam istaec flagitia tua   pati
78  patior  I  magis multo   patior  facilius verba : verbera ego odi
79  patior  I  neque ridiculus esse neque plagas pati    possum
80  patior  I    patior  facile iniuriam , si est vacua a contumelia
81  patior  I  quem contumeliae aculeum  pati    … viri boni difficillime possunt
82  patior  I  si hoc vectigal aratio tolerare , hoc est sicilia ferre ac    pati    potest
83  patior  I  aliae nationes servitutem pati    possunt , populi romani est propria libertas
84  patior  I  si dolores eosdem tolerabilius    patiuntur   qui excipiunt eos pro patria quam qui leviore
    de causa
85  patior  I  panaetius cum … de dolore patiendo    scriberet
86  patior  I  qui non turbulente humana patiantur
87  patior  I  servire et    pati    contumelias … odero
88  patior  I  senes callium difficultatem ac montium arduitatem … non facile ferunt , quod  patiundum
    est pastoribus . et passim
89  patior  I  nec caelum    patior  nec aquis adsuevimus istis
90  patior  I  pisces … , qui salem non  patiuntur
91  patior  I  quamlibet viam iumenta    patiuntur   , quorum durata … ungula est
92  patior  I  mullus raro … vivarii claustra    patitur
93  patior  I  fluvii cuiusdam gurgitem periuri negantur pati    velut flammam
94  patior  I  quidam equi melius equitem    patiantur   , quidam iugum
95  patior  I  insueta … arma non    passurae    manus
96  patior  I  exercita … membra vides mea ; disce a .   pati
97  patior  I  pondera regni non inflexa cervice pati
98  patior  I  cum de tribus unum est optandum , aut facere iniuriam nec accipere , aut et facere et
    accipere , aut neutrum , optumum est facere impune … , secundum nec facere nec  pati    , miserrimum
    digladiari semper tum faciendis tum accipiendis iniuriis
99  patior  I  imminentia fraudis , quam quis vel facturus cuipiam vel   passurus    est
```

Figure 2: Flattened, sense-labeled WSD data for BERT, derived from the TLL article and its sense inventory, for the lemma *patior*.

[2] https://tll.degruyter.com/about

[3] The Bavarian Academy of Sciences and Humanities plans to make the complete TLL data open source by 2030.

[4] Currently headwords are prepared till letter R.

[5] https://github.com/dbamman/latin-bert

2 Exploratory Data Analysis

2.1 B&B Data

The B&B dataset comprises 8,354 instances for a total of 201 dictionary headwords (lemmas). The source of B&B data is the bilingual dictionary of L&S[6] that is a translation of Freund's dictionary from the 19th century, reflecting edition techniques from 200 years ago.

2.2 TLL Data

The ongoing TLL compilation project started in 1900; its editorial principles have changed every once in a while[7]. Within each TLL article, a contrastive, nested (thus: semantically additive) structure is pursued that can descend as deep as 10+ levels.

Sense groups on the same level are aimed to be of the same sense granularity but to feature mutually exclusive parameters of syntactic or semantic nature or their combination. This implies that the TLL structure does not reflect sense distinctions that depend on their translatability to another language, but its goal is a dichotomic arrangement (which is not always limited to two sense groups on the highest level) of word attestations (quotes from Latin texts) while staying within the same language.

The TLL data was available to us in TEI XML format. Just like B&B, we generated the data from within a single dictionary entry, by definition excluding homonymy, and we only considered the first two main senses of a lemma, labeling all text snippets that are longer than 4 words with the corresponding highest-level sense label (see Figure 2), by recursively descending into – thus flattening – the nested structure of the printed article (see Figure 1). Our TLL data points correspond to 25,227 text snippets for the subset of 40 lemmas, whose part-of-speech distributions are: 40% verbs, 22.5% adjectives, 10% nouns, 27.5% others (adverb, pronoun, preposition, conjunction, particle).

Starting from letter C, in the articles a large amount of words – by definition the lemma onset itself, but also other tokens – are heavily and somewhat irregularly abbreviated, which we had to resolve by extensive human-in-the-loop procedures, e.g. by identifying patterns and writing replacement rules for omitted subword material in a per-lemma fashion. Reconstructing the omitted subword parts of the inflected lemma forms was mandatory for running meaningful WSD experiments because the lemma forms supply a core piece of information to the learning algorithms.

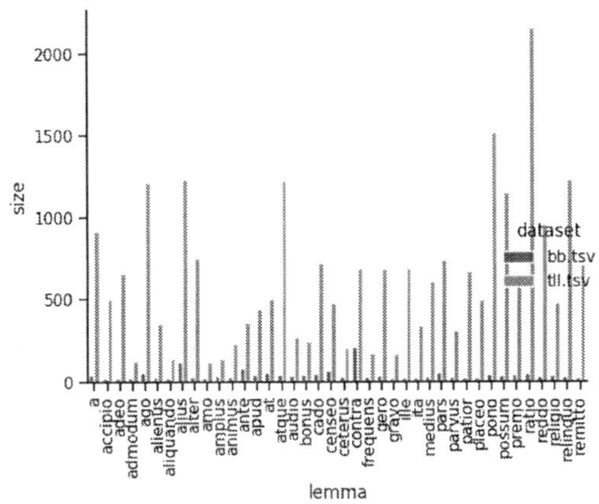

Figure 3: Data size per lemma per dataset. Blue: B&B data. Orange: TLL data.

2.3 Analysis of the Derived Sense Classes

We observed a number of important phenomena about sense classes as derived from the dictionaries.

1. Semantically motivated separation between senses Often, sense separation is mutually exclusive, e.g. the lemma *relinquo* demonstrates that out of the first two main TLL sense groups, I pertains to 'relocation in physical space', as opposed to II that describes 'movement in a figurative sense'.

2. Artificial dichotomy of senses The separation of senses can often be rather artificially constructed, e.g. in *ratio*, and L&S uses such separation practices, e.g. by container labels such as "in general" vs. "in particular", even though the latter split oftentimes does not yield a semantically or syntactically homogeneous group.

3. Lemma vs. Sublemma Classes can also be split on certain grammatical phenomena in L&S, e.g. on participle perfect used as an adjective (cf. *remitto* where this usage makes up class II for B&B), whereas the TLL renders such usage as a so-called sublemma and treats it structurally elsewhere than in the main article, thus the Latin quotes in it do not get extracted into the TLL WSD data.

4. Temporal and domain diversity The TLL has a uniquely wide temporal scope spanning nearly 1000 years from Old and Classical Latin till late antiquity and Christian Latin (cca. AD 700),

[6]http://www.perseus.tufts.edu/hopper/

[7]For an impression see https://publikationen.badw.de/de/thesaurus/lemmata

and encompasses genres beyond the domain of literature, such as legal and medical texts and inscriptions. Thereby, it delivers markedly different semantic representation proportions than (a) the pretrained BERT that saw texts spanning cca. 2000 years, seeing attestation from Middle Latin and Humanism, or (b) the B&B finetuned BERT that saw texts from cca. 200 years, focused on a subset of canonical classical authors. As an example: *religio* in the contemporary sense of *religion* as 'a dogmatic system of faith based on revelation' did not exist before the rise of Christianity; for "pagan" Romans, *religio* denoted 'feelings of awe, fear, respect towards the gods or strictly defined forms of (liturgical) worship'.[8]

5. Truthfulness to sources In both the B&B and the TLL data, their antique sources are not always literally cited, but the quotes are often edited. The TLL maintains more strictness, e.g. no syntactic changes are allowed. In the B&B (aka L&S) data, one regularly finds modified or artificially inserted constructions that diverge from the sources.

3 WSD Experiments

Finetuning BERT is a technique that takes its pretrained language model and explicitly trains it for the WSD task, i.e., in our case on Latin quote – typically on the subsentential level – that are labeled to have class I or class II, as assigned based on the TLL sense inventory. This yields a classification model that can distinguish exactly two meanings for the token that designates the focus lemma. This is certainly a simplified WSD setup, nevertheless helpful for pilot studies to assess the power of newly constructed data for disambiguating between two major senses (or usage contexts) of words. The finetuning task is in contrast with what already took place in the first phase of creating lexical representations, the so-called pretraining. There the task was that BERT's Latin language model learns as many senses of a word as possible.

3.1 Training and Testing Setup

The setup across our WSD experiments on a machine with GPU running Linux Ubuntu 18 is listed below. Splitting the data into partitions for training, development, and testing was done by the method and Github code of Bamman and Burns (2020).

[8]We aim to utilize TLL data for chronological analyses, characterizing and training the recognition of e.g. semantic drift, but this goes beyond the scope of the current paper.

Dataset	Model	mean F-macro	stdev
B&B	biLSTM	.613	.205
	BERT	.695	.213
TLL	biLSTM	.705	.132
	BERT	.794	.143

Table 1: Mean performance scores over 40 lemmas.

- 100 epochs (training rounds) per lemma
- Training and testing performed per lemma
- B&B used cross entropy loss without class weights for training. Since in our data the two classes are imbalanced per lemma, we calculated the weights for each class for the cross entropy loss function
- Performance was evaluated in terms of the unweighted macro F1-score per lemma using Pedregosa et al. (2011). Accuracy would be suboptimal to use as it does not transparently express how well we perform on the two classes and it does not correct for class imbalance
- For each epoch, macro F1 was calculated on the development set
- For each lemma, the best performing development epoch's parameters were used to measure macro F1 on the heldout test set
- As baseline model we used from B&B[9] 200-dimensional static word2vec embeddings (Mikolov et al., 2013) in a biLSTM classifier
- Enclitica were not separated from words since BERT's wordpiece tokenizer[10] was assumed to account for these.

3.2 Evaluation

B&B Dataset We reproduced the B&B WSD study with a similar accuracy score as they report (.737). Next, we derived from the B&B aggregated dataset a per-lemma dataset, on which we trained both classifier models, using the B&B code that we amended with the settings listed in Section 3.1. The results are shown in Table 1. We observe that the B&B per-lemma data are small (cf. Figure 3) and yield statistically unreliable results as standard deviation values are large; this variability is also illustrated by the whiskers of the boxplot (cf. Figure 4). While Table 1 reports the means and the standard deviations, the boxplots show the median.

[9]https://github.com/dbamman/latin-bert/blob/cd6bea9f7ff84ff4b18c172f3d5719d1d3198e69/case_studies/pos_tagging/scripts/download_static_vectors.sh

[10]https://ai.googleblog.com/2021/12/a-fast-wordpiece-tokenization-system.html

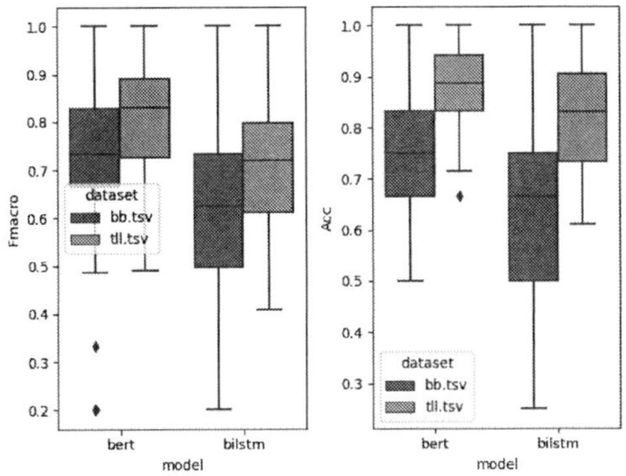

Figure 4: Performance distribution boxplots: F-macro and accuracy across lemmas per dataset per model.

TLL Dataset Due to the data preparation overhead, thus far we processed a subset of 40 lemmas. The WSD performance scores on TLL data are also listed in Table 1: BERT attains a nearly .80 F-score and outperforms the baseline biLSTM model with a large margin (for both datasets). Figure 4 also indicates that the median of the scores for TLL data is higher than for B&B data.

4 Summary and Conclusion

Our study aimed to confirm the impact of Latin BERT (Bamman and Burns, 2020) and to point out an important new Latin WSD resource. We constructed a large dataset from the TLL that holds quotes labeled with the first two highest-level senses of a headword. These likely incorporate senses that the B&B dataset did not include. We experimentally validated that the nested dictionary structure of the TLL is able to deliver WSD data for finetuning contextual representations in a transformer architecture. The WSD models yielded a large improvement above the static embeddings baseline, when evaluated on held-out data from our new, TLL-based dataset. We plan to scale up this study and to release a benchmark dataset and trained models for Latin WSD in future work.

References

David Bamman and Patrick J. Burns. 2020. Latin BERT: A Contextual Language Model for Classical Philology. *CoRR*, abs/2009.10053.

Michele Bevilacqua, Tommaso Pasini, Alessandro Raganato, Roberto Navigli, et al. 2021. Recent trends in word sense disambiguation: A survey. In *Proceedings of the Thirtieth International Joint Conference on Artificial Intelligence, IJCAI-21*. International Joint Conference on Artificial Intelligence, Inc.

Jacob Devlin, Ming-Wei Chang, Kenton Lee, and Kristina Toutanova. 2018. BERT: Pre-training of deep bidirectional transformers for language understanding. *arXiv preprint arXiv:1810.04805*.

Greta Franzini, Andrea Peverelli, Paolo Ruffolo, Marco Passarotti, Helena Sanna, Edoardo Signoroni, Viviana Ventura, and Federica Zampedri. 2019. Nunc est aestimandum: Towards an evaluation of the Latin WordNet. In *CLiC-it*.

Tomas Mikolov, Kai Chen, Greg Corrado, and Jeffrey Dean. 2013. Efficient estimation of word representations in vector space. *arXiv preprint arXiv:1301.3781*.

Roberto Navigli. 2009. Word Sense Disambiguation: A Survey. *ACM Computing Surveys*, 41(2).

F. Pedregosa, G. Varoquaux, A. Gramfort, V. Michel, B. Thirion, O. Grisel, M. Blondel, P. Prettenhofer, R. Weiss, V. Dubourg, J. Vanderplas, A. Passos, D. Cournapeau, M. Brucher, M. Perrot, and E. Duchesnay. 2011. Scikit-learn: Machine learning in Python. *Journal of Machine Learning Research*, 12:2825–2830.

Bianca Scarlini, Tommaso Pasini, and Roberto Navigli. 2020. SENSEMBERT: Context-enhanced sense embeddings for multilingual word sense disambiguation. In *Proceedings of The Thirty-Fourth AAAI Conference on Artificial Intelligence (AAAI-20)*.

Putting WordNet's Dictionary Examples in the Context of Definition Modelling: An Empirical Analysis

Fatemah Almeman[*] **Luis Espinosa-Anke**[*◇]
[*]CardiffNLP, School of Computer Science and Informatics, Cardiff University, UK
[◇]AMPLYFI, UK
{almemanf, espinosa-ankel}@cardiff.ac.uk

Abstract

Definition modeling is the task to generate a valid definition for a given input term. This relatively novel task has been approached either with no context (i.e., given a word embedding alone) and, more recently, as word-in-context modeling. Despite their success, most works make little to no distinction between resources and their specific features (e.g., type and style of definitions, or quality of examples) when used for training. Given the high diversity lexicographic resources exhibit in terms of topic coverage, style and formal structure, it is desirable for downstream definition modeling to better understand which of them are better suited for the task. In this paper, we propose an empirical evaluation of the well-known lexical database WordNet, and specifically, its dictionary examples. We evaluate them both directly, by matching them against criteria for *good* dictionary writing, and indirectly, in the task of definition modeling. Our results suggest that WordNet's dictionary examples could be improved by extending them in length, and incorporating prototypicality.

1 Introduction

Definition modeling (DM), as introduced by Noraset et al. (2017), is the task of generating a dictionary definition for a given word. This task was made possible by the adoption in NLP of sequence-to-sequence architectures based on RNNs (Gardner et al., 2022). Recently, DM systems have shown impressive performance in several intrinsic and downstream tasks, mostly thanks to being able to go from context-less (Noraset et al. only used the definiendum[1] as a conditioning token at all timesteps) to a contextually richer setting, e.g., by conditioning the generated definition to an example of usage of the target word (Ni and Wang, 2017; Gadetsky et al., 2018; Chang et al., 2018; Zhu et al., 2019; Mickus et al., 2019; Ishiwatari et al., 2019).

Recently, a notable leap in DM was achieved in Bevilacqua et al. (2020), who fine-tuned BART (Lewis et al., 2019) on example-definition pairs, and reported high results in intrinsic benchmarks and, more importantly, used their DM system for downstream NLP, specifically word sense disambiguation (WSD) and word-in-context classification. DM has also been explored from other perspectives, e.g., generating definitions with appropriate specificity using re-ranking mechanisms (Huang et al., 2021), or extending the generation cross-entropy loss with a reconstruction objective (Kong et al., 2022) (reminiscent of works that used dictionary definitions for improving word embeddings via autoencoders (Bosc and Vincent, 2018) or LSTMs (Hill et al., 2016)). Moreover, Barba et al. (2021) explore a BART-based model for performing the reverse task to DM, i.e., *exemplification modeling*, or generating a dictionary example given a term and its definition. Other applications of DM range from the aforementioned lexical semantics tasks to reverse dictionary (predict a word given a definition), interpretability, or for clarifying technical and medical terminology (Chen and Zhao, 2022; August et al., 2022), whereas recent applications of BART to tasks not originally designed to be solved generatively are semantic role labeling (Bevilacqua et al., 2020), relation extraction (Cabot and Navigli, 2021) or entity linking (De Cao et al., 2020).

Despite the above successes, little attention has been paid so far to the quality of the dictionary examples (or *contexts*) used for fine-tuning these models. In fact, most existing DM systems train on WordNet (**WN**) (Miller, 1995), which is the defacto lexical database for English. However, we are not aware of previous work that has explored the quality (and hence, suitability for DM) of WN examples. Therefore, in this paper, we first inves-

[1]The *genus-et-differentia* Aristotelian definitions follows an *A is a B which Z* structure, with *A* being the *definiendum*, *B* the *genus* and Z the *definiens* or *differentia specifica*.

Proceedings of the Workshop on Cognitive Aspects of the Lexicon, pages 42–48
November 20, 2022. ©2022 Association for Computational Linguistics
https://doi.org/10.26615/978-954-452-056-4_006

tigate the quality of WN examples by evaluating against the GDEX (Good Dictionary Examples) set of criteria (Kilgarriff et al., 2008), and use as a point of comparison a widely adopted open dataset used in DM, which is primarily based on the Oxford Dictionary (Chang and Chen, 2019) (**CHA**). It is worth noting, however, that these two resources were built for different objectives, as the initial purpose behind creating WN was to explain how lexical meaning is stored in the mind (Broda et al., 2009), and its primary use may be as a sense inventory (Agirre and Edmonds, 2007). However, with this caveat in mind, and given how lexicographic resources are currently converging into useful pretraining and fine-tuning datasets for lexical semantics, we also propose to extrinsically test these two resources in the DM task. Specifically, in our second set of experiments we fine-tune a BART-based model on WN and CHA, and show that generally speaking, results of models fine-tuned on WN perform slightly worse than if fine-tuned on CHA. Our preliminary results suggest that WN's examples sometimes do not provide enough context, making it difficult to learn a good representation for the word being contextualized. We also report an experiment comparing DM modeling results on WN nouns vs. WN verbs; which suggests that a DM model trained on WN nouns performs slightly better.

2 Data

WordNet (WN) is an electronic lexical dictionary for English that describes words (11,7097 nouns, 11,488 verbs, 22,141 adjectives, and 4,601 adverbs) organized in groups of synonyms called "synsets" (Miller, 1995; Fellbaum, 2013). Each synset is described by its definition, lemmas, examples of usage (for some but not all words), and the relations between synsets, e.g., hypernymy (is-a), meronymy (is-part) or troponymy (manner-of). WN has typically been used in lexicographic and language learning settings (Morato et al., 2004), but more importantly, also in NLP, e.g., as a natural language interface for optimizing the precision of search engines, WSD or query expansion (Moldovan and Mihalcea, 2000; Banerjee and Pedersen, 2002). Moreover, relations in WN have been used extensively, for example for improving word embeddings via retrofitting (Faruqui et al., 2014; Espinosa-Anke et al., 2016; Vulić and Mrkšić, 2017; Mrkšić et al., 2017).

CHA (Chang and Chen, 2019), the other resource we consider in this paper, is based on Oxford Dictionaries. It was released with two splits, namely *seen*, where definitions in the training set also exist in the test set, and *unseen*, which contains a set of words not available in the training set (Bevilacqua et al., 2020). This is similar to the lexical splits (as opposed to random splits) present in other analogous tasks such as graded lexical entailment (Shwartz et al., 2016; Vulić et al., 2017). In this paper, we are concerned with the quality of examples in WN (and how they compare with CHA), i.e., sentences where a target word appears, and which should be informative enough to convey the necessary contextual information to clarify fully or partially the word's meaning (encoded in a natural language definition or gloss, instead of e.g., a word embedding).

We show in Table 1 examples from WN and CHA, where it becomes apparent that WN examples have a different pattern, e.g., they are much shorter, and are crucially limited in the contextual information they provide, as opposed to the examples in CHA, which features, first, full-fledged grammatical examples, and second, associated vocabularies that help position the target word in the mental lexicon, which is crucial for word access (Zock et al., 2010).

Data	Lemma	Definition	Example
WN	**people**	(plural) any group of human beings (men or women or children) collectively	old people
CHA	**people**	human beings in general or considered collectively	each day he has looked at a key issue facing us as a nation as a people as frail human beings
WN	**sheet**	any broad thin expanse or surface	a sheet of ice
CHA	**sheet**	a large rectangular piece of cotton or other fabric used on a bed to cover the mattress and as a layer beneath blankets when these are used	Mary quietly got off the bed and covered him with the sheet and blanket
WN	**tall**	great in vertical dimension; high in stature	tall people
CHA	**tall**	of great or more than average height especially with reference to an object relative to width	the elevator came to a stop and the doors slid open revealing the sixth floor of the tall building

Table 1: WN vs CHA definitions and examples for a given lemma (in bold).

3 Experiments

In this section, we introduce the two sets of experiments we perform. First, the descriptive comparison between WN and CHA examples using GDEX as a proxy (Section 3.1). Second, we describe the setting for the DM experiment, where we test WN as supervision signal (Section 3.2).

3.1 GDEX-based comparison

As a proxy for determining the quality of dictionary examples in WN, and given that there is no manually annotated dataset for this purpose, we used GDEX (Good Dictionary Examples) criteria. GDEX is a system that added around 8,000 new example sentences to Macmillan English Dictionary by automatically finding good examples in corpora using a set of rules of thumb (Kilgarriff et al., 2008; Bejoint, 2014).

In our work, we used some of the features that are introduced in GDEX, specifically:

- **sentence length**: according to Kilgarriff et al. (2008), good dictionary examples should range between 10 and 25 words, and thus we penalize shorter or longer dictionary examples proportionally (the more an example deviates from the acceptable minimum or maximum, the more it is penalized).
- **word frequency**: a sentence is penalized for each non-frequent word that is not in the list of the top 20,000 most frequent words in English Wikipedia.
- **anaphoric references**: we penalize the number of pronouns in the dictionary example, normalized by sentence length.
- **sentence probability**: we use the GPT-2 (Radford et al., 2019) language model to score the probability of dictionary examples. Intuitively, this can be a useful metric for semantic coherence and fluency.

3.2 Definition Modeling

The general formulation of DM is as follows. To generate a gloss g that defines a target lemma t in a context c, the standard sequence-to-sequence conditional generation probability is computed by factorising it auto-regressively (Bevilacqua et al., 2020):

$$P(g|c,t) = \prod_{k=1}^{|g|} P(g_k|g_{0:k-1}, c, t) \qquad (1)$$

where g_k is the kth token of g and g_0 is a special start token (Bevilacqua et al., 2020). We fine-tune BART, a pre-trained encoder-decoder system, to perform the definition generation task by taking the pair (context, target lemma) as an input to produce the corresponding definition. The dataset includes (c, t, g) triples where t is the target word (lemma) in a context c (example) and g is the gold gloss which defines t in c (definition). We encode the input as (t, c) pairs and special tokens are used to identify the target lemma in each context such as *The cherry tree <target> bloomed </target>*., with the lemma "bloom" as the target word in this context.

Exp. 1 (WN vs CHA) Since we are concerned with using WN in definition modeling, we trained and tested the definition generation model (BART) on WN lemmas that have examples (44,351 lemmas) using an 80/20 split for training and testing. Additionally, we trained the same model using a CHA-derived training set of the same size as our WN training set, and tested it on the same WN test set. We ensured that no duplicates/leakage occured between sets in both experiments. We train both models with a maximum of 50 epochs with early stopping[2].

Exp. 2 (WN Nouns vs WN Verbs) We trained and tested the same BART model with same hyperparameters as in the WN vs CHA experiment on random 10k noun lemmas and 10k verb lemmas from WN separately (using again an 80/20 ratio for training and testing) to evaluate whether there are noticeable differences between these two grammatical categories.

4 Analysis

In this section, we discuss the results of our two experiments, namely GDEX-wise comparison between WN and CHA, and WN's stress test in the DM task.

[2]We implemented our experiments using the `simpletransformers` (`http://simpletransformers.ai/`) library, a wrapper on top of `transformers` (Wolf et al., 2020).

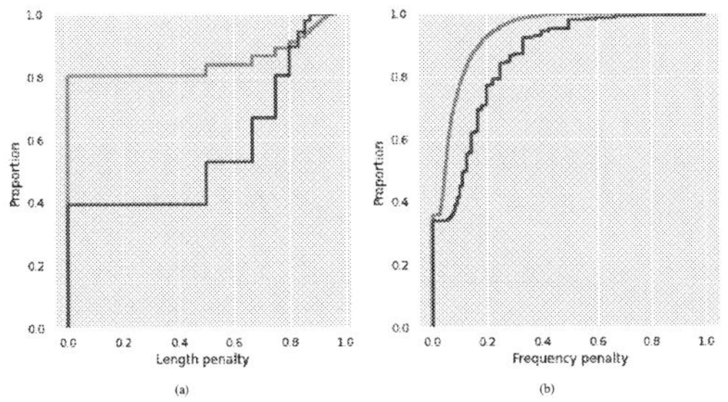

Figure 1: Empirical distribution functions between WN (blue) and CHA (orange) for length (a) and frequency (b) penalties.

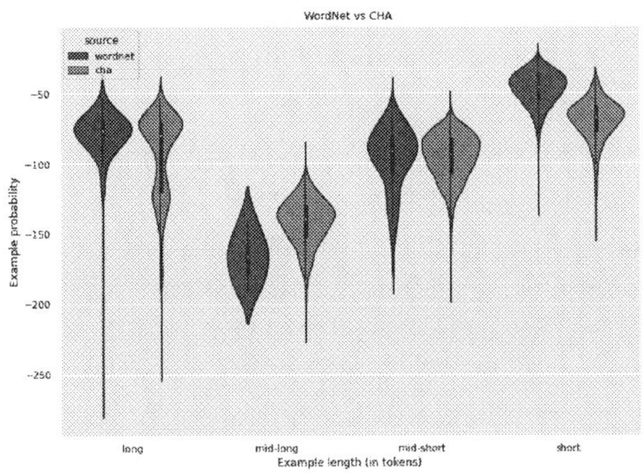

Figure 2: Violin plot showing the difference in log-likelihood assigned by GPT-2 to WN vs CHA examples (higher is better).

4.1 GDEX score

Since Kilgarriff et al. did not specify an optimal weighting for the different factors they took into account in the GDEX metric, we look individually at each of the four factors discussed in Section 3.1. We leave for future work investigating optimal weighting for these and other metrics, for example, by tuning them on downstream applications. When comparing these scores for both WN and CHA examples, Figure 1 (lower is better in both metrics) shows that WN has generally higher penalties both for example length and for usage of infrequent words. Specifically, for instance, we found that 80% of CHA's examples have a length penalty of .6 or less, whereas for the same proportion, the length penalty reaches more than .8 in WN. In a subsequent analysis, we found that these differences, if studied between WN's nouns and verbs, clearly favour nouns, that is, WN's nouns are in general accompanied by better examples. Specifically, we found that, on average, the length penalty is .49 for nouns, and .62 for verbs, and that the frequency penalty is .10 for nouns and .15 for verbs.

Finally, while the **sentence probability** is a valid metric, we observe that it is more likely that shorter sentences exhibit lower perplexity, and therefore will be scored higher by a language model. To further investigate this, we conduct an analysis where we split WN's and CHA's examples into 4 bins, namely *short*, *mid-short*, *mid-long* and *long*, with *short* examples containing between 1 and 15 tokens, *mid-short* up to 30 tokens, *mid-long* up to 45 tokens, and *long* above 45 tokens. Then, we compared the probability assigned by the language model to these examples, and verified that, indeed, WN has better short and mid-short examples, but worse mid-long examples. It also important to note that among the *long* examples, most of them were close to 45 tokens for WN, while for CHA they are much longer. To (perhaps anecdotally) illustrate this point, the longest dictionary example in WN is only 46 tokens long, while the longest in CHA is 141. Finally, in terms of usage of anaphoric references, we did not find significantly different results between WN and CHA.

4.2 Definition Modeling

Evaluating the quality of the generated definitions is a subjective matter, as delivering the meaning of words can take many forms. Table 2 shows examples of the predicted definitions generated by a WN-trained model and a CHA-trained model. When analysing these definitions and annotating the error types (following the typification proposed in Noraset et al. (2017)), it seems that the predicted definitions generated by the WN-trained model show evidence of under-specificity (first and second rows), since in each case the definition represents the general idea, but where part of the meaning of the target lemma in context is lost. In the third row, the generated definition falls into the self-reference type of error, since it refers to the same lemma in a circular way.

We also noticed that, generally speaking, the CHA-trained model learned to explicitly mention the prototypical concept or the idea to which a definition applies, and this is interesting from a commonsense learning point of view, which has recently received considerable attention (Gajbhiye et al., 2022; Nguyen et al., 2022). Therefore, given that CHA has many definitions that start with the prototypical concept/entity that embodies that prop-

No.	Lemma	Example	Gold definition	PD_WN	PD_CHA
(1)	accelerate	The car accelerated	move faster	become more powerful or efficient	of a vehicle or aircraft move forward at a high rate of speed
(2)	appear	Did your latest book appear yet?	be issued or published	have a physical form or appearance	of a book or other product reach the shelves of a bookstore or other store
(3)	immigrate	Many people immigrated at the beginning of the 20th century	come into a new country and change residency	become immigratory	of a person move to a foreign country to settle permanently

Table 2: Sample of predicted definitions generated by WN-trained model and CHA-trained model. PD_WN: predicted definition by WN-trained model, PD_CHA: predicted definition by CHA-trained model

	WN	CHA
BLEU	0.18	00.16
METEOR	12.28	14.89
ROUGE-L	16.49	17.37

Table 3: DM evaluation results for WN and CHA

	Nouns	Verbs
BLEU	3.67	0.47
METEOR	20.66	14.13
ROUGE-L	26.85	18.72
Average	1 7.06	11.12

Table 4: DM evaluation results for WN Nouns vs WN Verbs

erty (e.g., "*accelerate*" having a definition starting with "*of a vehicle*"), for the future, this resource could be helpful to map prototypical features to concepts, using dictionary examples as additional contexts.

We evaluated the definitions intrinsically using automatic string matching measures, specifically BLEU, ROUGE-L and METEOR. BLEU is a metric used for machine translation evaluation and compares n-grams matches of the candidate sentence with the reference sentence (Papineni et al., 2002) (we used the default BLEU-4). Rouge-L measures the longest common sub-sequence between the candidate sentence with the reference sentence (Lin, 2004). METEOR is another improved machine translation evaluation metric that matches uni-grams based on their surface forms, stemmed forms, and meanings (Lavie and Agarwal, 2007).

Exp. 1 (WN vs CHA) Table 3 shows the average BLEU, METEOR and ROUGE-L scores for the definitions generated by WN-trained model and CHA-trained model. The results show that the overall scores for evaluating the definition generation model that uses WN examples are low in general, even when comparing it with the model that uses CHA examples for training.

Exp. 2 (WN Nouns vs WN Verbs) Finally, with regards to the WN nouns vs WN verbs experiment, Table 4 shows the results of the three metrics used for evaluating the generated definitions. When comparing these results and the average of the scores, we can see that the quality of generated definitions of nouns is generally better than that of verbs. We leave for future work to further explore the differences between WN's noun vs verb examples, and why nouns seem to be easier to learn.

5 Conclusion

Definition modeling is the task to generate a dictionary definition given an input word and, optionally, some context. While different lexicographic resources are used as supervision for DM systems, there is little work analyzing their intrinsic quality. Our evaluation is focused on the examples available in WordNet and the Oxford Dictionary, where we train a sequence-to-sequence definition modeling architecture based on BART using these two dictionaries. We found that WN's dictionary examples are written in a style that may make them hard to learn (especially verbs), and that they are, generally, (perhaps too) short. For the future, we would like to explore extrinsic evaluations and perform additional experiments with other datasets and language models.

6 Acknowledgements

We thank the anonymous reviewers for their insightful comments. The experiments were executed using the computational facilities of the Advanced Research Computing @Cardiff (ARCCA) at Cardiff University.

References

Eneko Agirre and Philip Edmonds. 2007. *Word sense disambiguation: Algorithms and applications*, volume 33. Springer Science & Business Media.

Tal August, Catharina Reinecke, and Noah Smith. 2022. generating scientific definitions with controllable commplexity.

Satanjeev Banerjee and Ted Pedersen. 2002. An adapted lesk algorithm for word sense disambiguation using wordnet. volume 2276, pages 136–145.

Edoardo Barba, Luigi Procopio, Caterina Lacerra, Tommaso Pasini, and Roberto Navigli. 2021. Exemplification modeling: Can you give me an example, please? In *Proceedings of the Thirtieth International Joint Conference on Artificial Intelligence, IJCAI-21*, pages 3779–3785. International Joint Conferences on Artificial Intelligence Organization.

Henri Bejoint. 2014. The bloomsbury companion to lexicography edited by howard jackson. *Dictionaries: Journal of the Dictionary Society of North America*, 35:374–381.

Michele Bevilacqua, Marco Maru, and Roberto Navigli. 2020. Generationary or "how we went beyond word sense inventories and learned to gloss". In *Proceedings of the 2020 Conference on Empirical Methods in Natural Language Processing (EMNLP)*, pages 7207–7221, Online. Association for Computational Linguistics.

Tom Bosc and Pascal Vincent. 2018. Auto-encoding dictionary definitions into consistent word embeddings. In *EMNLP*, pages 1522–1532.

Bartosz Broda, Maciej Piasecki, and Stan Szpakowicz. 2009. A wordnet from the ground up. *Oficyna Wydawnicza Politechniki Wrocławskiej*.

Pere-Lluís Huguet Cabot and Roberto Navigli. 2021. Rebel: Relation extraction by end-to-end language generation. In *Findings of the Association for Computational Linguistics: EMNLP 2021*, pages 2370–2381.

Ting-Yun Chang and Yun-Nung Chen. 2019. What does this word mean? explaining contextualized embeddings with natural language definition. In *Proceedings of the 2019 Conference on Empirical Methods in Natural Language Processing and the 9th International Joint Conference on Natural Language Processing (EMNLP-IJCNLP)*, pages 6064–6070, Hong Kong, China. Association for Computational Linguistics.

Ting-Yun Chang, Ta-Chung Chi, Shang-Chi Tsai, and Yun-Nung Chen. 2018. xsense: Learning sense-separated sparse representations and textual definitions for explainable word sense networks.

Pinzhen Chen and Zheng Zhao. 2022. A unified model for reverse dictionary and definition modelling. *arXiv preprint arXiv:2205.04602*.

Nicola De Cao, Gautier Izacard, Sebastian Riedel, and Fabio Petroni. 2020. Autoregressive entity retrieval. In *International Conference on Learning Representations*.

Luis Espinosa-Anke, Jose Camacho-Collados, Sara Rodríguez Fernández, Horacio Saggion, and Leo Wanner. 2016. Extending wordnet with fine-grained collocational information via supervised distributional learning. In *Proceedings of COLING 2016: Technical Papers. The 26th International Conference on Computational Linguistics; 2016 Dec. 11-16; Osaka (Japan).[place unknown]: COLING; 2016. p. 900-10.* COLING.

Manaal Faruqui, Jesse Dodge, Sujay Jauhar, Chris Dyer, Eduard Hovy, and Noah Smith. 2014. Retrofitting word vectors to semantic lexicons.

Christiane Fellbaum. 2013. Wordnet. In Carol Chapelle, editor, *The encyclopedia of applied linguistics*, pages 6739–6746. Blackwell Publishing Ltd.

Artyom Gadetsky, Ilya Yakubovskiy, and Dmitry Vetrov. 2018. Conditional generators of words definitions. In *Proceedings of the 56th Annual Meeting of the Association for Computational Linguistics (Volume 2: Short Papers)*, pages 266–271, Melbourne, Australia. Association for Computational Linguistics.

Amit Gajbhiye, Luis Espinosa-Anke, and Steven Schockaert. 2022. Modelling commonsense properties using pre-trained bi-encoders.

Noah Gardner, Hafiz Khan, and Chih-Cheng Hung. 2022. Definition modeling: literature review and dataset analysis. *Applied Computing and Intelligence*, 2(1):83–98.

Felix Hill, Kyunghyun Cho, Anna Korhonen, and Yoshua Bengio. 2016. Learning to understand phrases by embedding the dictionary. *Transactions of the Association for Computational Linguistics*, 4:17–30.

Han Huang, Tomoyuki Kajiwara, and Yuki Arase. 2021. Definition modelling for appropriate specificity. In *Proceedings of the 2021 Conference on Empirical Methods in Natural Language Processing*, pages 2499–2509, Online and Punta Cana, Dominican Republic. Association for Computational Linguistics.

Shonosuke Ishiwatari, Hiroaki Hayashi, Naoki Yoshinaga, Graham Neubig, Shoetsu Sato, Masashi Toyoda, and Masaru Kitsuregawa. 2019. Learning to describe unknown phrases with local and global contexts. In *Proceedings of the 2019 Conference of the North American Chapter of the Association for Computational Linguistics: Human Language Technologies, Volume 1 (Long and Short Papers)*, pages 3467–3476, Minneapolis, Minnesota. Association for Computational Linguistics.

Adam Kilgarriff, Miloš Husák, Katy McAdam, Michael Rundell, and Pavel Rychlý. 2008. Gdex: Automatically finding good dictionary examples in a corpus.

In *Proceedings of the 13th EURALEX International Congress*, pages 425–432, Barcelona, Spain. Institut Universitari de Linguistica Aplicada, Universitat Pompeu Fabra.

Cunliang Kong, Yujie Wang, Ruining Chong, Liner Yang, Hengyuan Zhang, Erhong Yang, and Yaping Huang. 2022. Blcu-icall at semeval-2022 task 1: Cross-attention multitasking framework for definition modeling. *arXiv preprint arXiv:2204.07701*.

Alon Lavie and Abhaya Agarwal. 2007. Meteor: An automatic metric for mt evaluation with high levels of correlation with human judgments. pages 228–231.

Mike Lewis, Yinhan Liu, Naman Goyal, Marjan Ghazvininejad, Abdelrahman Mohamed, Omer Levy, Veselin Stoyanov, and Luke Zettlemoyer. 2019. Bart: Denoising sequence-to-sequence pre-training for natural language generation, translation, and comprehension.

Chin-Yew Lin. 2004. ROUGE: A package for automatic evaluation of summaries. In *Text Summarization Branches Out*, pages 74–81, Barcelona, Spain. Association for Computational Linguistics.

Timothee Mickus, Denis Paperno, and Matthieu Constant. 2019. Mark my word: A sequence-to-sequence approach to definition modeling. In *Proceedings of the First NLPL Workshop on Deep Learning for Natural Language Processing*, pages 1–11, Turku, Finland. Linköping University Electronic Press.

George Miller. 1995. Wordnet: A lexical database for english. *Communications of the ACM*, 38:39–.

D.I. Moldovan and Rada Mihalcea. 2000. Using wordnet and lexical operators to improve internet searches. *Internet Computing, IEEE*, 4:34 – 43.

Jorge Morato, Miguel Marzal, Juan Llorens, and Jos Moreiro. 2004. Wordnet applications. *Proceedings of the 2nd Global Wordnet Conference*, 2004.

Nikola Mrkšić, Ivan Vulić, Diarmuid O Séaghdha, Ira Leviant, Roi Reichart, Milica Gašić, Anna Korhonen, and Steve Young. 2017. Semantic specialization of distributional word vector spaces using monolingual and cross-lingual constraints. *Transactions of the association for Computational Linguistics*, 5:309–324.

Tuan-Phong Nguyen, Simon Razniewski, Julien Romero, and Gerhard Weikum. 2022. Refined commonsense knowledge from large-scale web contents. *IEEE Transactions on Knowledge and Data Engineering*, pages 1–16.

Ke Ni and William Yang Wang. 2017. Learning to explain non-standard English words and phrases. In *Proceedings of the Eighth International Joint Conference on Natural Language Processing (Volume 2: Short Papers)*, pages 413–417, Taipei, Taiwan. Asian Federation of Natural Language Processing.

Thanapon Noraset, Chen Liang, Larry Birnbaum, and Doug Downey. 2017. Definition modeling: Learning to define word embeddings in natural language. pages 3259–3266.

Kishore Papineni, Salim Roukos, Todd Ward, and Wei-Jing Zhu. 2002. Bleu: A method for automatic evaluation of machine translation. In *Proceedings of the 40th Annual Meeting on Association for Computational Linguistics*, ACL '02, page 311–318, USA. Association for Computational Linguistics.

Alec Radford, Jeffrey Wu, Rewon Child, David Luan, Dario Amodei, and Ilya Sutskever. 2019. Language Models are Unsupervised Multitask Learners.

Vered Shwartz, Yoav Goldberg, and Ido Dagan. 2016. Improving hypernymy detection with an integrated path-based and distributional method. *arXiv preprint arXiv:1603.06076*.

Ivan Vulić, Daniela Gerz, Douwe Kiela, Felix Hill, and Anna Korhonen. 2017. Hyperlex: A large-scale evaluation of graded lexical entailment. *Computational Linguistics*, 43(4):781–835.

Ivan Vulić and Nikola Mrkšić. 2017. Specialising word vectors for lexical entailment. *arXiv preprint arXiv:1710.06371*.

Thomas Wolf, Lysandre Debut, Victor Sanh, Julien Chaumond, Clement Delangue, Anthony Moi, Pierric Cistac, Tim Rault, Rémi Louf, Morgan Funtowicz, et al. 2020. Transformers: State-of-the-art natural language processing. In *Proceedings of the 2020 conference on empirical methods in natural language processing: system demonstrations*, pages 38–45.

Ruimin Zhu, Thanapon Noraset, Alisa Liu, Wenxin Jiang, and Doug Downey. 2019. Multi-sense definition modeling using word sense decompositions.

Michael Zock, Olivier Ferret, and Didier Schwab. 2010. Deliberate word access: an intuition, a roadmap and some preliminary empirical results. *International Journal of Speech Technology*, 13(4):201–218.

Exploring Nominal Coercion in Semantic Spaces with Static and Contextualized Word Embeddings

Chenxin Liu and **Emmanuele Chersoni**
The Hong Kong Polytechnic University
Department of Chinese and Bilingual Studies
Yuk Choi Road 11, Hung Hom, Kowloon, Hong Kong (China)
chenxin.liu@connect.polyu.edu.hk, emmanuelechersoni@gmail.com

Abstract

The distinction between *mass* nouns and *count* nouns has a long history in formal semantics, and linguists have been trying to identify the semantic properties defining the two classes. However, they also recognized that both can undergo meaning shifts and be used in contexts of a different type, via *nominal coercion*.

In this paper, we present an approach to measure the meaning shift in count-mass coercion in English that makes use of static and contextualized word embedding distance.

Our results show that the coercion shifts are detected only by a small subset of the traditional word embedding models, and that the shifts detected by the contextualized embedding of BERT are more pronounced for mass nouns.

1 Introduction

The literature in formal semantics has debated for long on the distinction between *count* nouns and *mass* nouns, which has often been described as an opposition between discrete, countable objects and substances that cannot instead be divided into subunits. A notorious formal characterization of this intuition is provided by Link (1983): mass nouns like *wine* are *non-quantized*, in the sense that each subpart of *wine* will still count as *wine*; on the other hand, count nouns like *cat* are *quantized*, because if you take a subpart of a *cat*, it will not count as a *cat* (Cheng, 1973). According to such view, in other words, the two types of nouns denote in different domains with different properties.

Chomsky (1965) proposed instead a lexicalist perspective on the problem, where nouns are marked with a binary feature $\pm$ COUNT determining the kind of syntactic context (mass or count) in which they can appear. Although the approaches adopt different criteria for defining the "countability" of the nouns, they both predict that count nouns will (mostly) appear in count contexts, and mass nouns will (mostly) appear in mass contexts.

However, cases like the following are extremely frequent in natural language:

1. There is *rabbit* in my soup. (count to mass)
2. Two *wines* at table four! (mass to count)

In 1., the count noun *rabbit* is interpreted as *rabbit meat*, while in 2. the plural form of the mass noun *wine* means *glasses of wine*. Both cases are examples of **coercion**, a semantic phenomenon occurring when the standard interpretation of an expression (in our case, the noun) yields an impossible conceptual representation (e.g. in 1. a rabbit swimming in the soup) (Wiese and Maling, 2005); consequently, a more plausible interpretation is retrieved by "enriching" the semantic representation with concepts that are associated to the standard interpretation of the target expression (*enriched composition*; see Jackendoff (1997)). The focus of this paper is specifically on nominal coercion of mass and count nouns.

Since it is rare to find nouns that occur exclusively in either mass or count contexts, it makes more sense to talk about predominantly count and predominantly mass nouns. Chierchia (2010) describes the idea of mass-count *elasticity*, meaning that any noun can be in principle mass or count, its status being determined at the level of the nominal phrase. When we say "predominantly" mass or count noun, therefore, we mean that a noun has the tendency to occur more frequently in one of the two context types. On such basis, the count-mass distinction can be intuitively seen as a continuum, with the nouns traditionally described in the literature being closer to one the two extremes (Katz and Zamparelli, 2012).

In this work, we investigate to what extent modern *Distributional Semantic Models* -which are nowadays the standard for the representation of lexical meaning in NLP- encode the meaning shifts caused by mass-count coercion. We run two different experiments, making use respectively of

Proceedings of the Workshop on Cognitive Aspects of the Lexicon, pages 49–57
November 20, 2022. ©2022 Association for Computational Linguistics
https://doi.org/10.26615/978-954-452-056-4_007

static and contextualized word embedding models to identify the meaning shifts, and we study some of the potential factors that might influence the extent to which a noun is shifting.

2 Related Work

Modern NLP widely adopts Distributional Semantic Models (DSMs) for the representation of lexical meaning, using vectors that are based on the co-occurrences patterns of words in large text corpora. Vector representations are usually compared using the cosine of the angle between them, and the smaller the angle between two words, the closer their meanings will be (Turney and Pantel, 2010).

The literature on DSMs has identified three generations of vector spaces (Lenci et al., 2022). The first generation is typically referred to as *count models* (Baroni et al., 2014), because the spaces are obtained from the extraction of co-occurrences between the target words and the linguistic contexts that are deemed relevant, then the co-occurrences are weighted via associations measures (Landauer and Dumais, 1997; Baroni and Lenci, 2010; Bullinaria and Levy, 2012).

A second family of models emerged in the early 2010s and became known as *word embeddings* or *prediction-based* models (Mikolov et al., 2013; Bojanowski et al., 2017). In such models, the learning of word vectors is generally framed as a supervised task: a neural network is trained to predict words given other context words, and the vectors are learned as parameters. Words that tend to cooccur will have similar vector representations.

However, a common feature of both families is that they produce *static* vector representations, in the sense that each word gets represented as a single vector, which makes it difficult to handle cases of ambiguity and polysemy. The most recent generation of distributional vectors is said instead to be *contextualized*, because word representations are generated in context on the basis of the activation states of a neural language model (Peters et al., 2018; Devlin et al., 2019). One of the advantages of models like BERT (Devlin et al., 2019) is that they allow generating a specific word embedding for each context in which target words occur, making them an interesting option for modeling contextual phenomena such as nominal coercion.

Concerning the modeling work on nominal coercion in Distributional Semantics, Katz and Zamparelli (2012) were the first, to our knowledge, to use DSMs to investigate the phenomenon. They considered pluralisation as a proxy of count usage, and built a traditional count model with separate vector representations for the singular and the plural of a list of candidate mass and count nouns. Consistently with their initial hypothesis, they found that the vector similarity between singular and plural is higher for count nouns than for mass nouns, since the latter undergo a meaning shift when they are pluralized (cf. example 2 in Section 1). Hürlimann et al. (2014) later analyzed the factors affecting the similarity scores in the data by Katz and Zamparelli (2012), reporting that abstract and highly polysemous nouns undergo greater semantic shifts as a consequence of pluralization.

Both these works are close in spirit to our research: in our first experiment, we will use several types of word embedding models to compare the distances between singular and plural forms of mass and count nouns; in our second experiment, we will use the contextualized vectors of BERT to observe how coercion changes the semantic representations of the nouns in mass and count contexts, which we automatically extract from the British National Corpus (Leech, 1992). To our knowledge, this is the first study specifically on mass-count nominal coercion including both static and contextualized embedding models, although other types of coercion have previously been investigated in the literature on DSMs, e.g. complement coercion (Zarcone and Padó, 2011; Chersoni et al., 2017; Rambelli et al., 2020; Chersoni et al., 2021; Ye et al., 2022) or classical metonymies (CONTAINER-FOR-CONTENT, PRODUCER FOR PRODUCT etc.) (Pedinotti and Lenci, 2020).

3 Experiment 1: Comparing the Singular-Plural Similarity in Static Embedding Spaces

In our first experiment, we follow Katz and Zamparelli (2012) in considering pluralisation as a reliable proxy of count usage and we compare the distributional representations of singular and plural forms of candidate mass and count nouns across the most popular word embedding spaces in the literature. If a model is able to detect the coercion meaning shift, then we expect to see that the average semantic similarity between singular and plural forms is *lower* for the mass nouns (see example 2 in Section 1). We use a list of predominantly count and predom-

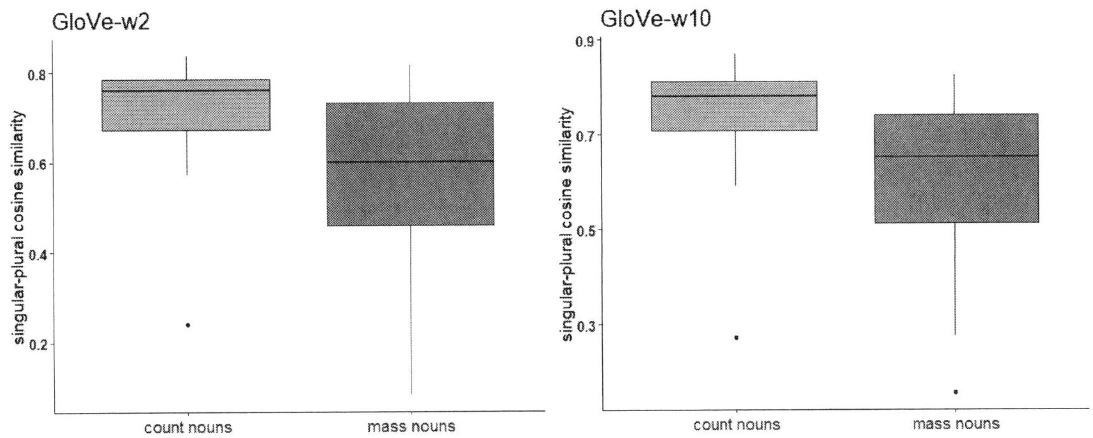

Figure 1: Cosine similarity scores for the singular-plural comparison of count and mass nouns in the GloVe-w2 (left) and in the GloVe-w10 model (right).

inantly mass nouns introduced in the same paper, identified via the selection of syntactic contexts:

- 1a. candidate mass nouns: *information, time, money, detail, space, fun, attention, info, part, work, interest, evidence, experience, energy, power, water, room, recipe, use, opportunity, effort, emphasis, support, research, trouble*;
- 1b. candidate count nouns: *time, year, day, way, person, place, bit, week, man, opportunity, problem, lot, thing, role, company, basis, child, look, one, report, month, book, area, approach, hour.*

The vectors of the target nouns and their corresponding plural forms are firstly extracted from different word embedding spaces. Our pool of models includes the following vector spaces: CBOW vectors (Mikolov et al., 2013), one model with window size 2 (**CBOW-w2**) and one with window size 10 (**CBOW-w10**); Skip-Gram vectors (Mikolov et al., 2013), one model with window size 2 (**SGNS-w2**) and one with window size 10 (**SGNS-w10**); GloVe vectors (Pennington et al., 2014), one model with window size 2 (**GloVe-w2**) and one with window size 10 (**GloVe-w10**); FastText vectors (Bojanowski et al., 2017), one model with window size 2 (**FastText-w2**) and one with window size 10 (**FastText-w10**). Finally, we also include two variants of the Skip Gram where the contexts are selected via syntactic dependency with the target word (Levy and Goldberg, 2014; Lenci et al., 2022), one with untyped dependencies (**SGNS-synf**) and one with typed dependencies (**SGNS-synt**) (e.g. in the first case, given the target *dog* and the context *big dog*, the model will just use the syntactic neighbor *big* as a context, while the second will also include the type of syntactic relation linking the two words, i.e. adjectival modifier). All models have been trained with default hyperparameters on a concatenation of the UkWac (Baroni et al., 2009), of the British National Corpus and of a 2018 dump of Wikipedia [1], and the semantic similarity is estimated via the classical cosine metric.

Model	Avg. mass	Avg. count	p
CBOW-w2	0.59	0.60	
CBOW-w10	0.54	0.56	
FastText-w2	0.66	0.68	
FastText-w10	0.69	0.74	$*$
GloVe-w2	0.56	0.71	$***$
GloVe-w10	0.60	0.75	$***$
SGNS-w2	0.64	0.66	
SGNS-w10	0.62	0.67	$*$
SGNS-synf	0.66	0.66	
SGNS-synt	0.67	0.65	

Table 1: Average of cosine similarity scores between singular and plural forms for each vector space, and p-values computed on the scores of mass and count nouns. Significant differences are reported as follows: $p < 0.05*$, $p < 0.01 **$, $p < 0.001 ***$.

We report the average similarity scores between singular and plural forms for both mass and count nouns in Table 1, and we use the Wilcoxon rank sum test to identify significant differences between the two groups. While for most models the scores are very close, 4 of them manage to identify a sig-

[1] The corpus was POS-tagged and parsed and contains syntactic annotations in the Universal Dependencies format (Nivre et al., 2016; De Marneffe et al., 2021).

nificant difference and in all cases the similarity is lower for the mass nouns. GloVe models are the ones finding the biggest differences, with the scores of mass nouns being significantly lower (see the boxplots in Figure 1). Interestingly, among the embedding models, GloVe is the only one belonging to the more traditional count-based types, and thus more similar to the ones used in the studies of Katz and Zamparelli (2012) and Hürlimann et al. (2014). This may suggest that the GloVe training method, based on global co-occurrence statistics, is a better fit for capturing fine-grained semantic differences than the vectors derived from the Word2Vec family, which are all trained on separate local context windows. Additionally, larger differences are found by the models with a larger window, suggesting that semantic shifts are better captured by vector spaces modeling topic/domain similarity (Turney, 2012). On the other hand, vector spaces modeling local contextual co-occurrences fail to find any difference between mass and count nouns.

4 Experiment 2: Modeling Mass/Count Coercion with BERT

In our second experiment, we extract sentences in which our mass and count nouns occur from the British National Corpus, and we use the patterns described in Katz and Zamparelli (2012) to divide them into mass contexts and count contexts, and then we use the BERT model to compare their contextualized representations. Using BERT allows us to take into account a wider variety of contexts rather than just using a pair of vectors for the singular and plural forms. In this case, we expect that both types of nouns, when they occur in different context types, will have a lower semantic similarity, because both of them will be undergoing semantic shifts (mass to count or count to mass).

The selected patterns are the following:

- 2a. mass: i) singular nouns immediately be preceded by *lots, plenty of, much, more, less, enough, most, sufficient, considerable, boundless, ample,* or *limited* that are not preceded by *a(n)*; ii) singular nouns directly following a verb;

- 2b. count: i) singular nouns immediately be preceded by *a, an, one, every, first, each, another*; ii) plural nouns.

In both contexts, the nouns are excluded if followed by another noun, adjective, or participle to avoid selecting noun-noun compounds. In mass contexts, we also exclude the cases where the target nouns directly follow a participle to prevent misclassification of the participle noun phrases, e.g. *the baked cake*. To increase the reliability of the sentences for the experiment, we manually filter the sentences containing cases of idiomatic usages, e.g. *day by day*. As a result, we extract a total of 614512 sentences. Only the candidate mass or count nouns occurring at least 20 times in both mass and count contexts are considered. Generally, count nouns have a higher average frequency in both contexts, and both count and mass nouns have a higher average frequency in count contexts. The frequency of count nouns in count context ranges from 49218 (*time*) to 6148 (*role*), with a mean of 27787.47, while the frequency in mass context ranges from 8211(*time*) to 20 (*role*), with a mean of 1245.53. For mass nouns, the width of frequency in mass context is from 9259 (*part*) to 45 (*recipe*) and the average frequency is 2110.43, whereas the mass nouns in count contexts have an average frequency of 6414.19, a maximum of 49598 (*time*) and a minimum of 34 (*information*). Notice that nouns can, in principle, occur both as count and as mass nouns, and their frequencies are computed separately as they have been extracted with different patterns. Among the target nouns, *time* and *opportunity* appear as both candidate count noun and candidate mass noun. Although the nouns may be argued as ambiguous, the syntactic patterns used to extract them are unambiguous and can correctly reflect their usage in the count contexts and mass contexts. [2] Therefore, they could still be included to compare the meaning shift a noun undergoes in the transition from the 'standard' context to coerced context.

Noun	Context	Avg. freq	Avg. freq	Min. freq
Count	Count	27787.47	49218	6148
Count	Mass	1245.53	8211	20
Mass	Mass	2110.43	9259	45
Mass	Count	6414.49	48598	34

Table 2: Statistics for the context extraction from the British National Corpus: average, max and min frequency for each noun-context type.

Then we use the BERT-BASE-UNCASED model and the MINICONS Python library (Misra, 2022) [3] to generate semantic representations of the target

[2] We thank the first anonymous reviewer for pointing out this issue.

[3] `https://github.com/kanishkamisra/minicons`

nouns in context: the idea is to measure the similarity scores of each (mass or count) noun to itself for randomly sampled sentences. We carry out the sampling either i) by selecting context pairs where the target noun occurs in both cases in its mass, or in its count contexts (within the same context type, which could be either count or mass); or ii) by selecting context pairs where the target noun occurs once in a mass context and once in a count context (*between* context types).

This means that each noun type will have its occurrences sampled in three different ways:

1. all context pairs sampled from its own type (mass nouns in mass contexts, count nouns in count contexts);

2. all context pairs sampled from the other type (mass nouns in count contexts, count nouns in mass contexts);

3. the context pair composed by one mass context and one count context.

The similarity comparison between 1) and 3) is the most relevant one for our study: we expect that similarities in 3) to be much lower than in 1), to an extent proportional to the meaning shift that the noun is undergoing. For each noun, we repeat the sampling 10 times from each group, and for each time we randomly extract 10 different context pairs to generate the vectors.

Notice that, differently from a big part of the literature, we use Spearman's rank correlation and not the cosine as a similarity metric for BERT vectors. Our choice is motivated by recent findings about the anisotropy of contextualized vector spaces, where a small number of 'rogue' dimensions dominate the cosine similarity scores (Ethayarajh, 2019; Timkey and van Schijndel, 2021). Timkey and van Schijndel (2021) showed that using postprocessing techniques like normalization or rank-based metrics such as Spearman's rank led to much better correlations with human similarity judgments. Moreover, rank-based metrics have been previously proven to be more robust than cosine in several similarity-related tasks (Santus et al., 2016a,b, 2017, 2018; Zhelezniak et al., 2019).

The results of Spearman's rank correlation experiment are reported in Table 3. The average correlation of context pairs where the target noun occurs in its typical kind of context (i.e. count nouns in count contexts, mass nouns in the mass ones) reflects how semantically similar the target noun is to itself when used in the 'standard' meaning, while the average correlation across different context types reflects the similarity between the standard and the coerced meaning. Therefore, the difference between the two correlations should quantify the meaning shift of the target noun when nominal coercion is imposed on the standard interpretation.

Noun	Context	Avg. corr
Count	Count	0.455
Count	Mass	0.466
Count	Both	0.360
Mass	Mass	0.550
Mass	Count	0.476
Mass	Both	0.391

Table 3: Average Spearman's rank correlation scores for each noun type under the six different sampling conditions.

Let us illustrate the statement with an example for the predominantly count noun *problem* and an example for the predominantly mass noun *water*, respectively.

s1. more, i believe, than would be acceptable to people, so that nuclear power in itself will never be the solution to our energy ***problems***. (count context)

s2. not surprisingly these devices are distributed with little or no instruction on correct use — thus increasing women's health ***problems***. (count context)

s3. current models seem to be auto-sensing, so there shouldn't be much ***problem***. (mass context)

The noun *problems* in s1 and s2 refer in both cases to a specific issue that needs to be resolved, while *problem* in s3 seems to be more generic and more similar to *trouble*. Accordingly, the correlation of s1 and s2 is 0.55, and the correlation of s1 and s3 is 0.33. The correlation difference between the s1-s2 pair and the s1-s3 pair should reflect the meaning shift that *problem* undergoes, changing from its standard "count" meaning to its coerced interpretation in a mass context.

s4. you can drink ***water*** freely during the course of the diet. (mass context)

s5. in the year to august 1992, the works used 22 per cent less ***water***, 18 per cent less nitrogen, 11 per cent less steam and nine per cent less electricity. (mass context)

s6. to the east of Venice lies Lido di Jesolo and Caorle, with miles of golden sand lapped by the warm ***waters*** of the Adriatic. (count context)

The noun *water* in s4 and s5 is used in mass contexts and it has the standard meaning of i) *water* as

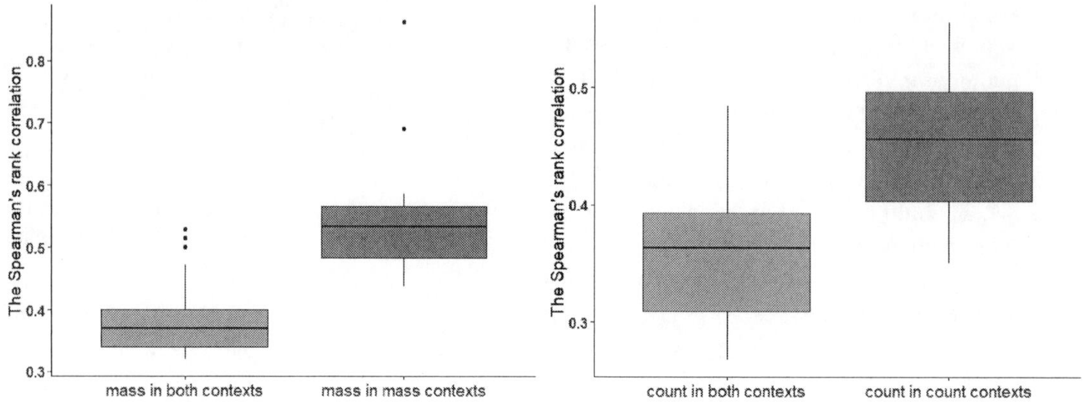

Figure 2: Spearman's rank correlations for mass (left) and count (right) nouns computed with BERT-BASE-UNCASED. The dark green box shows the correlations for the same group (mass in mass, count in count) context sampling, the light green box shows the correlations with one mass and one count context.

a liquid that can be drunk (s4); and ii) the amount of *water* usage in a hydraulic system (s5). On the other hand, in the last context (s6) *waters* is rather referring to a specific geographical/territorial unit. The correlation of the s4-s5 pair is 0.59, while the correlation of the s4-s6 pair is 0.41, and the correlation difference between the two pairs should reflect the meaning shift from mass to count usage.

It is immediately evident from Table that 3 count nouns generally have a lower average Spearman correlation score than mass nouns in either count or mass contexts, suggesting that the cluster of count nouns is less compact and their meanings are more varied and scattered across the semantic space. It should be noticed that many of the count nouns are highly frequent (e.g. *child, thing, way, man, one, place, time, day* all have more than 10K occurrences, more than any mass noun in our data), therefore they might display much more contextual variation in their usage, which could explain the relatively low similarity value. Indeed, the similarity of the count nouns when the contexts are sampled from the count or the mass groups does not differ significantly, with the latter being even slightly higher.

For both count and mass nouns, as we expected, we observe a lower similarity when the contexts are sampled from both groups (see also Figure 2): the average difference with the sampling within the same group is, respectively, of 0.1 and 0.16 correlation points, confirming the finding that mass nouns typically undergo a greater meaning shift (Hürlimann et al., 2014) even when patterns beyond pluralization are taken into account.

It is also noticeable that mass nouns have a relatively high similarity when they are sampled in count contexts, which could be explained by the fact that many of these nouns have systematic secondary meanings that are more compatible with a count usage (nouns denoting drinkable liquids are typically undergoing a shift from the liquid to the container, e.g. *beers* $\rightarrow$ *pints of beer*, or from the liquid to the variety, e.g. *wines* $\rightarrow$ *varieties of wine*). In sum, the results of our experiment provide further support to the view that the mass/count distinction should be seen as a continuum, and that the syntactic context is the strongest cue to the type of denotation (Chierchia, 2010). Moreover, even with more varied mass and count contexts than the ones used in previous studies (Katz and Zamparelli, 2012; Hürlimann et al., 2014), we also find that coercion makes mass nouns undergo a greater semantic shift than count nouns.

We also analyze some of the factors mentioned as relevant by Hürlimann et al. (2014) to predict the meaning shift of the nouns: frequency, polysemy, and concreteness. For polysemy, we simply use the WordNet synsets (Fellbaum, 2010) of a noun as an indicator of the number of word senses, while for concreteness we use the values from the English norms by Brysbaert et al. (2014).

Unfortunately, we do not find any significant correlation between the average differences in the Spearman correlations that we computed with BERT and the above-mentioned factors, probably because of the small size of our set of nouns. Table 4 presents the statistics for the top-5 most shifting count and mass nouns (i.e. the nouns with the

Noun	Freq.	WordNet Synsets	Concreteness
company	18792	9	4.11
child	43018	4	4.78
thing	47655	12	3.17
way	29644	12	2.34
area	26273	6	3.72
information	3199	5	2.87
attention	2323	6	2.30
trouble	1051	6	2.25
support	308	11	2.83
money	4947	3	4.54

Table 4: Frequency, synsets and concreteness for the top-5 most shifting count (**bold**) and mass (*italic*) nouns.

highest average correlation difference). Despite the lack of significance of the correlation scores, it can still be noticed that: i) regarding polysemy, the most shifting nouns tend to have a relatively high number of word senses; ii) as for concreteness, the most shifting count nouns have relatively high values, while the most shifting mass nouns tend to denote more abstract entities. More studies with a larger set of predominantly mass and count nouns are needed to confirm the finding.

4.1 A Final Note about Polysemy

With reference to our *rabbit meat* example (see Section 1) and as a general methodological consideration, Reviewer 2 points out that the, given the polysemy of the word *rabbit*, which is also attested in dictionaries, this example cannot be considered as a case of coercion, but it just corresponds to a different word sense. As a consequence, the polysemy of the target nouns should be identified in advance, because otherwise we risk to confuse coercion with occurrences of different word senses.

Since we are adopting the perspective of distributional approaches, in our view the main issue is whether linguistic distributions are *determined* by the inventory of senses of a word, or they are *determining* what we conceive as their inventory of senses, in accordance to the so-called strong versions of the Distributional Hypothesis (Miller and Charles, 1991; Lenci, 2008). In cases such the above-mentioned one, coercion itself might be responsible the emergence of new meanings and senses. Keeping the *rabbit meat* example, one could imagine that, following the same pattern, the speakers of a language at some point could start using the name for its meat in similar mass contexts, and that would undoubtedly qualify as a case of coercion because the coerced meaning will be an innovation, and thus it would not be attested in any dictionary. Only when the usage of the name of the animal for its meat will have become frequent enough to be conventional, then dictionaries will start including it as a secondary sense.

This does not detract from the validity of the reviewer's objection. But we would like to clarify that, in our approach, we consider the word senses annotated in dictionaries and lexicographic resources as possibly consequential to shifts in linguistic distributions, and not the other way around.

5 Conclusion

In this paper, we have presented two experiments on modeling nominal coercion of mass and count nouns with two different typologies of Distributional Semantic Models. In the first experiment, we compared the vector representations of singular and plural mass/count nouns across several popular word embedding models. Perhaps surprisingly, we found that i) the count-based GloVe models and ii) the Word2Vec-like models with larger contextual windows were the most successful in identifying significant differences between singular and plural representations of mass nouns, whose meanings shifted more when they were pluralized, while the most of the other models did not detect any shift. We hypothesized, therefore, that such semantic shifts are better captured by semantic spaces that focus on modeling similarities of topic/domain, rather than similarity of co-occurrence in the same local contexts.

In the second experiment, we compared the vectors generated by BERT in different context types. We found that the self-similarity of the nouns sharply decreased when contexts of different types were sampled to generate the contextualized representations and that the shifts of predominantly mass nouns were more pronounced. Our qualitative analyses suggested that factors such as polysemy and concreteness of the nouns might play a role in predicting semantic shifts, although more studies with a larger set of nouns are necessary.

Another promising direction for future research would be using DSMs to model the effects of nominal coercion in human sentence processing, since psycholinguistic studies proved that, in several languages (e.g. English, German, Mandarin Chinese), coerced nouns lead to increased reading times and longer eye fixations (McElree et al., 2001; Traxler et al., 2002; Pylkkanen and McElree, 2006; Zarcone et al., 2017; Xue et al., 2021). In this sense, integrating DSMs-derived similarity metrics in the current computational models could lead to better estimation of reading difficulties induced by coercion operations.

Acknowledgements

This research was made possible by the start-up research fund (1-BD8S) at the Hong Kong Polytechnic University. We would also like to thank the two anonymous reviewers for their comments.

References

Marco Baroni, Silvia Bernardini, Adriano Ferraresi, and Eros Zanchetta. 2009. The WaCky Wide Web: a Collection of Very Large Linguistically Processed Web-crawled Corpora. *Language Resources and Evaluation*, 43(3):209–226.

Marco Baroni, Georgiana Dinu, and Germán Kruszewski. 2014. Don ' t Count, Predict! a Systematic Comparison of Context-counting vs. Context-predicting Semantic Vectors. In *Proceedings of ACL*.

Marco Baroni and Alessandro Lenci. 2010. Distributional Memory: A General Framework for Corpus-based Semantics. *Computational Linguistics*, 36(4):673–721.

Piotr Bojanowski, Edouard Grave, Armand Joulin, and Tomas Mikolov. 2017. Enriching Word Vectors with Subword Information. *Transactions of the Association for Computational Linguistics*, 5:135–146.

Marc Brysbaert, Amy Beth Warriner, and Victor Kuperman. 2014. Concreteness Ratings for 40 Thousand Generally Known English Word Lemmas. *Behavior Research Methods*, 46(3):904–911.

John A Bullinaria and Joseph P Levy. 2012. Extracting Semantic Representations from Word Co-occurrence Statistics: Stop-lists, Stemming, and SVD. *Behavior Research Methods*, 44(3):890–907.

Chung-Ying Cheng. 1973. Response to Moravcsik. *Approaches to Natural Language*.

Emmanuele Chersoni, Alessandro Lenci, and Philippe Blache. 2017. Logical Metonymy in a Distributional Model of Sentence Comprehension. In *Proceedings of *SEM*.

Emmanuele Chersoni, Enrico Santus, Alessandro Lenci, Philippe Blache, and Chu-Ren Huang. 2021. Not All Arguments Are Processed Equally: A Distributional Model of Argument Complexity. *Language Resources and Evaluation*, 55(4):873–900.

Gennaro Chierchia. 2010. Mass Nouns, Vagueness and Semantic Variation. *Synthese*, 174(1):99–149.

Noam Chomsky. 1965. *Aspects of the Theory of Syntax*. MIT Press.

Marie-Catherine De Marneffe, Christopher D Manning, Joakim Nivre, and Daniel Zeman. 2021. Universal Dependencies. *Computational Linguistics*, 47(2):255–308.

Jacob Devlin, Ming-Wei Chang, Kenton Lee, and Kristina Toutanova. 2019. BERT: Pre-training of Deep Bidirectional Transformers for Language Understanding. In *Proceedings of NAACL*.

Kawin Ethayarajh. 2019. How Contextual Are Contextualized Word Representations? Comparing the Geometry of BERT, ELMo, and GPT-2 Embeddings. In *Proceedings of EMNLP*.

Christiane Fellbaum. 2010. Wordnet. In *Theory and Applications of Ontology: Computer Applications*, pages 231–243. Springer.

Manuela Hürlimann, Raffaella Bernardi, and Denis Paperno. 2014. Nominal Coercion in Space: Mass/Count Nouns and Distributional Semantics. In *Proceedings of CLiC-it*.

Ray Jackendoff. 1997. *The Architecture of the Language Faculty*. 28. MIT Press.

Graham Katz and Roberto Zamparelli. 2012. Quantifying Count/Mass Elasticity. In *Proceedings of the West Coast Conference on Formal Linguistics*.

Thomas K Landauer and Susan T Dumais. 1997. A Solution to Plato's Problem: The Latent Semantic Analysis Theory of Acquisition, Induction, and Representation of Knowledge. *Psychological Review*, 104(2):211.

Geoffrey Neil Leech. 1992. 100 Million Words of English: The British National Corpus (BNC). *Language Research*.

Alessandro Lenci. 2008. Distributional Semantics in Linguistic and Cognitive Research. *Italian Journal of Linguistics*, 20(1):1–31.

Alessandro Lenci, Magnus Sahlgren, Patrick Jeuniaux, Amaru Cuba Gyllensten, and Martina Miliani. 2022. A Comparative Evaluation and Analysis of Three Generations of Distributional Semantic Models. *Language Resources and Evaluation*, pages 1–45.

Omer Levy and Yoav Goldberg. 2014. Dependency-based Word Embeddings. In *Proceedings of ACL*.

Godehard Link. 1983. *The Logical Analysis of Plurals and Mass Terms: A Lattice-theoretical Approach*, volume 127. Blackwell Oxford.

Brian McElree, Matthew J Traxler, Martin J Pickering, Rachel E Seely, and Ray Jackendoff. 2001. Reading time evidence for enriched composition. *Cognition*, 78(1):B17–B25.

Tomas Mikolov, Kai Chen, Greg Corrado, and Jeffrey Dean. 2013. Efficient Estimation of Word Representations in Vector Space. *arXiv preprint arXiv:1301.3781*.

George A Miller and Walter G Charles. 1991. Contextual Correlates of Semantic Similarity. *Language and Cognitive Processes*, 6(1):1–28.

Kanishka Misra. 2022. minicons: Enabling Flexible Behavioral and Representational Analyses of Transformer Language Models. *arXiv preprint arXiv:2203.13112*.

Joakim Nivre, Marie-Catherine De Marneffe, Filip Ginter, Yoav Goldberg, Jan Hajic, Christopher D Manning, Ryan McDonald, Slav Petrov, Sampo Pyysalo, and Natalia Silveira. 2016. Universal Dependencies v1: A Multilingual Treebank Collection. In *Proceedings of LREC*.

Paolo Pedinotti and Alessandro Lenci. 2020. Don ' t Invite BERT to Drink a Bottle: Modeling the Interpretation of Metonymies Using BERT and Distributional Representations. In *Proceedings of COLING*.

Jeffrey Pennington, Richard Socher, and Christopher Manning. 2014. Glove: Global Vectors for Word Representation. In *Proceedings of EMNLP*.

Matthew E. Peters, Mark Neumann, Mohit Iyyer, Matt Gardner, Christopher Clark, Kenton Lee, and Luke Zettlemoyer. 2018. Deep Contextualized Word Representations. In *Proceedings of NAACL*.

Liina Pylkkanen and Brian McElree. 2006. The Syntax-semantics Interface: On-line Composition of Sentence Meaning. *Handbook of Psycholinguistics*, pages 539–579.

Giulia Rambelli, Emmanuele Chersoni, Alessandro Lenci, Philippe Blache, and Chu-Ren Huang. 2020. Comparing Probabilistic, Distributional and Transformer-Based Models on Logical Metonymy Interpretation. In *Proceedings of AACL-IJCNLP*.

Enrico Santus, Emmanuele Chersoni, Alessandro Lenci, and Philippe Blache. 2017. Measuring Thematic Fit with Distributional Feature Overlap. In *Proceedings of EMNLP*.

Enrico Santus, Emmanuele Chersoni, Alessandro Lenci, Chu-Ren Huang, and Philippe Blache. 2016a. Testing APsyn against Vector Cosine on Similarity Estimation. In *Proceedings of PACLIC*.

Enrico Santus, Tin-Shing Chiu, Qin Lu, Alessandro Lenci, and Chu-Ren Huang. 2016b. What a Nerd! Beating Students and Vector Cosine in the ESL and TOEFL Datasets. In *Proceedings of LREC*.

Enrico Santus, Hongmin Wang, Emmanuele Chersoni, and Yue Zhang. 2018. A Rank-Based Similarity Metric for Word Embeddings. In *Proceedings of ACL*.

William Timkey and Marten van Schijndel. 2021. All Bark and No Bite: Rogue Dimensions in Transformer Language Models Obscure Representational Quality. In *Proceedings of EMNLP*.

Matthew J Traxler, Martin J Pickering, and Brian McElree. 2002. Coercion in Sentence Processing: Evidence from Eye-movements and Self-paced Reading. *Journal of Memory and Language*, 47(4):530–547.

Peter D Turney. 2012. Domain and Function: A Dual-space Model of Semantic Relations and Compositions. *Journal of Artificial Intelligence Research*, 44:533–585.

Peter D Turney and Patrick Pantel. 2010. From Frequency to Meaning: Vector Space Models of Semantics. *Journal of Artificial Intelligence Research*, 37:141–188.

Heike Wiese and Joan Maling. 2005. Beers, Kaffi, and Schnaps: Different Grammatical Options for Restaurant Talk Coercions in Three Germanic Languages. *Journal of Germanic Linguistics*, 17(1):1–38.

Wenting Xue, Meichun Liu, and Stephen Politzer-Ahles. 2021. Processing of Complement Coercion With Aspectual Verbs in Mandarin Chinese: Evidence From a Self-Paced Reading Study. *Frontiers in Psychology*.

Bingyang Ye, Jingxuan Tu, Elisabetta Jezek, and James Pustejovsky. 2022. Interpreting Logical Metonymy through Dense Paraphrasing. In *Proceedings of CogSci*.

Alessandra Zarcone, Ken McRae, Alessandro Lenci, and Sebastian Padó. 2017. Complement Coercion: The Joint Effects of Type and Typicality. *Frontiers in Psychology*.

Alessandra Zarcone and Sebastian Padó. 2011. Generalized Event Knowledge in Logical Metonymy Resolution. In *Proceedings of CogSci*.

Vitalii Zhelezniak, Aleksandar Savkov, April Shen, and Nils Hammerla. 2019. Correlation Coefficients and Semantic Textual Similarity. In *Proceedings of NAACL*.

A Frame-Based Model of Inherent Polysemy, Copredication and Argument Coercion

Long Chen and **Laura Kallmeyer** and **Rainer Osswald**
Heinrich Heine University Düsseldorf
Germany
{chen.long,laura.kallmeyer,rainer.osswald}@hhu.de

Abstract

The paper presents a frame-based model of inherently polysemous nouns (such as 'book', which denotes both a physical object and an informational content) in which the meaning facets are directly accessible via attributes and which also takes into account the semantic relations between the facets. Predication over meaning facets (as in 'memorize the book') is then modeled as targeting the value of the corresponding facet attribute while coercion (as in 'finish the book') is modeled via specific patterns that enrich the predication. We use a compositional framework whose basic components are lexicalized syntactic trees paired with semantic frames and in which frame unification is triggered by tree composition. The approach is applied to a variety of combinations of predications over meaning facets and coercions.

1 Introduction

The lexical representation of inherently polysemous nouns and the variable evocation of their meaning facets by the predications in which they occur continue to be topics of ongoing research. Two questions are of particular interest in this context: (i) What are the mechanisms that underlie *copredication constructions* in which two or more predicates that aim at different meaning facets are applied to the same nominal argument? (ii) How does facet selection for inherently polysemous nouns differ from cases of *argument coercion* in which an apparent mismatch between the semantic type of an argument expression and the requirements of the predicate is resolved by an extended mode of composition that draws on additional pieces of lexical or contextual information?

Examples of inherent polysemy classes are given by nouns such as 'book' and 'letter', which have a physical facet and an information facet, and by nouns such as 'documentation' and 'classification', which have a process and a result facet. The sentence in (1a) illustrates a verb-verb copredication construction in which 'memorize' addresses the information facet of the letter while 'burn' targets its physical facet.

(1) a. Before leaving Rome he had *memorized* and *burned* a nine-page *letter* from Moscow.[1]
 b. [...] and she *ripped* the *offending letter* to shreds.[2]
 c. Although Kafur *burned* the *poem* without having read it, [...][3]

In verb-adjective copredication constructions like (1b), it is the argument-taking verb and the modifying adjective that address different facets of the noun. The example in (1c), by contrast, would count as a case of coercion if we assume that poems do not inherently come with physical facets.

The examples in (2), retrieved via Sketch Engine's interface to the ACL Anthology Reference Corpus (Bird et al., 2008), show an analogous pattern with respect to the evocation of process and result facets. In (2a), 'conducted' addresses the process facets of the classifications while 'evaluated' (most probably) refers to their result facets. Likewise, the modifying adjective 'correct' targets the result facet in (2b).

(2) a. [...] all *classifications* are *conducted* and *evaluated* on the basis of individual instances.[4]
 b. [...] while still *performing correct classification*.[5]
 c. The model generates *automatic summaries* of topics [...][6]

[1] Forsyth, 1996: *Icon.* (Google Books)
[2] Marshall, 2013: *Margaret Fuller - A New American Life.* (Google books)
[3] Larkin, 2012: *Al-Mutanabbi.* (Google Books)
[4] Feng & Hirst, 2012: *Text-level discourse parsing with rich linguistic features.*
[5] Goldstein & Uzuner, 2010. *Does negation really matter?*
[6] Ramage et al., 2009: *Labeled LDA: A supervised topic model for credit attribution in multi-labeled corpora.*

Proceedings of the Workshop on Cognitive Aspects of the Lexicon, pages 58–67
November 20, 2022. ©2022 Association for Computational Linguistics
https://doi.org/10.26615/978-954-452-056-4_008

The example in (2c), on the other hand, would count again as a coercion since the noun 'summary' (in contrast to 'summarization') does not lexically provide reference to a process or event. For instance, 'summary' does not combine well with verbs like 'perform' nor does it go together with 'process' in noun compounds (*'summary process' vs. 'summarization process').

A more systematic approach to distinguishing coercion from polysemy would draw on empirical data from corpus studies and psycholinguistic experiments. As to the former type of approach, Jezek and Vieu (2014) argue that inherent polysemy can be distinguished from coercion by looking at the variability of the co-occuring predicates in copredication constructions, where high variability is taken as an indicator of polysemy. From a psycholinguistic point of view, the hypothesis is that complement coercion comes with higher processing costs (Traxler et al., 2002) than just selecting a lexically provided facet of a polysemous noun. (See Murphy (2021) for a more recent overview of the relevant experiments.) The primary goal of the present paper is not so much to provide a strong empirical basis for the distinction in question but to introduce a formal cognitive model that allows us to represent the postulated semantic differences in a sufficiently fine-grained way.

A good part of the more recent formal modeling approaches for inherent polysemy and coercion rely on some sort of advanced type-theoretical framework such as Type Composition Logic (Asher, 2011), Type Theory with Records (Cooper, 2011), Montagovian Generative Lexical Theory (Mery and Retoré, 2015), Unifying Theory of dependent Types (Chatzikyriakidis and Luo, 2015), and Dependent Type Semantics (Kinoshita et al., 2017, 2018). Most if not all of them were at least partly driven by the aim to overcome what was seen as formal limitations of Pustejovsky (1995)'s original proposal. Notably Asher (2011, p. 87) regards the typed feature structure formalism used by Pustejovsky and feature structure unification as inadequate for modeling copredication and coercion.

In this paper, we present a *frame-semantic* model of inherent polysemy and argument coercion. A central assumption of frame semantics is that *attributes* (*features*) play a crucial role for the structured representation of meaning (Barsalou, 1992; Löbner, 2014). Our approach builds on the framework of Kallmeyer and Osswald (2013), where (i) frames are defined as *generalized typed feature structures*, (ii) semantic frames are linked with syntactic trees, and (iii) frame unification is guided by syntactic tree operations; cf. Section 2 for details.

Babonnaud et al. (2016) describe a first application of this framework to the analysis of polysemy and coercion. They pursue an "eliminative" strategy with respect to complex types and objects in that they avoid positing special "dot objects" that jointly represent the different meaning facets of an inherently polysemous noun. Their idea is that a frame-based representation of the facets and the semantic relations between them is sufficient for explaining the flexible behavior of polysemous nouns. For instance, they do not introduce a "dot type" *physical-object • information* (*phys-obj • info*, for short) for characterizing the class of polysemous nouns comprising 'book', 'letter', etc. Instead, these nouns are lexically classified as denoting entities of type *info(rmation)-carrier*, which is introduced as a subtype of *phys-obj* together with the constraint that its instances have an attribute CONT(ENT) whose value is of type *info*. More succinctly, in the formal frame description language used in the present paper: *info-carrier* $\Rrightarrow$ *phys-obj* $\wedge$ CONT : *info*.

Babonnaud et al.'s eliminative strategy has the following two issues: (i) It is usually necessary to decide on a "primary" facet of which the other facet is value of an attribute. (ii) In order to access the "non-primary" facet of a polysemous noun, the predicate has to anticipate the underlying attribute structure. To give an illustration, consider the two predications 'memorized the letter' and 'burned the letter'. If 'letter' has the type *info-carrier* then the NP 'the letter' is compatible with the selectional restrictions of the PATIENT argument of the verb 'burned', which requires an argument of type *phys-obj*. Figure 1 sketches how argument substitution would lead to the integration of the NP argument frame into the verb frame in this case. (The specific choice of the syntactic category labels will be explained in Section 2.)

Combining 'the letter' with 'memorized' by NP substitution, on the other hand, calls for more flexible selectional restrictions on the direct object of the verb: the object NP can have the type *info* or the type *info-carrier*. This is shown in Figure 2 where 'memorized' comes with a disjunctive specification: either the direct object is of type *info* and can directly provide the THEME or the THEME is the value of the direct object's CONT attribute. How-

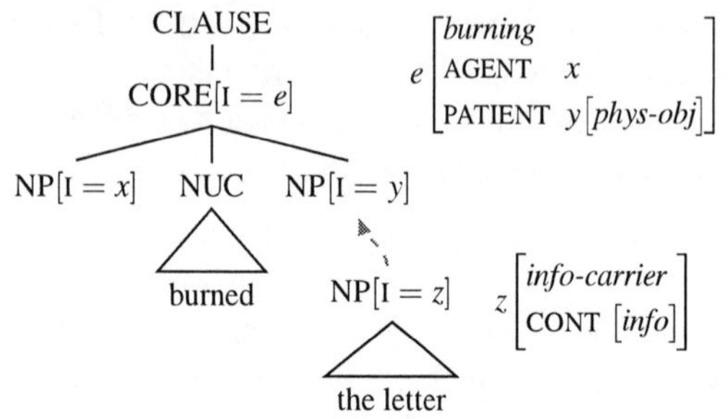

Figure 1: Syntactic and semantic composition for 'burned the letter' (preliminary version)

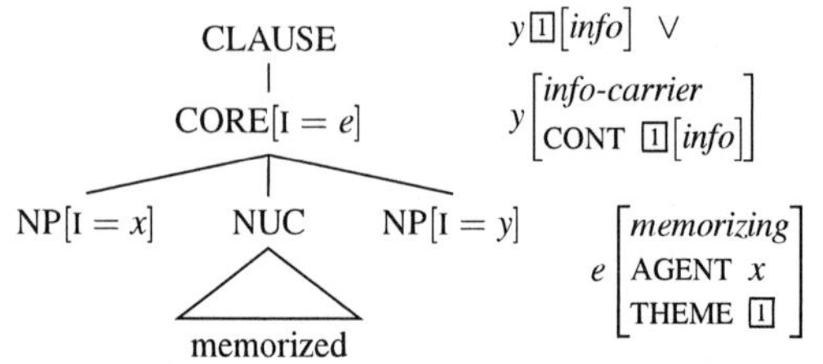

Figure 2: Lexicalized construction for 'memorized' along the lines of Babonnaud et al. (2016)

ever, since having different meaning facets is a lexical property of the polysemous noun, access to them should be provided by the noun entry as well.

A related issue is that Babonnaud et al. (2016) employ the same kind of disjunctive encoding for modeling coercion. However, there should be a distinction between coercion mechanisms (linked to the predicate) and accessing different meaning facets (provided by the noun). An example where the difference matters is the selection of the object of 'perform'. Assuming that in 'perform an annotation', the frame of 'perform' picks the creation event of the 'annotation' frame, and assuming that such an event is also present in the frame of 'summary', it is not clear why the latter cannot be targeted by 'perform'. The crucial difference is that in "perform an annotation" a meaning facet is targeted ('annotation' is a *process • result* dot type noun), while "perform a summary" requires a coercion. The unavailability of 'perform a summary' might therefore be due to the absence of an event facet for 'summary' and, furthermore, the unavailability of an adequate coercion pattern for 'perform'.

The goal of the present paper is to show how a non-eliminative strategy for modeling polysemous nouns by means of frames can overcome the described issues. To this end, dot types are added as proper members of the type hierarchy. They are not related to their component types by inheritance but rather by functional relations, i.e., by attributes. For example, instances of type *phys-obj • info* have two attributes OBJ(ECT)-FACET and INFO(RMATION)-FACET whose values are of type *info-carrier* and *info*, respectively. The two facets are related by the CONT attribute as before:

(3) $$\begin{aligned} \textit{phys-obj} \bullet \textit{info} \Rrightarrow\ & \text{OBJ-FACET} : \textit{info-carrier} \wedge \\ & \text{INFO-FACET} : \textit{info} \wedge \\ & \text{OBJ-FACET} \cdot \text{CONT} \doteq \text{INFO-FACET} \end{aligned}$$

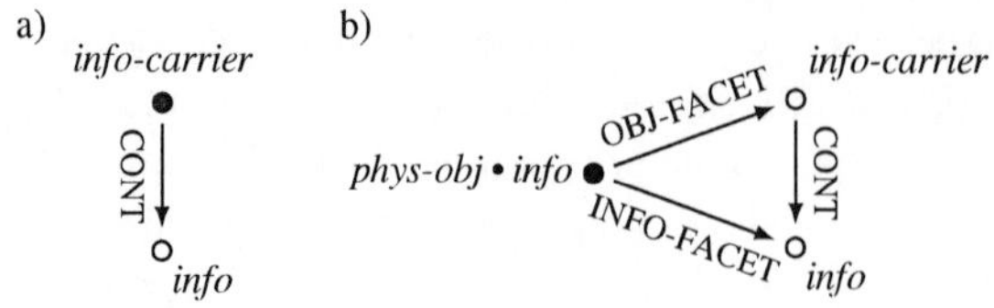

Figure 3: Eliminative (a) and non-eliminative (b) frame representations for inherently polysemous nouns like 'letter' and 'book'

Figure 3 depicts the two frame representations for the eliminative and the non-eliminative strategy side by side. Argument coercion, on the other hand, does not involve facet selection but is analyzed via additional patterns that can be used to augment the semantics of a predicate.

2 Background: Syntax-driven frame composition

The formalization of frame semantics used in the present paper is a slightly modified version of the one proposed by Kallmeyer and Osswald (2013). Frames are understood as *generalized feature structures*. Instead of requiring a distinguished root node from which every other node is accessible via a finite attribute sequence, the generalized version allows for multiple labeled nodes under the condition that each node is accessible from at least one of the labeled nodes. Correspondingly, frame unification does not require the identification of designated root nodes but relies on the identification of nodes with the same label. Frames can be defined as *minimal models* of conjunctive attribute-value formulas. The underlying logic is described in Appendix A.

Kallmeyer and Osswald (2013) combine frame semantics with Tree Adjoining Grammars (TAG). The basic components of this approach are *elementary constructions*, which are pairs of elementary syntactic trees and semantic frames where (some of) the constituent nodes of the tree are linked to nodes of the frame. The link is encoded by an I(NDEX)

Constraints for dot types and their meaning facets:

phys-obj • *info* $\Rrightarrow$ OBJ-FACET : *info-carrier* $\wedge$ INFO-FACET : *info* $\wedge$ OBJ-FACET · CONT $\doteq$ INFO-FACET
process • *result* $\Rrightarrow$ EVENT-FACET : *process* $\wedge$ EVENT-FACET · RESULT · CREATION $\doteq$ EVENT-FACET
process • *result* $\wedge$ EVENT-FACET · RESULT · OBJ-FACET $\Rrightarrow$ EVENT-FACET · RESULT · OBJ-FACET $\doteq$ OBJ-FACET
process • *result* $\wedge$ EVENT-FACET · RESULT · INFO-FACET $\Rrightarrow$ EVENT-FACET · RESULT · INFO-FACET $\doteq$ INFO-FACET

Constraints for single types and their meaning facets:

phys-obj $\Rrightarrow$ OBJ-FACET $\doteq$ SELF   *event* $\Rrightarrow$ EVENT-FACET $\doteq$ SELF   *info* $\Rrightarrow$ INFO-FACET $\doteq$ SELF

Subtype constraints:

info-carrier $\Rrightarrow$ *phys-obj*	*sheet* $\Rrightarrow$ *phys-obj*	*poem* $\Rrightarrow$ *info*
book $\Rrightarrow$ *phys-obj* • *info*	*letter* $\Rrightarrow$ *phys-obj* • *info*	*summary* $\Rrightarrow$ *phys-obj* • *info*
annotation $\Rrightarrow$ *process* • *result*	*classification* $\Rrightarrow$ *process* • *result*	*process* $\Rrightarrow$ *event*

Specification of attributes depending on types:

annotation $\Rrightarrow$ EVENT-FACET · RESULT : *phys-obj* • *info*   *classification* $\Rrightarrow$ EVENT-FACET · RESULT : *phys-obj* • *info*

Type incompatibilites:

phys-obj $\wedge$ *info* $\Rrightarrow$ $\bot$ *phys-obj* $\wedge$ *event* $\Rrightarrow$ $\bot$ *event* $\wedge$ *info* $\Rrightarrow$ $\bot$

Type-attribute incompatibilites:

phys-obj $\wedge$ INFO-FACET : $\top$ $\Rrightarrow$ $\bot$	*event* $\wedge$ INFO-FACET : $\top$ $\Rrightarrow$ $\bot$	*info* $\wedge$ EVENT-FACET : $\top$ $\Rrightarrow$ $\bot$
phys-obj $\wedge$ EVENT-FACET : $\top$ $\Rrightarrow$ $\bot$	*event* $\wedge$ OBJ-FACET : $\top$ $\Rrightarrow$ $\bot$	*info* $\wedge$ OBJ-FACET : $\top$ $\Rrightarrow$ $\bot$

Figure 4: Selected universal AV constraints

feature at the constituent nodes. Tree composition then gives rise to the identification of index values and, thereby, to specific constraints on how the associated semantic frames are unified. For example, the composition of the two constructions in Figure 1 leads to the identification of y and z, i.e. $y \doteq z$.

The syntactic side of the approach is not restricted to TAG but generalizes to other tree rewriting formalisms. In this paper, we use the formalism of Tree Wrapping Grammars (TWG) together with grammatical concepts of Role and Reference Grammar (RRG; Van Valin 2005), for which TWG has been developed (Kallmeyer et al., 2013).

RRG provides an elaborate theory of clause linkage, which comes in handy for the analysis of copredication constructions, among others. Instead of an X-bar scheme, RRG assumes a layered structure consisting of *nucleus*, *core* and *clause*. The nucleus contains the main predicate, the core contains the nucleus and the (non-extracted) syntactic arguments, and the clause includes the core and extracted arguments. Each layer can have a *periphery* of adjuncts. Grammatical *operators*, that is, closed-class elements encoding tense, modality, aspect, etc., attach to different layers depending on their scope.

Concerning complex constructions, RRG draws not only a distinction between coordination and subordination but assumes in addition *cosubordination* constructions, which are dependent but non-embedded structures of the general form $[[\ ]_X\ [\ ]_X]_X$. In such constructions, operators that apply to category X are usually realized only once but have scope over both X-daughters.

The tree composition operations of TWG are *(simple) substitution* (replacing a non-terminal leaf by a tree, as in Figure 1), *sister adjunction* (adding a tree as a subtree of a non-leaf, see the adjunction of 'and' in Figure 9) and *wrapping substitution* (splitting the new tree at a dominance-edge, filling a substitution node with the lower part and adding the upper part to the root of the target tree, cf. Figure 9).

3 Predications over meaning facets

In this section, we develop an analysis of predications that target existing meaning facets (either of dot type nouns or of single type nouns).

Universal constraints. As already mentioned, we introduce attributes for meaning facets and specific types for dot types. Meaning facets occur systematically for certain types, and they are therefore introduced by universal attribute-value constraints of the form $\varphi \Rrightarrow \psi$. (Cf. the appendix for the formal background). Some of the relevant constraints for dot types *phys-obj* • *info* and *process* • *result* are given in Figure 4. They specify available meaning facets together with the specific relations that hold between the different facets: For *phys-obj* • *info*, the CONT value of the OBJ-FACET is the INFO-FACET, while for *process* • *result*, the CREATION value of the OBJ-FACET is the EVENT-FACET and the RESULT of the EVENT-FACET is the OBJ-FACET. For sin-

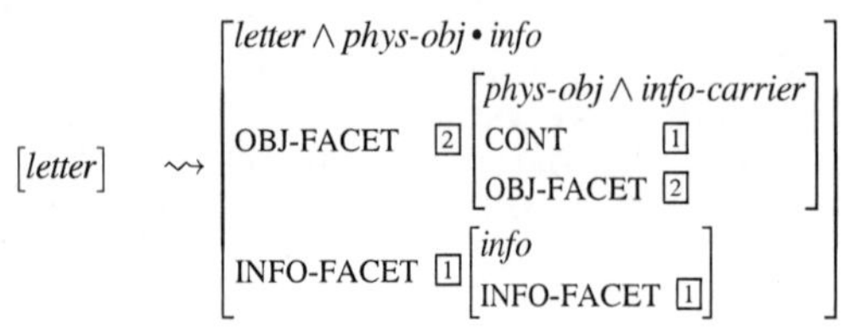

Figure 5: Application of universal constraints to the lexical entry of *letter*

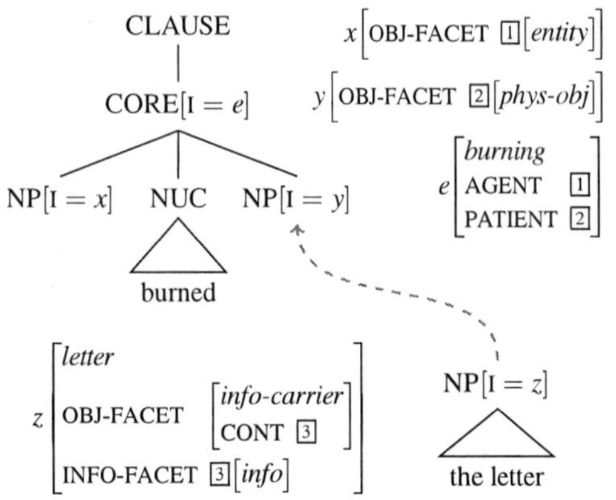

Figure 6: Revised syntactic and semantic composition for 'burned the letter' (cf. Figure 1)

gle types, the frame node is its own corresponding meaning facet (with SELF denoting the identity function properly restricted). The third group of constraints specifies subtype relations, for instance every entity of type *book* is also of type *phys-obj • info*, and the last two groups detail incompatibilities between types (e.g., nothing can be of types *event* and *phys-obj* at the same time) and between types and attributes (e.g., nothing can be of type *phys-obj* while having an EVENT-FACET). Figure 5 shows the application of these constraints to the lexical frame of 'letter'.

Single verbal predications. (4) lists cases of verbs predicating over single meaning facets of their object nouns (the latter being single or dot type nouns).

(4) a. Kim burned the sheet/letter.
  b. Kim memorized the poem/letter.
  c. Kim performed the dance/annotation.
  d. Kim evaluated the essay/annotation.

The elementary constructions for the verbs describe the event and its participants and determine which facet of the respective arguments fills which semantic role; see the entry for 'burned' in Figure 6. In combination with the I features on the nodes, the frame encodes that the OBJ-FACET of the direct object is the PATIENT of the *burning* event. The derivation in Figure 6 leads to the frame in Figure 7. The constructions for 'memorized', 'performed' and 'evaluated' look similar, except that the THEME expressed by the direct object is provided by different facets. Due to the frame constraints for meaning facets in single type nouns, the analysis works there as well (as in 'burned the sheet').

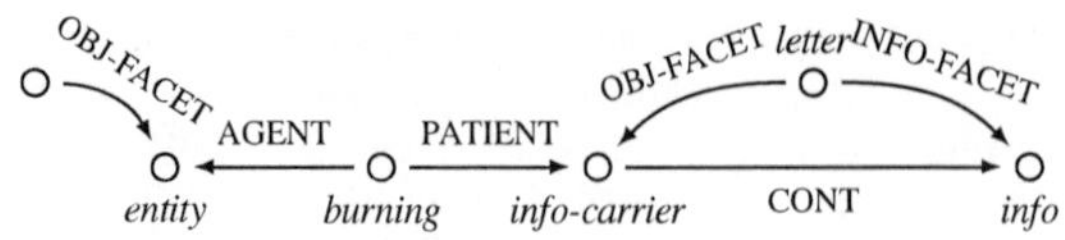

Figure 7: Resulting frame for 'burned the letter'

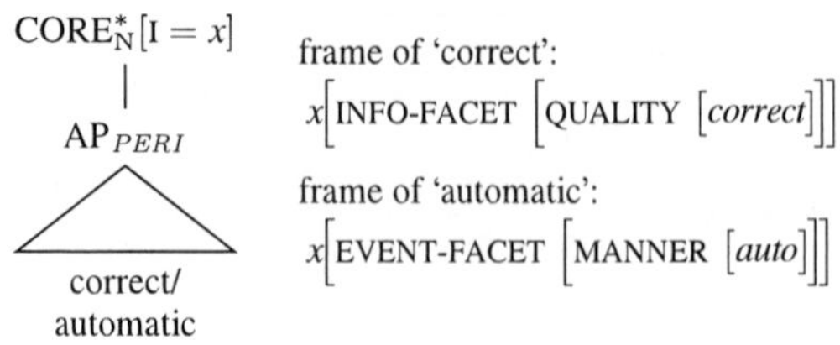

Figure 8: Tree frame pairs for 'correct' and 'automatic'

Adjectival predications. A second type of predication we consider in this paper are adjectival predications as in (5) where two adjectives modify a noun while targeting different facets of it.

(5) a. Where manual fine-grained annotation is unavailable, [...][7]
  b. the correct automatic annotation

The elementary constructions for 'correct' and 'automatic' in (5b) are given in Figure 8. The trees are added by sister adjunction to the CORE_N node of an NP tree. The CORE_N is the immediate daughter of NP, and both constituent nodes carry the same I feature. This way, the frame of the adjective unifies with the noun frame.

Multi-verb copredication. We now consider constructions of the form 'NP V_1 and V_2 NP', as in (6).

(6) a. Kim memorized and burned the letter.
  b. Kim performed and evaluated the annotation.

The two verbs in (6a) and (6b) share their arguments while targeting different facets of the object NP and assigning different semantic roles. They

[7]Abney and Bird, 2010. *The Human Language Project: Building a Universal Corpus of the World's Languages.*

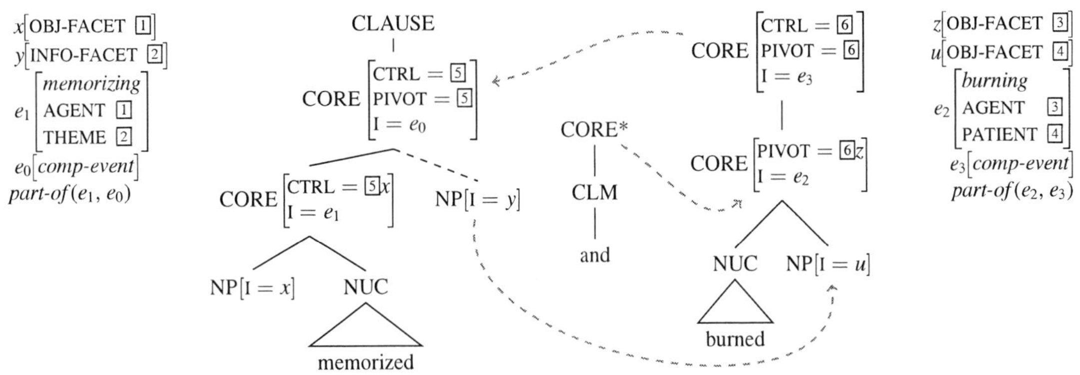

Figure 9: Derivation for 'memorized and burned'

constitute a complex event with a certain temporal structure, but they are still distinguishable within the complex event. We therefore analyze their syntactic structure as constituting a complex CORE consisting of two single COREs, i.e., a CORE cosubordination construction in RRG terms; see the tree in Figure 10. We capture the information about the shared subject by means of the features CONTROLLER (CTRL; for the CORE that provides the subject) and PIVOT (for the CORE that needs to retrieve an argument). The shared object NP, however, is present in the trees of both verbs, and the two NP nodes are merged via wrapping substitution (see Figure 9). The first CORE contains a dominance edge that leaves room between the upper CORE node and the shared object NP for inserting the second CORE while merging the object NP nodes.

We introduce a frame type *comp(lex)-event* for events that have several component events that all stand in a *part-of* relation to it. This relation between the complex event and its parts is specified in the corresponding unanchored elementary tree frame pairs, i.e., in the construction.

Figure 9 gives the tree-frame pairs for the two verbs. Each contributes an event that is part of a joint complex event. The first tree contributes the subject or, in more general RRG notions, the privileged syntactic argument (PSA). This is shared between all component events and, to this end, it is made available at the higher CORE node via a CTRL attribute. The second argument of the two trees is a shared NP node, where the sharing is realized via wrapping. Both the PSA and second NP argument can fill different semantic roles for the two events, and, furthermore, different facets of them can fill these roles. As a result of the adjunction, the frames

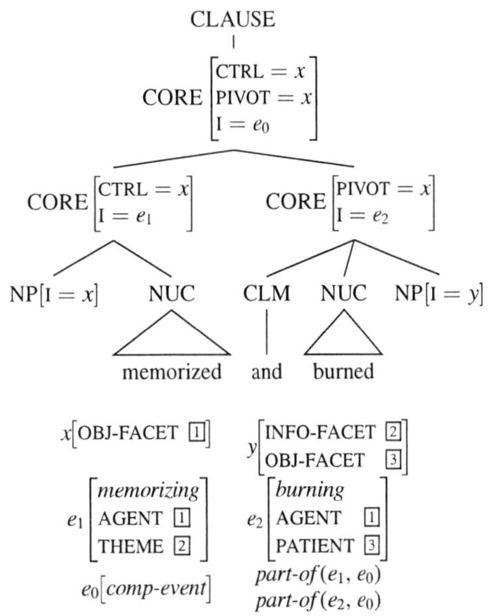

Figure 10: Result of the derivation in Figure 9

e_0 and e_3 unify, which yields a frame (Figure 10) that expresses that we have a complex event consisting of two part events, *memorizing* and *burning*, and that the subject filler provides the respective agents via its object facet, while the object NP filler provide the THEME of *memorizing* via its INFO-FACET and the PATIENT of *burning* via its OBJ-FACET.

For (6b), the analysis is similar, except for targeting different facets of the object NP.

4 Coercion

We now extend our analysis to cases of coercion as in (1c) ('burn the poem') and (2c) ('automatic summary'). The examples in (7) show that for the same predicate, depending on the context, different additional frame fragments are coerced, even for the same object nouns.

Frame for 'summary':

$$x\begin{bmatrix} \textit{summary} & \\ \text{INFO-FACET} & \boxed{1} \\ \text{OBJ-FACET} & \boxed{2} \\ \text{CREATION} & \begin{bmatrix} \textit{summarize} & \\ \text{AGENT} & [\ ] \\ \text{THEME} & [\ ] \\ \text{RESULT} & x\begin{bmatrix} \textit{phys-obj} \bullet \textit{info} & \\ \text{OBJ-FACET} & \boxed{2} \\ \text{INFO-FACET} & \boxed{1} \end{bmatrix} \end{bmatrix} \end{bmatrix}$$

Revised frame for 'automatic' (tree as in Figure 8):

$$y\Big[\text{EVENT-FACET}\ \big[\text{MANNER}\ [\textit{auto}]\big]\Big] \vee$$
$$y\Big[\text{CREATION}\ \big[\text{MANNER}\ [\textit{auto}]\big]\Big]$$

Figure 11: Frames for 'automatic summary'

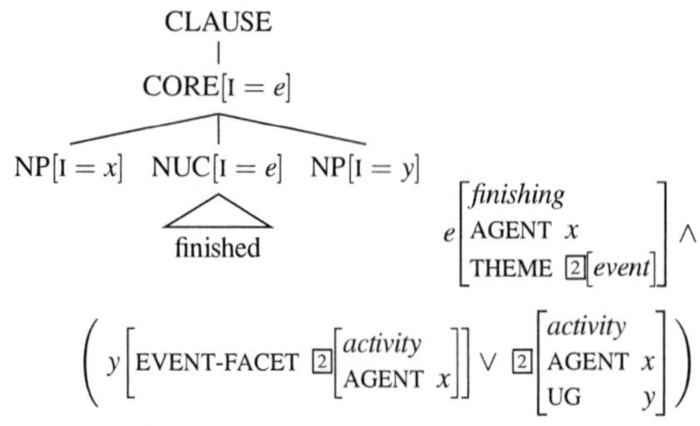

Figure 12: Tree-frame pair for 'finished'

(7) a. [...] Mr. Darcy had much better *finish his letter*.[8]

b. [...] once we start to translate words in a zone, we have to *finish all its words* before moving outside again.[9]

Let us start by discussing 'automatic summary'. If the modified noun has an event facet, we can apply 'automatic' directly. Otherwise, we have to coerce an event. This could simply be done by adding an attribute EVENT-FACET on the fly via unification. But this would predict that we target always the same event, which is not the case. The event facet (if existent) is unique, but not the coerced events. For example, let us assume that Kim has to grade a number of manually and automatically produced summaries. In this situation, 'finished' in sentence (8) may refer to the process of grading the summary while 'automatic' refers to creating it.

(8) Kim just *finished* a bad *automatic summary*.

In 'automatic summary', the noun does not have an event facet, while the adjective adds a manner specification to a process, in this case to the creation of the summary, which is part of the frame of 'summary' (see Figure 11).[10] This type of coercion, namely targeting the creation event, is common among manner adjectives, so we assume that there is a coercion pattern for this, that can be applied to manner modifications in general. Coercion patterns are defined as separate classes in the metagrammar (a factorized description of elementary tree frame pairs) and then combined in a disjunction with the basic pattern. Since coercion patterns are metagrammar classes, they can be (re)used in different constructions. Figure 11 shows the resulting disjunction of frames for 'automatic'. The first frame is used when combining with a noun that has an event facet, while the second is used when combining with a noun that has a CREATION attribute. (Note that, technically, this disjunction is part of the metagrammar and will therefore already be compiled out when computing the elementary constructions.) The composition of 'automatic summary' ($x \doteq y$ in Figure 11) necessarily chooses the coercion option, since a *summary* cannot have an event facet. Coercion can easily be combined with predications over existing meaning facets, as in 'evaluate the automatic summary' since the meaning facets of the noun are not changed by the coercion patterns.

As we have seen, 'automatic' in 'automatic summary' follows an existing path in the noun frame in order to retrieve its argument. This is different for 'finish' in (7). When triggering a coercion, 'finish' creates a new *event* frame (the coerced event) which embeds the denotation of the noun as a participant, more concretely as an undergoer. This is expressed in the frame in Figure 12 where the disjunction contains the basic pattern (the THEME $\boxed{2}$ is the existing EVENT-FACET) and a coercion pattern ($\boxed{2}$ is a newly created event). An aspect that is missing here is that the coerced event tends to be of a type that corresponds to the telic qualia of the noun (e.g., *writing* in (7a); cf. Pustejovsky 1995). One could model this within frames by including frame types as proper frame objects. We leave this for future research.

With this analysis, we can apply more than one coercion leading to different coerced frame elements of the same type, as in (8). And we can

[8]Jane Austen, 1813: Pride and Prejudice.

[9]Koehn & Haddow, 2009. Analysing the effect of out-of-domain data on SMT systems.

[10]Our classification of 'summary' as a dot object noun may be disputable. However, the coercion mechanism presented here would apply in the same way if 'summary' had an INFO-FACET only.

also apply coercion to dot type nouns, creating new frame nodes in addition to the available facets, even when one of the facets matches the type requirements. For example, if we replace 'summary' in (8) by 'annotation' then 'automatic' refers to the event facet of 'annotation'. In this case, the basic pattern as well as the coercion pattern are possible.

5 Conclusion

In this paper, we proposed a frame-based analysis of dot objects, predications over their meaning facets, and, in contrast to this, coercion. A crucial aspect of our analysis is that the meaning facets are modeled as attributes in the lexical frames of dot type nouns, while coercion involves the application of coercion patterns that are defined in the metagrammar. Their application is constrained by lexical properties, but the meaning components added by coercion are not part of the lexical entries and are in particular not meaning facets. This accounts for the high flexibility of coercion, i.e., the possible variability of the coerced meaning components.

Acknowledgments

This work has been carried out as part of the research project 'Coercion and Copredication as Flexible Frame Composition' funded by DFG (German Science Foundation). Parts of the research were also funded by the European Research Council (ERC) project TreeGraSP and by the multilingualism part of the European project UNIVERSEH. We would like to thank the anonymous reviewers for their valuable comments.

Appendix: Attribute-value logic of frames

The appendix describes the attribute-value (AV) logic that underlies the frame approach of this article; see also Kallmeyer and Osswald (2013), who in turn build on Hegner (1994). The logic makes use of two kinds of expressions: *AV formulas* and *AV descriptions*.

AV descriptions are evaluated at frame nodes, formulas on whole frames. AV expressions are defined over a vocabulary $\langle \mathsf{Attr}, \mathsf{Typ}, \mathsf{Rel}, \mathsf{Nnam}, \mathsf{Nvar} \rangle$ consisting of a finite set Attr of *attribute symbols*, a finite set Typ of *type symbols*, a finite set $\mathsf{Rel} = \bigcup_n \mathsf{Rel}_n$ of *relation symbols* (where Rel_n are n-ary relation symbols), a finite set Nnam of *node names* (or *nominals*), and a countably infinite set Nvar of *node variables*. The members of $\mathsf{Nlab} = \mathsf{Nnam} \cup \mathsf{Nvar}$ are referred

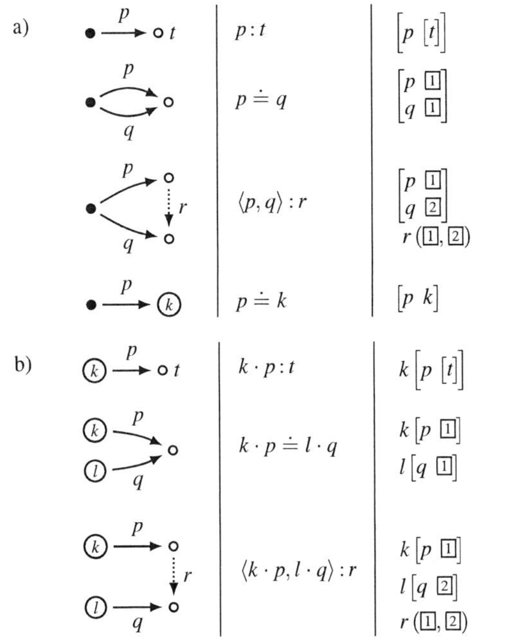

Figure 13: The middle column shows primitive AV descriptions (a) and formulas (b), their notation as AV matrices (right columns), and the structures they denote (left columns)

to as *node labels*. The *primitive AV descriptions* consist of the following expressions:

(9) $t \mid p{:}t \mid p \doteq q \mid \langle p_1,\ldots,p_n\rangle : r \mid p \doteq k$

with $t \in \mathsf{Typ}$, $r \in \mathsf{Rel}$, $p, q, p_i \in \mathsf{Attr}^*$, and $k \in \mathsf{Nlab}$. The intended meaning of these expressions is depicted in Figure 13a, which also shows the equivalent matrix style notations. The filled circles indicate the nodes at which the expressions are evaluated. Node labels are depicted inside nodes, type symbols are depicted at the outside of nodes.

The set of *primitive AV formulas* is defined as follows:

(10) $k \cdot p : t \mid k \cdot p \doteq l \cdot q \mid \langle k_1 \cdot p_1, \ldots, k_n \cdot p_n \rangle : r$

with $t \in \mathsf{Typ}$, $r \in \mathsf{Rel}$, $p, q, p_i \in \mathsf{Attr}^*$, and $k, l, k_i \in \mathsf{Nlab}$. AV formulas state that there are certain labeled nodes that have certain properties. The intended meaning of AV formulas is sketched in Figure 13b.

Formally, the satisfaction of AV expressions is defined relative to a *structure* $\langle V, \mathcal{I}, g \rangle$ over the given vocabulary consisting of a set V, the *universe* of "nodes", an *interpretation function* $\mathcal{I}$ defined on $\mathsf{Attr} \cup \mathsf{Typ} \cup \mathsf{Rel} \cup \mathsf{Nnam}$, and a partial *variable assignment* function g from Nvar to V. The function $\mathcal{I}$ takes members of Attr to partial functions on V, members of Typ to subsets of V, members of Rel_n to n-ary relations on V, and members of Nnam to members of V. Let $\mathcal{I}_g$ be the partial function from Nlab to V that takes k to $\mathcal{I}(k)$ if $k \in$ Nnam and to $g(k)$ if $k \in \mathrm{dom}(g)$. The members of the image of $\mathcal{I}_g$ are called *labeled nodes*. The interpretation of attributes extends naturally to an interpretation of attribute paths such that $\mathcal{I}(p \cdot f) = \mathcal{I}(f) \circ \mathcal{I}(p)$ for $f \in$ Attr and $p \in \mathsf{Attr}^+$. Due to lack of space, we spell out the fairly canonical definitions of satisfaction only for a few cases. For example, primitive descriptions of the form $p : t$ are satisfied at a node v of a structure $\langle V, \mathcal{I}, g \rangle$, in symbols, $\langle V, \mathcal{I}, g \rangle, v \models p : t$, iff $v \in \mathrm{dom}(\mathcal{I}(p))$ and $\mathcal{I}(p)(v) \in \mathcal{I}(t)$. By comparison, primitive formulas of the form $k \cdot p \doteq l \cdot q$ are satisfied by a structure $\langle V, \mathcal{I}, g \rangle$ iff $\{k, l\} \subseteq \mathrm{dom}(\mathcal{I}_g)$, $\mathcal{I}_g(k) \in \mathrm{dom}(\mathcal{I}(p))$, $\mathcal{I}_g(l) \in \mathrm{dom}(\mathcal{I}(q))$, and $\mathcal{I}(p)(\mathcal{I}_g(k)) = \mathcal{I}(q)(\mathcal{I}_g(l))$. The AV descriptions and formulas include $\top$ and $\bot$ and are closed under all Boolean operators. The satisfaction relation $\models$ can be extended correspondingly in the usual way.

A *frame* is a structure $\langle V, \mathcal{I}, g \rangle$ in which every node is accessible from a labeled node by finitely many applications of attribute functions; that is, for every node v there is a node label k and a finite attribute sequence p such that $v = \mathcal{I}(p)(\mathcal{I}_g(k))$.

Given two frames $F = \langle V, \mathcal{I}, g \rangle$ and $F' = \langle V', \mathcal{I}', g' \rangle$ over $\langle$Attr, Typ, Rel, Nnam, Nvar$\rangle$, F *subsumes* F', or F' *is more informative than* F, in symbols, $F \sqsubseteq F'$, if there is a function h from V to V' that preserves the labeling and the typing in the frame F as well as its attribute structure and the relations between its nodes. For instance, preservation of the attribute structure of F by h means that $h(v) \in \mathrm{dom}(\mathcal{I}'(f))$ and $\mathcal{I}'(f)(h(v)) = h(\mathcal{I}(f)(v))$ for $f \in$ Attr and $v \in \mathrm{dom}(\mathcal{I}(f))$. It is easy to see that if such a function h exists, it is uniquely determined by these conditions. The *unification* $F \sqcup F'$ of two frames F and F' is their least upper bound with respect to subsumption, if existent.

A frame F is a *model* of an AV formula α iff F satisfies α. It is not difficult to see that every finite conjunction of primitive AV formulas has a unique frame model (up to isomorphism) that is *minimal* with respect subsumption. Vice versa, every frame is the minimal model of a finite conjunction of primitive AV formulas.

Frame representations of a certain domain are usually subject to a number of *(universal) AV constraints* that express implicational relations between types and attributes: Types may be (i) subtypes of other types, (ii) imply the presence of certain attributes (and vice versa), etc. Universal constraints have the general form $\forall\varphi$, with φ a Boolean AV description. A frame (or structure) satisfies $\forall\varphi$ if each of its nodes satisfies φ. If φ is a Horn description, $\forall\varphi$ is called a *Horn constraint*. Instead of $\forall(\varphi \rightarrow \psi)$, we write $\varphi \Rrightarrow \psi$. Given a frame F and a finite set of Horn constraints (which do not generate infinite structures),[11] there is a unique frame F' subsumed by F that satisfies all the constraints.

References

Nicholas Asher. 2011. *Lexical meaning in context: A web of words*. Cambridge University Press.

William Babonnaud, Laura Kallmeyer, and Rainer Osswald. 2016. Polysemy and coercion – a frame-based approach using LTAG and Hybrid Logic. In *Logical Aspects of Computational Linguistics, 9th International Conference*, Lecture Notes in Artificial Intelligence 10054, pages 18–33, Berlin. Springer.

Lawrence W. Barsalou. 1992. Frames, concepts, and conceptual fields. In Adrienne Lehrer and Eva Feder Kittay, editors, *Frames, Fields, and Contrasts*, pages 21–74. Lawrence Erlbaum Associates, Hillsdale, NJ.

Steven Bird, Robert Dale, Bonnie Dorr, Bryan Gibson, Mark Joseph, Min-Yen Kan, Dongwon Lee, Brett Powley, Dragomir Radev, and Yee Fan Tan. 2008. The ACL anthology reference corpus: A reference dataset for bibliographic research in computational linguistics. In *Proceedings of the sixth international conference on language resources and evaluation (LREC'08)*.

Stergios Chatzikyriakidis and Zhaohui Luo. 2015. Individuation criteria, dot-types and copredication: A view from modern type theories. In *Proceedings of the 14th Meeting on the Mathematics of Language (MoL 14)*, pages 39–50.

Robin Cooper. 2011. Copredication, quantification and frames. In Sylvain Pogodalla and Jean-Philippe Prost, editors, *Logical Aspects of Computational Linguistics, 6th International Conference*, Lecture Notes in Artificial Intelligence 6736, pages 64–79. Springer, Berlin.

Stephen J. Hegner. 1994. Properties of Horn clauses in feature-structure logic. In C. J. Rupp, Michael A. Rosner, and Rod L. Johnson, editors, *Constraints, Language and Computation*, pages 111–147. Academic Press, San Diego, CA.

[11] See Kallmeyer and Osswald (2013, p. 323) for more information about this restriction.

Elisabetta Jezek and Laure Vieu. 2014. Distributional analysis of copredication: towards distinguishing systematic polysemy from coercion. *Distributional analysis of copredication: towards distinguishing systematic polysemy from coercion*, pages 219–223.

Laura Kallmeyer and Rainer Osswald. 2013. Syntax-driven semantic frame composition in Lexicalized Tree Adjoining Grammars. *Journal of Language Modelling*, 1(2):267–330.

Laura Kallmeyer, Rainer Osswald, and Robert D. Van Valin, Jr. 2013. Tree wrapping for Role and Reference Grammar. In *Formal Grammar (FG 2012/2013)*, number 8036 in Lecture Notes in Computer Science, pages 175–190. Springer.

Eriko Kinoshita, Koji Mineshima, and Daisuke Bekki. 2017. An analysis of selectional restrictions with dependent type semantics. In Setsuya Kurahashi, Yuiko Ohta, Sachiyo Arai, Ken Satoh, and Daisuke Bekki, editors, *New Frontiers in Artificial Intelligence. JSAI-isAI 2016 Workshops. Revised Selected Papers*, number 10247 in Lecture Notes in Computer Science, pages 19–32. Springer, Cham.

Eriko Kinoshita, Koji Mineshima, and Daisuke Bekki. 2018. Coercion as proof search in dependent type semantics. *Oslo Studies in Language*, 10(2):143–162.

Sebastian Löbner. 2014. Evidence for frames from human language. In Thomas Gamerschlag, Doris Gerland, Rainer Osswald, and Wiebke Petersen, editors, *Frames and Concept Types*, number 94 in Studies in Linguistics and Philosophy, pages 23–67. Springer, Dordrecht.

Bruno Mery and Christian Retoré. 2015. Are books events? ontological inclusions as coercive sub-typing, lexical transfers as entailment. In *LENLS: Logic and Engineering of Natural Language Semantics*, pages 74–87.

Elliot Murphy. 2021. *Linguistic representation and processing of copredication*. Ph.D. thesis, UCL (University College London).

James Pustejovsky. 1995. *The Generative Lexicon*. MIT Press, Cambridge, MA.

Matthew J. Traxler, Martin J. Pickering, and Brian McElree. 2002. Coercion in sentence processing: Evidence from eye-movements and self-paced reading. *Journal of Memory and Language*, 47(4):530–547.

Robert D. Van Valin, Jr. 2005. *Exploring the Syntax-Semantics Interface*. Cambridge University Press, Cambridge.

VISCOSE – a Kanji Dictionary Enriched with VISual, COmpositional, and SEmantic Information

Werner Winiwarter
University of Vienna
Faculty of Computer Science
Währingerstraße 29
1090 Vienna, Austria
werner.winiwarter
@univie.ac.at

Bartholomäus Wloka
University of Vienna
Department for Translation Studies
Gymnasiumstraße 50
1190 Vienna, Austria
bartholomaeus.wloka
@univie.ac.at

Abstract

In this paper, we present a novel approach for building kanji dictionaries by enriching the lexical data of 3,500 kanji with images, structural decompositions, and semantically based cross-media mappings from the textual to the visual dimension. Our kanji dictionary is part of a Web-based contextual language learning environment based on augmented browsing technology. We display our multimodal kanji information as kanji cards in the Web browser, offering a versatile representation that can be integrated into other advanced creative language learning applications, such as memorization puzzles, creative storytelling assignments, or educational games.

1 Introduction

Learning a foreign language can be interesting and exciting. However, when we begin to feel overwhelmed by difficulties, or are faced with uninteresting learning material, it can become tedious and frustrating (Doughty and Long, 2003; VanPatten et al., 2020). Learning Japanese as an English speaker poses a particular challenge (Matsumoto, 2007). It requires extensive memorization due to the drastically different and complicated writing system (Paxton, 2019). The logographic characters called *kanji* make up its core and are supplemented by two syllabic scripts: *hiragana* and *katakana*. Kanji pose a significant challenge to students who are not aware of this concept (Mori, 2014). There are thousands of these characters and each of them has several possible meanings and pronunciations depending on the usage context (Hermalin, 2015). People born and educated in Japan learn 80-200 kanji per school year, and more advanced characters after high school. Therefore acquiring kanji is a lifelong process. Someone who decides to learn Japanese as a foreign language cannot fall back on this incremental and steady acquisition process, but has to memorize these characters quickly.

2 Related Work

In order to build effective methods for the study of kanji, extensive high quality digital resources are needed. The most predominant, freely available kanji dictionary is *KANJIDIC2* (Breen, 2004), which contains detailed information about 13,108 characters. *Wiktionary* data is even more comprehensive and accessible as LLOD (Linguistic Linked Open Data) via *Dbnary* (Sérasset and Tchechmedjiev, 2014; Sérasset, 2015).

Recently, lexical resources have been increasingly enhanced with **visual** representations. Prominent examples are *Wikipedia* thumbnails and other illustrations, also accessible via *DBpedia* (Lehmann et al., 2014). However, the number of images provided varies widely across language versions. *Babelfy* (Moro et al., 2014a,b) is another good example of such efforts, whereas Wiktionary contains comparatively few images so far.

On the other hand, Wiktionary displays *Ideographic Description Sequences* (IDS) from the *IDS data* set, which is derived from the CHISE project (Morioka, 2008) and is freely available on github[1]. We are aware of only one application that uses this **compositional** data for educational purposes: the *KanjiBuilder* component included in *Kanshudo*[2]. However, the entire content is proprietary, hence it is not available for academic use.

At the **semantic** level, efforts are equally limited. So far, to the best of our knowledge, there exists no approach that maps kanji to *WordNet* (Miller, 1995) *synsets*. However, there are ongoing efforts at the word level in the Japanese WordNet (Isahara et al., 2008). Regarding the mapping of images to WordNet synsets, there is the well-known *ImageNet* collection, which maps about 1,000 images to each synset (Deng et al., 2009). While this is undoubtedly an excellent resource for deep learn-

[1] https://github.com/cjkvi/cjkvi-ids
[2] https://www.kanshudo.com/

Proceedings of the Workshop on Cognitive Aspects of the Lexicon, pages 68–77
November 20, 2022. ©2022 Association for Computational Linguistics
https://doi.org/10.26615/978-954-452-056-4_009

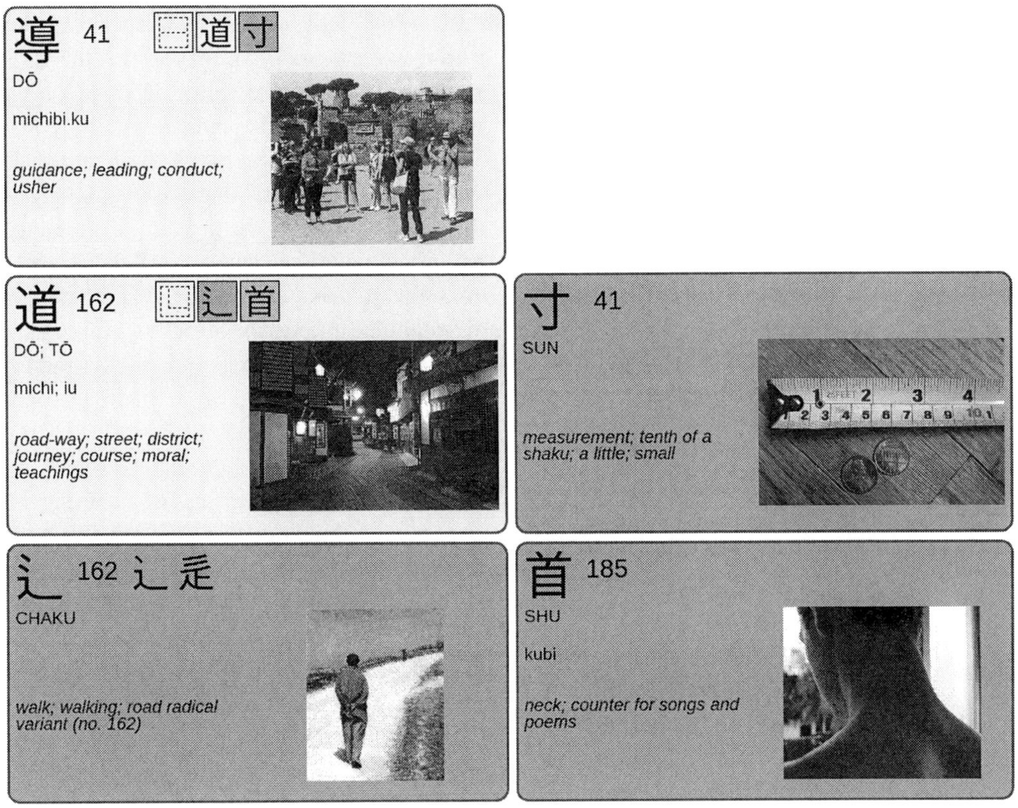

Figure 1: Example of decomposition of a kanji.

ing applications, it is not ideal for educational use, where we often need one well-chosen, representative image. Another effort to assign cliparts from *Openclipart*[3] to synsets was discontinued after illustrating only 581 synsets (Bond et al., 2009).

The use of flashcards has a long tradition in studying Japanese kanji (Diner and Prasetiani, 2015), e.g. available in *Anki* [4]. We integrate the display of our kanji data as kanji cards into our contextual language learning environment by using augmented browsing technology, as opposed to the traditionally isolated presentation. This way, we can offer advanced *creative learning* (Watts and Blessinger, 2017; Davies et al., 2013) solutions, such as storytelling (Windhaber, 2018) or educational games (Cornillie et al., 2012; Peterson, 2010). As stated very recently in (ELM Learning, 2021), creative learning is vital for several reasons:

- it stimulates **problem solving**, which can be further enhanced by *gamification* techniques;
- it develops **critical thinking** by leaving the study path up to the learners and enabling to change and shape the material to fit their patterns of thinking;
- it **promotes risk-taking** by leaving the difficulty level up to the student;
- the choice of the learning context encourages a **curious mindset** for the subject matter, fusing the acquisition of new, exciting information with acquisition of language;
- the study of more natural, context-oriented material **increases confidence levels** in everyday usage of the study material.

We included these insightful considerations and combine them with our experience from our long-lasting and ongoing research efforts in refining the structure and presentation of enriched kanji cards (Winiwarter, 2017; Wloka and Winiwarter, 2021b,c). We considered the feedback, critique, and comments we received in the course of this research to develop the novel design of kanji cards presented in this paper.

[3] https://openclipart.org/

[4] https://apps.ankiweb.net/

Our enriched kanji dictionary *VISCOSE* lays the foundation for a novel and innovative method that contributes a vital stimulus for second language acquisition of Japanese. We believe that this will greatly alleviate the difficulty of memorizing kanji for beginners (Kubota, 2017) and keep advanced students motivated.

3 Building an Enhanced Kanji Dictionary

We have implemented our kanji dictionary in *SWI-Prolog* (Wielemaker et al., 2012) because it is an optimal choice for natural language processing tasks as well as the management and retrieval of linguistic data. It is suitable for efficient processing of large XML and RDF files and provides a scalable Web server solution (Wielemaker et al., 2008). We use the latter to generate dynamic Web content for creative language learning scenarios via augmented browsing. We chose to render the kanji information in the Web browser as *kanji cards* because this is an aesthetically pleasing representation, which can be flexibly adapted to many language learning applications, including quizzes and educational games.

The kanji cards in Fig. 1 contain the following information: the radical number, variant forms, on'yomi and kun'yomi readings (described below), glosses, an image, and the ideographic description sequence. The *radical* is the main component of the kanji used for lookup in a paper kanji dictionary. There are 214 radicals in total.

The *on'yomi* readings are displayed in uppercase, they descend from approximations of original Chinese pronunciations. In contrast, *kun'yomi* readings are based on pronunciations of native words approximating the meaning of the kanji when it was introduced. Some kanji do not have on'yomi, they are so-called *kokuji*, having been newly created in Japan. We extracted all this lexical data from KANJIDIC2. So far, we performed 460 corrections and additions using mainly Wiktionary as supplementary resource for the 3,500 kanji in our dictionary.

The images displayed on the kanji cards add essential **visual information**. They were all collected manually and exclusively from Wikipedia pages due to licensing reasons and to guarantee access to valuable contextual and ontological data via DBpedia datasets.

We have also added **compositional information** to the kanji cards, represented as an ideographic description sequence (IDS). We spent extensive editorial work to meticulously check the IDS data resulting in 581 corrections. One reason for this high number was our goal of creating consistent and complete decompositions of all kanji as shown in Fig. 1. This means that we recursively follow the IDS data down to the level of radicals and some additional individual strokes. All the intermediary components have to be valid characters, i.e. they are included in our set of 3,500 kanji. In our visual representation, the kanji cards for radicals are red, same as the radical of the kanji if it occurs in the IDS. Additional radical kanji in the IDS are highlighted in orange.

During the arduous process of gathering suitable images for kanji cards, we soon identified successful strategies for finding visual representations of abstract concepts. We also observed that we often covered several aspects of the lexical data in one image, which sometimes happened even subconsciously. Often these hidden associations were discovered in a review process by a second person. These experiences were the main motivation to start annotating this mapping process to be able to preserve a formalized representation of the image acquisition task. This **semantic information** is a valuable resource for many more advanced language learning applications. However, to reap its full benefit we also had to address the issue of *word sense disambiguation* by assigning each mapping to the correct WordNet synset.

Figure 2: Resources used for the information on a kanji card.

A graphical representation of the integrated resources and an example depiction of a kanji card are shown in Fig. 2.

Figure 3 shows an example of three mappings for a kanji card with verbal descriptions and WordNet synset definitions. We have converted this representation into a more formal annotation format as

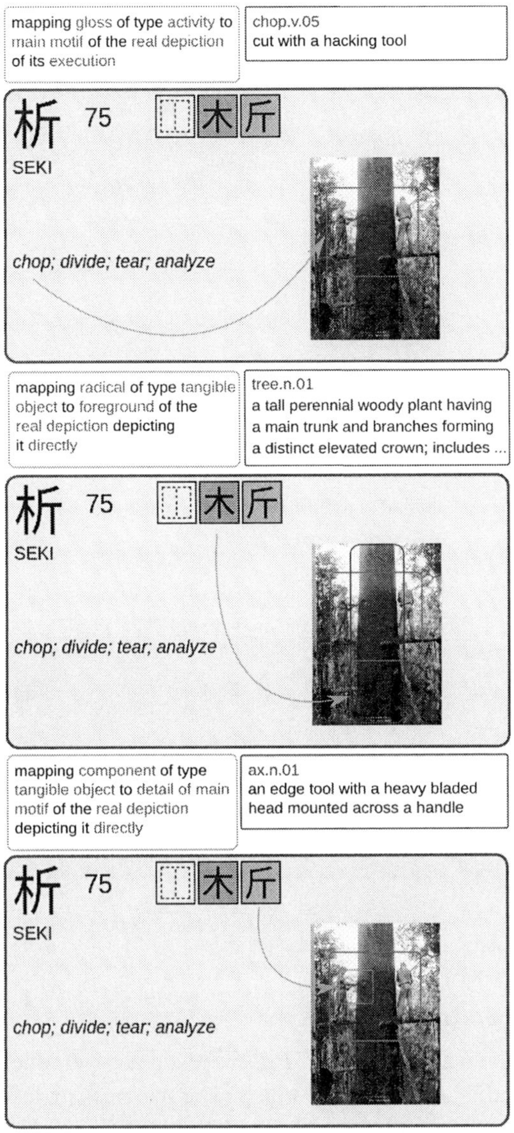

Figure 3: Example of mappings.

a set of septuples:

{(LexicalData,SourceType,InformationType, TargetRegion,DepictionType,MappingType,Synset)}

For instance, the mappings in Fig. 3 would be translated into:

{(chop,gloss,activity,main motif, real depiction,execution,chop.v.05), (tree,radical,tangible object,foreground, real depiction,direct,tree.n.01), (axe,component,tangible object,detail of main motif, real depiction,direct,ax.n.01)}.

Of course, we actually use one-letter codes for the values of the five features to guarantee the efficient storage and processing of the annotation data. The features are explained in detail in Sect. 4.

We have created annotations for all 3,500 kanji in our dictionary resulting in a total number of 4,282 annotated mappings. We used altogether 45 different feature values, which are introduced in the next section and summarized later in Table 1.

4 Annotation Examples

In the following subsections, we present detailed examples of annotations for all values of the five features that are used to represent the mappings from the textual kanji information to its visual representation.

4.1 Source Type

The first example in Fig. 4 shows the mapping of the *gloss* (G) "time", an *intangible object* (I), to the *real depiction* (R) of a sundial, which is the *main motif* (M) of the image. The connection between the two concepts is established through the *association* (A) that a sundial is used to measure the time of day. If we look at the *radical* (R) 日 (sun), we can see an association because the sunlight produces the shadow that indicates the time. Similarly, we can find an association with the indirect *component* (C) 寸 (measurement):

$$\{(\text{time},G,I,M,R,A,\text{clock\_time.n.01}), (\text{sun},R,I,M,R,A,\text{sunlight.n.01}), (\text{measurement},C,I,M,R,A,\text{measurement.n.01})\}.$$

Figure 4: Example of source types G, R, and C.

The kanji card in Fig. 5 is an example of mapping a *partial gloss* (P) "tea kettle", a *tangible object* (T), *directly* (D) to its visual representation as *detail of the main motif* (D). Partial glosses mainly concern radicals and a few more exotic cases:

$$\{(\text{kettle lid radical (no. 8)},P,T,D,R,D,\text{lid.n.02})\}.$$

Figure 5: Example of source type P.

There are numerous Japanese words that have become English loanwords over the years. In such cases we usually have a mapping from the *kun'yomi* (K) reading to the image as in the example in Fig. 6. We can also detect a *component* (C) or part meronym relation from the radical 木 (tree) to the fruit as well as an association with the component 市 (market) where the fruit is sold:

$$\{(\text{persimmon},G,T,M,R,D,\text{persimmon.n.02}),\\ (\text{kaki},K,T,M,R,D,\text{japanese\_persimmon.n.01}),\\ (\text{tree},R,T,M,R,C,\text{tree.n.01}),\\ (\text{market},C,T,M,R,A,\text{marketplace.n.02})\}.$$

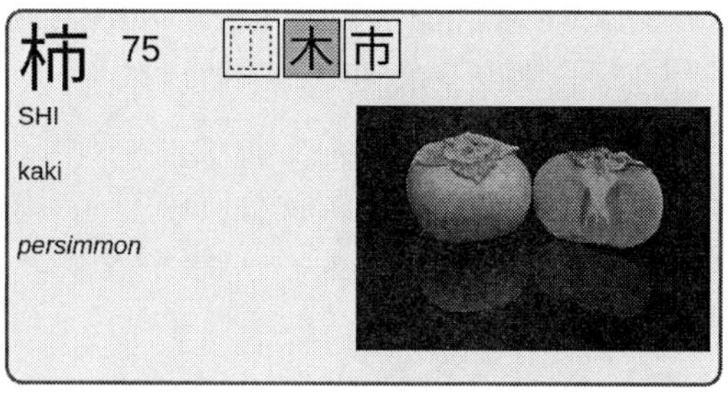

Figure 6: Example of source type K.

Similarly, there exist some mappings of *on'yomi* (O) readings, like in the example in Fig. 7. Conveniently, the string "SEN" is also printed on the coin, therefore, we have a *literal* (L) mapping:

$$\{(.01\ \text{yen},G,I,M,R,A,\text{sen.n.01}),\\ (\text{coin},G,T,M,R,D,\text{coin.n.01}),\\ (\text{money},G,I,M,R,A,\text{money.n.03}),\\ (\text{SEN},O,I,D,R,L,\text{sen.n.01})\}.$$

Finally, for some kanji we can match the *glyph* (G) of its *logogram* (L) with shapes, lines, or curves in the image. Figure 8 illustrates such an example for the kanji 爻. The image shows a famous *film scene* (F) from the "The Great Dictator" in which the "double cross" symbol can be seen on

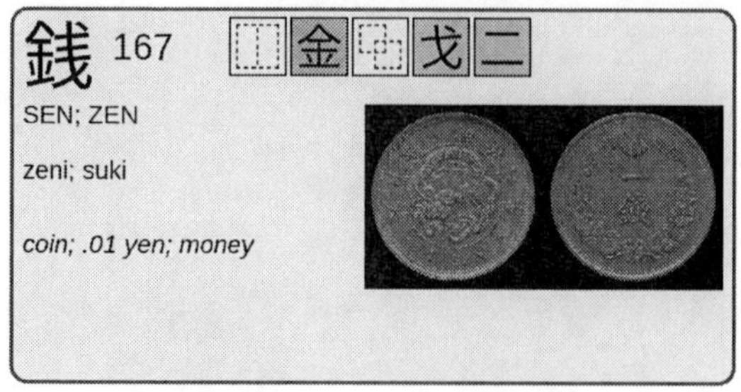

Figure 7: Example of source type O.

Charlie Chaplin's cap. Therefore, in this case, we have a *full match* (F):

$$\{(\text{double X radical (no. 89)},P,I,D,F,L,\text{x.n.02}),\\ (\varnothing,L,G,D,F,F,\varnothing)\}.$$

Figure 8: Example of source type L.

4.2 Information Type

The feature values I, T, G were already introduced in Fig. 4, Fig. 5, and Fig. 8. The two missing information types are *activities* (A) and *properties* (P). Both can be seen in the annotation for Fig. 9. The image shows a detail from the mural *painting* (P) entitled "Labor". The two men are shown during the *execution* (E) of the activity "toil". From their hard manual work we can infer that they presumably possess the *property* (P) "diligent" as well as being "strong" as indicated by the radical 力:

$$\{(\text{toil},G,A,M,P,E,\text{labor.v.02}),\\ (\text{diligent},G,P,M,P,P,\text{diligent.a.02}),\\ (\text{strong},R,P,M,P,P,\text{strong.a.01}\}.$$

4.3 Target Region

So far, we have encountered the feature values M in Fig. 4 and D in Fig. 5. The missing four target regions, which occur less often, are mappings to the *background* (B), the *foreground* (F), a *secondary motif* (S), and the *whole image* (W).

Figure 9: Example of information types A and P.

In Fig. 10 we map the radical 山 (mountain) to the background of the image:

$$\{(\text{beach},G,T,M,R,D,\text{beach.n.01}),$$
$$(\text{mountain},R,T,B,R,D,\text{mountain.n.01}\}.$$

Figure 10: Example of target region B.

If you look at the landscape in the foreground of Fig. 11, it gives you the impression of vastness:

$$\{(\text{vast},G,P,F,R,P,\text{huge.s.01})\}.$$

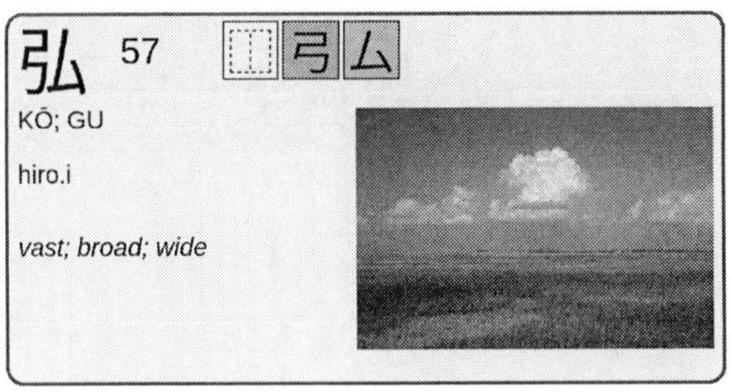

Figure 11: Example of target region F.

In Fig. 12, the main motif is the tape measure to represent the intangible objects "measurement" and "tenth of a shaku" because the latter is about 3.03 cm. In addition, there are the two "small" coins as secondary motif:

$$\{(\text{measurement},G,I,M,R,A,\text{measurement.n.01}),$$
$$(\text{tenth of a shaku},G,I,M,R,A,\text{unit\_of\_measurement.n.01}),$$
$$(\text{small},G,P,S,R,P,\text{minor.s.10}\}.$$

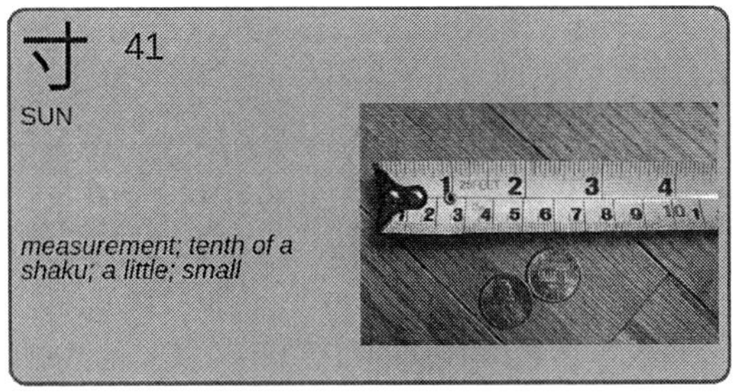

Figure 12: Example of target region S.

Finally, Fig. 13 shows a commemorative stamp depicting a *drawing* (D) that illustrates the well-known scene from the *narration* (N) "Sleeping Beauty". The *whole image* (W) is an excellent visual explanation of the intangible concept "curse":

$$\{(\text{curse},G,I,W,D,N,\text{hex.n.01})\}.$$

Figure 13: Example of target region W.

4.4 Depiction Type

In the previous subsections we have already used the depiction types R, F, P, D in Fig. 4, Fig. 8, Fig. 9, and Fig. 13. There are five additional, more specific depiction types. The first one is *bills* (B), such as posters or flyers. Figure 14 is a perfume advertisement, which also uses *textual* (T) information to make it easier to associate the image with the property "fragrant":

$$\{(\text{fragrant},G,P,W,B,T,\text{fragrant.a.01})\}.$$

A related category to bills regarding visual design are *covers* (C) of magazines, books, etc. Figure 15 shows the cover of the November 1924 issue of "Vanity Fair" magazine, which offers a literal hint towards the correct intangible object:

$$\{(\text{vanity},G,I,S,C,L,\text{amour\_propre.n.01})\}.$$

Another long tradition of transferring immaterial objects to perceivable artifacts are *monumental sculpture* (M) and any other form of three-dimensional visual arts. Right from the beginning,

Figure 14: Example of depiction type B.

Figure 15: Example of depiction type C.

ancient advanced civilizations used anthropomorphic *metaphors* (M), in particular personifications, for this purpose. In many polytheistic religions, abstract concepts were also attributed to deities. Figure 16 is such an example using goddess Justitia with her three symbolic items balance, sword, and blindfold: $\{(\text{justice},G,I,M,M,M,\text{justice.n.01})\}$.

The banner in Fig. 17 is an example of a *sign* (S), which contains the word "bribe" to demonstrate against bribery: $\{(\text{bribe},G,I,D,S,L,\text{bribe.n.01})\}$.

A special type of signs are *traffic signs* (T). They often use *icons* (I), also called pictograms. Their meaning is interpreted through their resemblance to a real object. Figure 18 is a warning sign from Poland to alert the driver to the danger of a steep upward slope: $\{(\text{slope},G,I,W,T,I,\text{gradient.n.02})\}$.

Finally, Fig. 19 shows the *result* (R) of the activ-

Figure 16: Example of depiction type M.

Figure 17: Example of depiction type S.

Figure 18: Example of depiction type T.

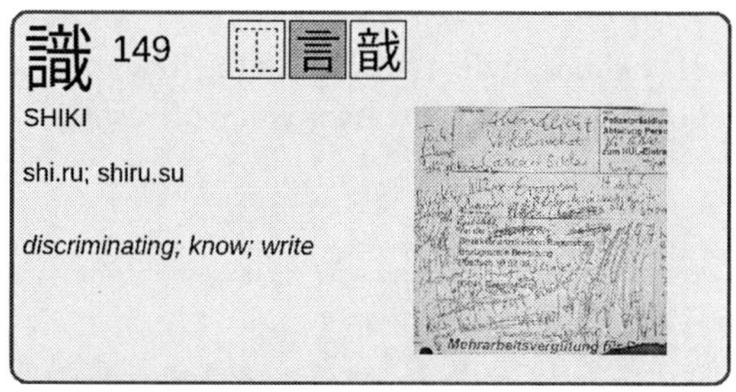

Figure 19: Example of depiction type W.

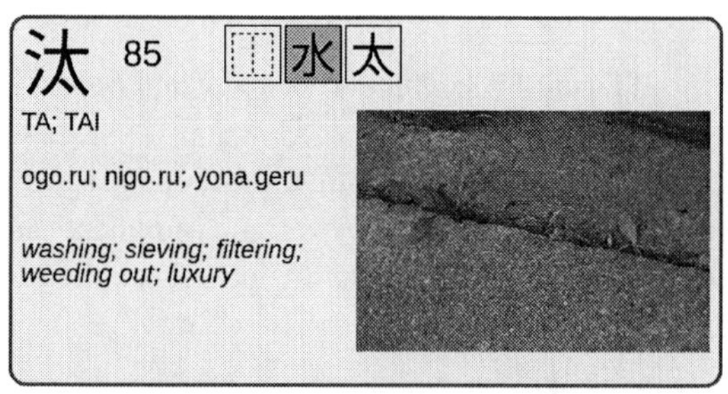

Figure 20: Example of mapping type O.

Figure 21: Example of mapping type S.

Figure 22: Example of mapping type V.

ity "write", a page filled with scribbled words. The page is an instance of a *written material* (W), the words are textual representations of the intangible object "word" referred to by the radical 言 (word):

$$\{(\text{write},G,A,W,W,R,\text{write.v.02}),$$
$$(\text{word},R,I,W,W,T,\text{word.n.01})\}.$$

4.5 Mapping Type

Most of the mapping types have already been discussed in the preceding subsections. There is one remaining feature value specifically for activities in addition to E and R. In some situations we visualize the *original state* O before executing an activity, e.g. in Fig. 20 before literally "weeding out": $\{(\text{weeding out},G,A,W,R,O,\text{weed.v.01})\}$.

One important semantic relation is the *substance* (S) holonym relation, e.g. in Fig. 21 the radical 木 indicates the material used to manufacture the table (and the chair) in the image:

$$\{(\text{table},G,T,D,R,D,\text{table.n.02}),$$
$$(\text{wood},R,T,M,R,S,\text{wood.n.01})\}.$$

Regarding the mapping of glyphs (see Fig. 8), we not only annotate full matches but also more *vague resemblances* (V) as shown in Fig. 22 for the athlete's legs:

$$\{(\text{legs radical (no. 10)},P,T,D,R,D,\text{leg.n.01}),$$
$$(\varnothing,L,G,D,R,V,\varnothing)\}$$

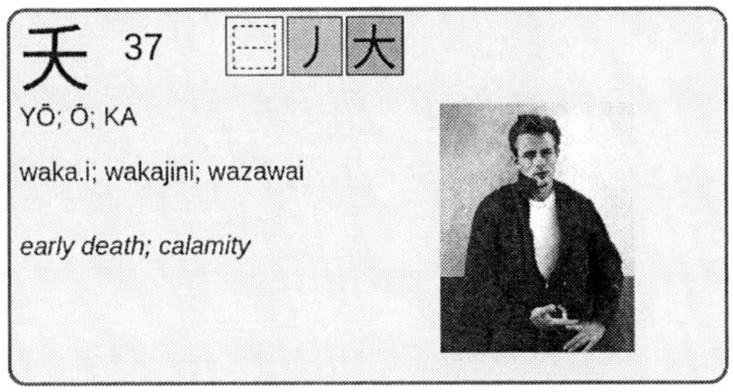

Figure 23: Example of mapping type W.

Finally, two very successful strategies to establish associations is to use knowledge and conceptions about *well-known personalities* (W) and *zoological subjects* (Z), i.e. animals. Figure 23 is a typical example where we can derive the following mapping from some basic biographical information about the life of the actor James Dean:

$$\{(\text{early death},G,I,M,R,W,\text{death.n.01})\}.$$

The last image in Fig. 24 is an example of the second strategy. It shows two dogs who seem to be quite happy: $\{(\text{happiness},G,I,M,R,Z,\text{happiness.n.01})\}$. For easier reference, we add an overview of all feature values introduced in this section in Table 1.

Figure 24: Example of mapping type Z.

5 Conclusion

In this paper we presented VISCOSE, an enhanced kanji dictionary with detailed visual, compositional, and semantic annotations. We described our motivation and the steps involved in building this lexical resource. Our main contribution is a formal representation of semantically grounded cross-media mappings from the textual to the visual dimension. We drew upon years of experience and many iterations of designs to optimize the presentation of the many details on the kanji cards.

The current version of the annotation was done by the authors, who both have a higher educational

Source Type	Information Type	Target Region	Depiction Type	Mapping Type
C component	A activity	B background	B bill	A association
G gloss	G glyph	D detail of main motif	C cover	C component
K kun'yomi	I intangible object	F foreground	D drawing	D direct
L logogram	P property	M main motif	F film scene	E execution
O on'yomi	T tangible object	S secondary motif	M monumental sculpture	F full match
P partial gloss		W whole image	P painting	I icon
R radical			R real depiction	L literal
			S sign	M metaphor
			T traffic sign	N narration
			W written material	O original state
				P property
				R result
				S substance
				T textual
				V vague resemblance
				W well-known personality
				Z zoological subject

Table 1: Overview of feature values.

background in computer science, linguistics, and Japanese studies, as well as long research and teaching experience in natural language processing including several projects on lexicographic and terminological topics. Future research will focus on editorial work and writing a comprehensive annotation guide. We will make a preliminary version available as soon as possible, before publishing our resource at LRE Map. We also plan to involve students in the process of refining and extending the annotations as class room assignments, and evaluate the annotation agreement. In this context we plan to measure the improvement regarding language acquisition in comparison with other approaches, as well as get feedback on usability, entertainment factors and the often related engagement level.

We already envision many interesting future use cases. One example is the use of kanji cards to replace thematic cards in strategic games based on feature value agreements and synset similarities. Another idea is to create cross-media analogies for memorization puzzles, such as guessing the correct gloss based on an image and an analogous kanji card. Finally, we also want to put the structural information to good use by applying our decomposition diagrams to creative storytelling to collect mnemonic sentences for improved kanji retention.

Finally, we will continue our ambitious research efforts towards integrating the kanji cards into multifaceted annotations of Japanese sentences at the lexical, syntactic, conceptual, and relational level (Wloka and Winiwarter, 2021a).

All these implementations will be evaluated in graduate courses with students in translation studies. We will follow recent suggestions in evaluation approaches (Heuer and Buschek, 2021) by putting learners in the center of the evaluation process and giving them an active role in the further development of our environment. We will solicit feedback at the beginning, during, and at the end of the evaluation to incorporate criticism and suggestions into the continued development of VISCOSE.

References

Francis Bond, Hitoshi Isahara, Sanae Fujita, Kiyotaka Uchimoto, Takayuki Kuribayashi, and Kyoko Kanzaki. 2009. Enhancing the Japanese WordNet. In *Proceedings of the 7th Workshop on Asian Language Resources (ALR7)*, pages 1–8, Suntec, Singapore. Association for Computational Linguistics.

Jim Breen. 2004. Multiple indexing in an electronic kanji dictionary. In *Proceedings of the Workshop on Enhancing and Using Electronic Dictionaries*, pages 1–7, Geneva, Switzerland. COLING.

Frederik Cornillie, Steven L. Thorne, and Piet Desmet. 2012. Digital games for language learning: From hype to insight? *ReCALL*, 24:243–256.

Dan Davies, Divya Jindal-Snape, Chris Collier, Rebecca Digby, Penny Hay, and Alan Howe. 2013. Creative learning environments in education – a systematic literature review. *Thinking Skills and Creativity*, 8:80–91.

Jia Deng, Wei Dong, Richard Socher, Li-Jia Li, Kai Li, and Li Fei-Fei. 2009. ImageNet: A Large-Scale Hierarchical Image Database. In *2009 IEEE Conference on Computer Vision and Pattern Recognition (CVPR)*, Miami, FL.

Lispridona Diner and Dyah Prasetiani. 2015. The effectiveness of use the kanji cards in kanji shokyu learning. *Jurnal Pnelitian Pendidikan*, 32(1):37–40.

Catherine J. Doughty and Michael H. Long, editors. 2003. *The Handbook of Second Language Acquisition*. Blackwell Publishing Ltd, Malden, MA.

ELM Learning. 2021. The difference between creativity vs. creative learning (and how to harness both). elmlearning.com/blog/creativity-vs-creative-learning/. Accessed: 2022-08-18.

Noah Hermalin. 2015. The processing and structure of kanji and their implications for kanji acquisition: A theoretical approach to kanji literacy. Technical report, Carnegie Mellon University.

Hendrik Heuer and Daniel Buschek. 2021. Methods for the design and evaluation of HCI+NLP systems. *arXiv*, 2102.13461 [cs.CL].

Hitoshi Isahara, Francis Bond, Kiyotaka Uchimoto, Masao Utiyama, and Kyoko Kanzaki. 2008. Development of the Japanese WordNet. In *Sixth International Conference on Language Resources and Evaluation (LREC)*, Marrakech, Morocco.

Maki Kubota. 2017. Post study abroad investigation of kanji knowledge in Japanese as a second language learners. *System*, 69:143–152.

Jens Lehmann, Robert Isele, Max Jakob, Anja Jentzsch, Dimitris Kontokostas, Pablo Mendes, Sebastian Hellmann, Mohamed Morsey, Patrick Van Kleef, Sören Auer, and Christian Bizer. 2014. DBpedia - a large-scale, multilingual knowledge base extracted from Wikipedia. *Semantic Web Journal*, 6.

Hiroshi Matsumoto. 2007. Peak learning experiences and language learning: A study of American learners of Japanese. *Language Culture and Curriculum - LANG CULT CURRIC*, 20:195–208.

George A. Miller. 1995. WordNet: A lexical database for English. *Commun. ACM*, 38(11):39–41.

Yoshiko Mori. 2014. Review of recent research on kanji processing, learning, and instruction. *Japanese Language and Literature*, 48(2):403–430.

Tomohiko Morioka. 2008. CHISE: Character processing based on character ontology. In *Large-Scale Knowledge Resources. Construction and Application*, pages 148–162, Berlin, Heidelberg. Springer Berlin Heidelberg.

Andrea Moro, Francesco Cecconi, and Roberto Navigli. 2014a. Multilingual Word Sense Disambiguation and Entity Linking for Everybody. In *Proceedings of the 13th International Semantic Web Conference, Posters and Demonstrations (ISWC 2014)*, pages 25–28, Riva del Garda, Italy.

Andrea Moro, Alessandro Raganato, and Roberto Navigli. 2014b. Entity Linking meets Word Sense Disambiguation: a Unified Approach. *Transactions of the Association for Computational Linguistics (TACL)*, 2:231–244.

Simon Paxton. 2019. Kanji matters in a multilingual Japan. *The Journal of Rikkyo University Language Center*, 42:29–41.

Mark Peterson. 2010. Computerized games and simulations in computer-assisted language learning: A meta-analysis of research. *Simulation & Gaming*, 41(1):72–93.

Gilles Sérasset. 2015. DBnary: Wiktionary as a lemon-based multilingual lexical resource in RDF. *Semantic Web*, 6(4):355–361.

Gilles Sérasset and Andon Tchechmedjiev. 2014. Dbnary : Wiktionary as Linked Data for 12 Language Editions with Enhanced Translation Relations. In *3rd Workshop on Linked Data in Linguistics: Multilingual Knowledge Resources and Natural Language Processing*, pages 67–71, Reykjavík, Iceland.

Bill VanPatten, Megan Smith, and Alessandro G. Benati. 2020. *Key Questions in Second Language Acquisition*. Cambridge University Press, Cambridge, United Kingdom.

Linda S. Watts and Patrick Blessinger. 2017. *Creative Learning in Higher Education*. Routledge, New York, NY.

Jan Wielemaker, Zhisheng Huang, and Lourens Van Der Meij. 2008. SWI-Prolog and the Web. *Theory and Practice of Logic Programming*, 8(3):363–392.

Jan Wielemaker, Tom Schrijvers, Markus Triska, and Torbjörn Lager. 2012. SWI-Prolog. *Theory and Practice of Logic Programming*, 12(1-2):67–96.

Kevin Windhaber. 2018. How interactive storytelling in a digital role-playing game can improve the learnability of Japanese kanji. Master's thesis, University of Skövde, School of Informatics.

Werner Winiwarter. 2017. Kangaroo – the kanji game room. In *Proceedings of the 19th International Conference on Information Integration and Web-based Applications & Services (iiWAS2017)*, pages 535–542, New York. Association for Computing Machinery (ACM).

Bartholomäus Wloka and Werner Winiwarter. 2021a. AAA4LLL – Acquisition, Annotation, Augmentation for Lively Language Learning. In *3rd Conference on Language, Data and Knowledge (LDK 2021)*, volume 93 of *Open Access Series in Informatics (OASIcs)*, pages 29:1–29:15, Dagstuhl, Germany. Schloss Dagstuhl – Leibniz-Zentrum für Informatik.

Bartholomäus Wloka and Werner Winiwarter. 2021b. DARE – a comprehensive methodology for mastering kanji. In *Proceedings of the 23rd International Conference on Information Integration and Web Intelligence (iiWAS2021)*, pages 427–435, New York. Association for Computing Machinery (ACM).

Bartholomäus Wloka and Werner Winiwarter. 2021c. ILEX – an integrated language learning experience. In *Proceedings of EdMedia + Innovate Learning 2021*, pages 544–553, Waynesville, NC. Association for the Advancement of Computing in Education (AACE).

Compositionality as an Analogical Process: Introducing ANNE

Giulia Rambelli
University of Pisa
giulia.rambelli@phd.unipi.it

Emmanuele Chersoni
The Hong Kong Polytechnic University
emmanuelechersoni@gmail.com

Philippe Blache
Aix-Marseille University/CNRS
philippe.blache@univ-amu.fr

Alessandro Lenci
University of Pisa
alessandro.lenci@unipi.it

Abstract

Usage-based constructionist approaches consider language a structured inventory of *constructions*, form-meaning pairings of different schematicity and complexity, and claim that the more a linguistic pattern is encountered, the more it becomes accessible to speakers. However, when an expression is unavailable, what processes underlie the interpretation? While traditional answers rely on the principle of compositionality, for which the meaning is built word-by-word and incrementally, usage-based theories argue that novel utterances are created based on previously experienced ones through *analogy*, mapping an existing structural pattern onto a novel instance.

Starting from this theoretical perspective, we propose here a computational implementation of these assumptions. As the principle of compositionality has been used to generate distributional representations of phrases, we propose a neural network simulating the construction of phrasal embedding as an analogical process. Our framework, inspired by word2vec and computer vision techniques, was evaluated on tasks of generalization from existing vectors.

1 Introduction

While the generative tradition has dominated linguistic research for over half a century, the last decades have seen the emergence of an alternative paradigm in linguistics and cognitive sciences, which goes under the name of *usage-based models of language* (Langacker, 1987; Croft, 1991, 2001; Givón, 1995; Tomasello, 2009; Bybee, 2010), a variety of approaches grounded on the idea that linguistic structures emerge and are shaped through the use of language. Their claim is that language is not different from any other cognitive domain: Linguistic structures are not the result of a specific-language function but are explainable as the implementation of domain-general processes (Ibbotson, 2013). The usage-based position shares the fundamental assumption of Construction Grammar (Hoffman and Trousdale, 2013): language consists of meaningful and symbolic form–meaning mappings, called *constructions*. Words, idiomatic expressions (e.g., *kick the bucket* —"to die" or *jog <someone's> memory* —"to refresh <someone's> memory") and highly general and productive syntactic patterns (e.g., ditransitive structures) are all constructions varying along a continuum of schematicity and complexity.

In particular, usage-based constructionist approaches emphasize the notion of frequency: combinations that are more frequently encountered become more accessible (perhaps because they are stored in memory) and are preferred. Indeed, if the language system derives from language use, it follows that how often a speaker encounters a particular linguistic expression will affect the system itself. This assumption implies that any sequence of words – if used frequently enough – can be a construction, even if there are no idiosyncrasies of form and meaning (Goldberg, 2006). However, it is impossible to store any possible word combinations a speaker has or will ever produce. The traditional answer relies on the *principle of compositionality*: the meaning of a complex expression is entirely determined by its structure and the meanings of its constituents – once we specify what the parts mean and how they are put together, there is no more leeway regarding the meaning of the whole (Partee, 2004). Usage-based theories favor a different explanation: novel utterances are created based on previously experienced utterances thanks to the cognitive process of *analogy*.

The ability to make analogies – that is, to map familiar relations from one domain of experience to another – is a fundamental ingredient of human intelligence and creativity (Hofstadter, 2001). In the linguistic domain, analogy depends on similarity in form and meaning between constructions,

Proceedings of the Workshop on Cognitive Aspects of the Lexicon, pages 78–96
November 20, 2022. ©2022 Association for Computational Linguistics
https://doi.org/10.26615/978-954-452-056-4_010

whether these constructions are of a concrete type or an abstract type: a novel instance is compared to those stored in our long-term memory to infer the new representation. In this perspective, the acceptability of a novel item is a gradient that depends on the extent of similarity to prior uses of a construction (Bybee, 2010). In a more radical stance, Ambridge (2020) proposed disregarding completely abstraction: unwitnessed forms are produced and comprehended "by on the fly analogy" across multiple stored exemplars. Without denying the existence of abstract representations, we also assume that analogical mechanisms play a key role in explaining systematic processes of language productivity.

This paper aims to articulate the hypotheses introduced above in computational terms. We address two interconnected questions: How can we represent (lexicalized) constructions? Is it possible to replicate the interpretation-as-analogy mechanism in computational terms? Specifically, we investigate how to model constructions as well as analogy-based compositionality using Distributional Semantic Models (DSMs). DSMs represent the lexicon in terms of vector spaces, where a lexical target is described in terms of a vector (also known as embedding) built by identifying in a corpus its syntactic and lexical contexts (Lenci, 2018).

As a first approximation, we decided to consider constructions any kind of frequent pairs of words linked by a syntactic relation. Traditionally, building distributional representations beyond individual words, such as phrases and sentences, is the focus of *Compositional Distributional Semantic Models*. Their proposed methodologies try to derive the meaning of an expression from the meanings of the sentence's constituents (Baroni et al., 2014): the simplest CSDMs represent words as vectors and obtain sentence vectors with sum or product operations between constituent vectors (Mitchell and Lapata, 2010), while more complex models represent predicates with matrices and tensors (Baroni and Zamparelli, 2010; Coecke et al., 2010; Baroni et al., 2014; Paperno et al., 2014) or reproduce the compositionality operation by means of a neural architecture learning so-called sentence embeddings (Socher et al., 2012; Cheng and Kartsaklis, 2015). It is interesting to notice that most distributional models for phrases/constructions/sentences assume more or less explicitly the principle of compositionality, while the idea that units above the word level could be stored and retrieved via analogy/similarity mechanisms has rarely been explored. [1]

The experiment presented here distances itself from these approaches, following a more usage-based perspective. Suppose frequently experienced word sequences are, to some extent, stored in memory, and the organization and productivity of language are understood as the result of analogical processes between form and meaning in this structured inventory of constructions. In that case, new phrases could be constructed by analogy with stored linguistic patterns. We propose a neural network model to infer a distributional representation of a new syntactic phrase by preserving the structural information encoded in the embeddings representing previously stored, high-frequency phrases.

As the main contributions of the paper, i) we introduce a new DSM in which both lemmas and syntactic relations in the form of <*head, dependent, syntactic role*> triples have a unique distributional representation; ii) we propose an analogical model to create the distributional embeddings of new relations by applying deep-learning techniques, and evaluate different architectures in terms of generalization and systematicity; iii) we discuss the implications of our analogical model from a theoretical and computational perspective.

2 Relational Embeddings

The first step consisted in developing a DSM for lexicalized constructions. We represent the meaning of phrases following a holistic approach (Turney, 2012): as a numeric vector can represent nouns like *space* and *race*, in the same way, phrases like *space race* are associated with a unique embedding. For our goal, we built embeddings corresponding to triples <*head, dependent, role*>, assuming that these vectors should keep track of the syntactic relation between words. For this reason, we called these **Relational Embeddings** (RelEmbs), and we assume they represent the meaning of lexicalized constructions.

We built our semantic space using `word2vecf` (Levy and Goldberg, 2014), a modification of the skip-gram model introduced by Mikolov et al. (2013a). While the original implementation assumes bag-of-words contexts, i.e., the model keeps

[1] Some partial exceptions are instance-based distributional models (Jones and Mewhort, 2007; Jamieson et al., 2018; Crump et al., 2020) and distributional models of event knowledge that store event occurrences in the form of syntactic graphs (Chersoni et al., 2019, 2021).

track of word counts and disregards the grammatical details and the word order, `word2vecf` allows us to use arbitrary context features. In detail, we extracted <target, context> occurrences from the concatenation of ukWaC and a 2018 dump of English Wikipedia, parsed using CoreNLP (Manning et al., 2014): targets are both words and *<head, dependent, role>* triples (e.g., *<bark, dog, nsubj>*), while context is always an open-class word (noun, verb, adjective) occurring with the target in the sentence within a window $\pm$ 10 (ten words before and ten words after the head of the relation excluding the dependent). Word2vecf parameters are reported in Appendix A. We built our DSM considering only words and relations with a frequency equal to or larger than 100 and filtering out <target, context> pairs with a frequency less than 20; lastly, we kept only *<head, dependent, role>* triples with a frequency $\geq$ 1,000, where both the head and the dependent lemmas have a frequency $\geq$ 10,000. This strategy is consistent with the idea that holistic representations of complex constructions are stored only for substantially frequent items. The final space contains 127,739 word embeddings and 173,496 RelEmbs, for a total of 301,235 items.

Semantic space evaluation We tested the quality of the semantic space over some most common benchmarks for the intrinsic evaluation of word and phrase embeddings. It is worth mentioning that we are not aiming at beating traditional DSMs, but rather at carrying out a general evaluation of the goodness of our distributional representations of lexicalized constructions.

For word embeddings, we ran the standard Word Similarity/Relatedness task using the well-known **WordSim-353** (Finkelstein et al., 2001) and **MEN** (Bruni et al., 2014). The task is to compute the cosine similarity between two words (e.g., *cup* and *mug*) and verify how their score correlates with the similarity rate given by humans. We also evaluated the DSM against **FAST** (Evert and Lapesa, 2021), a free associations dataset. The goal of this multiple-choice task is to determine the most frequent associate for a given stimulus among three candidates (e.g., which word between *neck, apple, wine* is most associated with *giraffe*?). As a baseline, we computed the performance of a DSM trained with the original word2vec Skip Gram model (Mikolov et al., 2013a) on the same concatenation of corpora.

Results are reported in Table 1. Considering the first task, we observe that Spearman's correlation scores for the baseline are a bit higher than our DSM in all settings, except for the MEN dataset. However, the differences are not statistically significant.[2] It is worth noticing that similarity results are better than relatedness results, showing the same trend reported in Agirre et al. (2009). We observe an opposite performance for the classification task: our space consistently beats the baseline, and the difference is statistically significant.

Dataset	RelEmbs.w	baseline	Coverage
WS353-all	0.684	0.721	333/353
WS353-sim	0.734	0.75	195/203
WS-353-rel	0.628	0.675	236/252
MEN	0.774	0.735	3000/3000
FAST-EAT	0.786***	0.737	5877/7610
FAST-USF	0.725***	0.719	4057/4719

Table 1: Word embeddings evaluation. On top: Spearman's correlation scores for Word Similarity/Relatedness task. Bottom: Accuracy scores for Free Association task. *** = p<0.01 using McNemar test.

Moving to the relational embeddings, we used the Mitchell et al. (2010) Phrase Similarity dataset (**ML10**), which includes 324 English phrase pairs, tripartite in noun phrases, verb phrases, and adjective phrases. Given two expressions (e.g., *general principle* and *basic rule*), the task consists in comparing the cosine similarity between the two corresponding vectors and then correlating the score with the human similarity rating. As a baseline, we represented the phrases as the sum of the word2vec vectors used for word embedding evaluation. Table 2 reveals that correlation scores are not homogeneous among the different sets: the noun phrase subset achieves a higher score (0.635) compared to the other two sets, whose score is lower than 0.5. Moreover, baseline results are consistently better than our model and are statistically significant for the AN subset.

Dataset	RelEmbs	baseline	Coverage
ML-vo	0.499	0.599	99/108
ML-nn	0.635	0.716	99/108
ML-an	0.462	0.683**	102/108

Table 2: Relational embeddings evaluation. Spearman's correlation scores for Phrase Similarity task. ** = p<0.01 using Fisher r-to-z transformation test.

[2] p>0.1, the p-value is computed with Fisher's r-to-z transformation, one-tailed test

Qualitative analysis Results in Table 2 suggest that RelEmbs perform worst than the baseline in the phrase similarity test. To gain more insight, we selected some problematic pairs from the ML10 dataset and manually inspected the k-nearest neighbors, i.e., the most similar words by cosine similarity. Let us look at the pair *reduce amount* and *cut cost*: the two expressions are judged very similar (6.55), but their cosine similarity is just 0.41. However, their distributional neighbors are coherent and somehow systematic in the sense that they are similar to relational embeddings in which the same head or dependent word occurs. So, *reduce amount* is mostly similar to *increase amount, reduce waste, a person reduce, large amount, high amount*; on the other hand, the neighbors of *cut cost* are *reduce cost, improve efficiency, increase profit, lower cost, save money*. Similar observations are for nominal phrases, like *government leader* and *health minister*. While ML10 reports a high score (4.95), the cosine similarity between the two is quite low (0.43). However, this is explainable by observing their neighbors. In the first case, *health minister* is similar to other types of ministers (*health secretary, transport minister, environment minister, minister for health*); conversely, *government leader* is more associated with situations (*invite a leader, include a leader*) or other offices (*chief whip, head of the committee, regional leader*) associated to leaders. In other words, while the phrases refer to government members, the two roles are not the same (and functions also differ).

To sum up, the qualitative analysis of the neighbors reveals that RelEmbs form a semantically coherent space, even though they do not outperform the baseline in the phrase similarity task.

3 Analogical Neural Network for Embeddings

Usage-based theories of language assume that systematic processes of language productivity can be explained mainly by analogical inferences rather than by sequential compositional operations. In this perspective, we present a system to expand the coverage of the RelEmbs space simulating the construction of phrasal meaning as an analogical process via deep learning techniques.

3.1 Architecture

We aim to infer a distributional representation of a new syntactic phrase (ANALOGICAL TARGET) by preserving the structural information encoded in an existing relational embedding (ANALOGICAL BASE). For simplicity, we represent this process using the familiar four-term formalism.[3] Approximately, solving the analogy A:B::C:? requires a system that generates an appropriate embedding to make a valid analogy: if we need to infer an embedding for the target phrase *drink cider* using *drink water* as the base, we can reformulate the analogy as: $water : drink\_water_{dobj} :: cider :?$

We framed the problem of analogy completion as a regression task: the aim is to build a phrasal vector given the embeddings of the other expressions in the analogy. While word embeddings have been widely employed to perform analogy by addition and subtraction of word embeddings (Mikolov et al., 2013b; Gladkova et al., 2016), we argue that directly training a deep neural network on the task of analogy completion could provide better results, as already proposed by Reed et al. (2015) for visual analogy-making. We named our novel neural network model as **Analogical Neural Network for Embeddings** (**ANNE**).

In detail, we implemented a feed-forward neural network architecture with one hidden layer: the model is trained to learn a function $f : R^{2D} \rightarrow R^{D}$ that maps an input vector x to a generated embedding y of dimension D (where D=300), preserving the structural properties of the selected base. The input vector x should incorporate the analogical base (e.g., *drink water*), and the new argument (e.g., *cider*). We tested two possible combinations: i) the input vector is the concatenation between the analogical base and the new argument (CONCAT, Figure 1a); ii) we compute the difference between the analogical base and the argument in the same relation; the resulting vector is concatenated to the new argument vector (DIFF; Figure 1b). The intuition below the DIFF input representation is that we apply some aspects of Mikolov's analogical operation with the nonlinearities and supervision offered by a neural network.

We developed several variants of this network, each with a distinct objective function. The basic architecture (SIMPLE) is trained to maximize the cosine similarity between the original and predicted embedding. However, ANNE should not simply create a vector similar to the actual instance in the DSM but also learn the relational structure

[3] It is, however, doubtful that linguistic analogies are computed in this way at the brain level (Bybee, 2010).

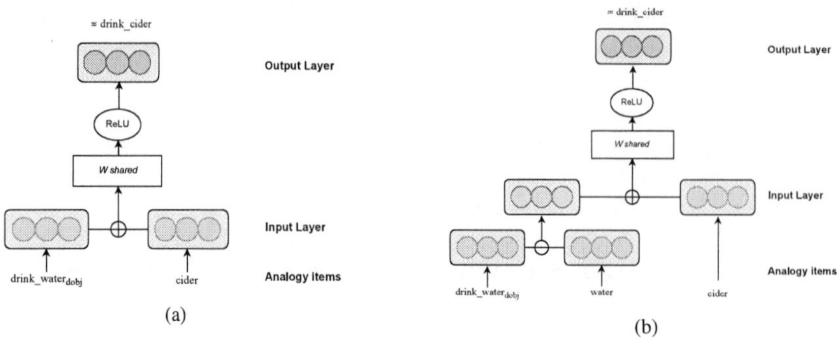

Figure 1: ANNE architecture with CONCAT (a) and DIFF (b) input. The $\bigoplus$ indicates a vector concatenation, while $\ominus$ indicates vector subtraction.

of the base and transpose it to the generated embedding. To this end, we implemented a multiple losses function, which combines the SIMPLE loss with a new loss aimed at minimizing the difference of the similarity between the relational vector and the embeddings of its words computed for the base and the target. For instance, if the similarity between *drink water* and *drink* is 0.60 and the similarity between *drink water* and *water* is 0.49, similar scores should be obtained by computing the similarity of the output vector with the vectors of *drink* and *cider*. Therefore, the network is trained to generate RelEmbs that preserve the same relations with its components as the ones in the analogical base. To compare the similarity scores we tested three functions (cf. Appendix B): the Mean Squared Error (MULTIMSE), the mean of the scores difference (MULTIAVG), or the hinge loss function (MULTIHINGE).

Training the network We selected analogical base-target pairs from the Relational Embeddings attested in space to train the neural network. We assembled the dataset as follows: given a relation *<head, dependent, syntactic relation>*, we selected all RelEmbs with the same head and syntactic relation and calculated the similarity between the arguments of each pair, keeping only those pairs with the cosine similarity between arguments ≥ 0.4 and the cosine similarity between RelEmbs ≥ 0.6. We chose the filter on similarity heuristically: the idea is that the candidate targets should be somehow similar with respect to their analogical bases but not the exact synonyms. The final dataset consisted of 350,404 items and was divided into **Train** and **Test** parts (respectively, 95% and 5%).

To verify the analogy-solving capability of the network, i.e., its ability to generalize from the base, we kept some analogical pairs out of the training step. The resulting data (named **Test-unseen**), comprises 3,201 pairs (cf. Appendix C). This dataset should verify the network's performance when encountering new relations, which is to say, evaluate the model's generalization ability. The training setup configurations are reported in Appendix D.

3.2 RSA Evaluation

A preliminary evaluation of ANNE consisted of computing the similarity between relational embeddings attested in the DSM and embeddings analogically generated from ANNE attested in the Test and the Test-unseen datasets. We applied the Representational Similarity Analysis (RSA; Kriegeskorte et al. (2008); Kriegeskorte and Kievit (2013)), a computational technique that allows us to compare heterogeneous representations in higher-order spaces. The core idea is simple: instead of directly correlating representations of stimuli in different representation spaces, we compute how similar representations are between pairs of stimuli in each space, and the resulting similarity matrices are then compared. As we are interested in understanding how similar the original and generated embeddings are, we created a pair of matrices where rows are the vectors representing the analogical targets from a test set and columns correspond to a subset of the RelEmbs vocabulary.[4] Following Lenci et al. (2022), we randomly sampled 100 disjoint sets of 1,000 lexemes, ran RSA analyses on each sample, and then computed the average score.

Table 3 reports Spearman's ρ between the similarity matrix computed with the original RelEmbs

[4]A matrix with 301,235 columns would be computationally too expensive.

and the matrix with vectors generated with ANNE. We can observe that the models reach similar results for the two test data, even if the Test-unseen scores are always slightly lower than those for the Test set. Overall, the SIMPLE model reaches the best scores (0.851 for Test and 0.835 for Test-unseen), while MULTIAVG performs the worst (reaching just 0.739 for Test-unseen with DIFF input). However, the average correlation of all models is significantly high. As a baseline, we also performed the vector offset method (Mikolov et al., 2013a). RSA correlation scores significantly drop (0.734 and 0.71 for the Test and Test-unseen, respectively). The worst architecture (MULTIAVG diff) is still better than the baseline for Test ($p < 0.1$), but not for Test-unseen. The best architecture (SIMPLE_{concat}) is different from the baseline with $p < 0.001$.[5] This result corroborates our assumption that the ANNE architecture is better at generating analogical vectors than a simple vector operation.

	TEST	TEST-UNSEEN
simple_{concat}	0.851	0.835
simple_{diff}	0.848	0.834
$\text{multiHinge}_{concat}$	0.819	0.805
multiHinge_{diff}	0.806	0.788
multiAVG_{concat}	0.782	0.754
multiAVG_{diff}	0.77	0.739
multiMSE_{concat}	0.835	0.82
multiMSE_{diff}	0.824	0.804
baseline	0.734	0.71

Table 3: Average Spearman's correlation between original and analogically generated semantic spaces computed with RSA on 100 random samples of 1,000 words for Test and Test-unseen datasets.

4 Compositionality vs. Idiomaticity

Finally, we present a series of analyses to evaluate the meaning encoded in analogically-generated embeddings. We hypothesize that the best-generated embedding should keep the same relationship among components as the base (*systematicity*). As a counterproof, we also generated embeddings from idiomatic expressions. In this case, we expect analogies with idiomatic bases to give odd results in the semantic space because of their reduced compositionality and systematicity. The results should answer the following questions: What are the characteristics of analogically-generated embeddings? How does the type of input (concatenation or difference) affect the final representation? What loss functions are better at retaining the same structural relation of the base, while at the same time generalizing from the original embedding?

[5] p-values for Fisher's r-to-z transformation, one-tailed test.

Data The analogical bases employed are 44 verbal phrases (22 idioms from Libben and Titone (2008) + 22 compositional manually picked from frequent relations) and 24 nominal compounds (12 idiomatic + 12 compositional) selected from the Noun Compound Senses dataset (Cordeiro et al., 2019) and the dataset by Reddy et al. (2011).

For each phrase, we manually chose a relation similar to the base but not attested in the vocabulary space, with the same head and syntactic role. For example, given the relation <*market*$_N$, *fish*$_N$, *compound*> ("a fish market"), we replaced the noun *fish* (i.e., the dependent) with the noun *shrimp*; expressly, the relation <*market*$_N$, *shrimp*$_N$, *compound*> ("a shrimp market") is not attested in RelEmbs vocabulary. The final dataset consists of 68 analogical pairs, half with an idiomatic base and half with the compositional counterpart.

	Idiomatic → Target	Compositional → Target
VN	*break ice* → *break chunk*	*break bone* → *break finger*
NC	*loan shark* → *credit shark*	*reef shark* → *atol shark*

Table 4: Examples of analogical pairs (the idiomatic/compositional base on the left, the target on the right of the arrow).

4.1 Analysis 1: Correlation of the Similarities with the Components

To evaluate if and how the ANNE configurations are generating embeddings systematically, we observed if the similarities between the relational embedding and those of the component words are similar for both the analogical base and the generated target. The assumption is that the embedding generated by ANNE should have the same internal structure as the base from which it is inferred: that is, the relationship between the phrase meaning and the meaning of its components should be systematically retained in the generated distributional vector. This idea can be approximated by the similarities between the RelEmbs and its parts: if the similarity between *break (a) bone* and *break* is 0.4 (*simHead* score) and the similarity with the dependent *bone* is 0.42 (*simDep* score), comparable scores should be obtained computing the similarities of *break (a) finger* with *break* and *finger*, respectively.

We computed the cosine similarity scores for all ANNE implementations. We assume that the best architecture (i.e., the one that best fits our theoretical hypothesis) should be the one that has i) comparable similarity distributions for compositional bases and derived targets (for both word components), and ii) different (or incoherent) similarity distributions for targets generated from idiomatic bases. By looking closely at the plots in Appendix E, we observe that each architecture produces different outputs. Among all models, MULTIAVG is the one performing worse (plots in (c) and (d)): the generated embeddings have high similarities with the dependent component in both idiomatic and compositional cases, possibly because they retain too much distributional information from dependent words used to generate the new embedding. The MULTIMSE (plots in (e) and (f)) and the SIMPLE (plots in (a) and (b)) losses show a similar behavior: they give a high *simHead* and *simDep* to vector generated from idiomatic targets. This result shows that, when deriving a new literal phrase meaning from a figurative one should be impossible, the models largely rely on attribute similarity instead of truly learning a relation. In this sense, the MULTIMSE$_{diff}$ (plots in (f)) model is the only one that perfectly respects our hypothesis (distributions should be the same for targets from compositional bases but different for targets with idiomatic bases). Conversely, the MULTIHINGE model (plots in (g) and (h)) reduces the impact of the dependent word, as proved by the fact that the mean similarity of *simDep* is lower for the target (orange) than for the base (blue).

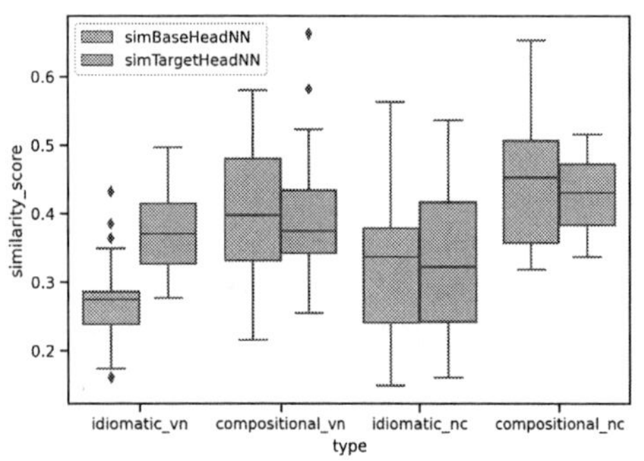

Figure 2: Distribution of the similarities between RelEmbs and their head for MULTIMSE$_{diff}$. Blue boxplots refer to the base embedding, orange to the analogically-generated ones.

4.2 Analysis 2: Intersection of Neighbors

As a complementary measure to cosine similarity, we computed the intersection between the 50-nearest neighbors of i) the base and the generated target, and ii) the generated target and the respective head/dependent.[6] The first measure tells us how much information the analogical embedding retains from its base: the higher the value, the higher their similarity, so it could be that the network did not generalize from the input. The second measure should say how much the analogy moved the distribution towards the component meanings. Appendix F reports the results as a series of heatmaps.

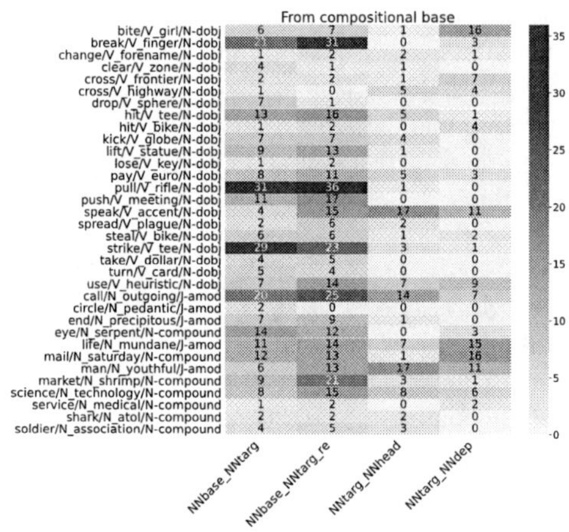

Figure 3: Heatmap for MULTIMSE$_{concat}$ shows the intersection between the neighbors of the analogically-generated embedding and the base ($NN_{base}NN_{targ}$, **re* only RelEmbs)), the head ($NN_{targ}NN_{head}$), and the dependent ($NN_{targ}NN_{dep}$).

Embeddings generated from idiomatic bases have no shared neighbors with the vectors of their heads or dependents: as the network was not trained on this type of analogies (which are impossible), we expected the neural model to fail. What we can add, however, is that sometimes it generates a new embedding that has no common neighbors with either its base or components, sometimes it resolves the analogy by copying the distributional signature of the base. The only exception to this trend is MULTIAVG (subfigures (c) and (d)): we notice that some items, such as *shark credit*, *cockroach market*, and *gastropod mail*, partake many neighbors with their dependent, revealing that this

[6]For head and dependent embeddings, we only considered neighbors that are RelEmbs to limit the variability.

model is not generalizing correctly.

A more complex scenario appears if we consider the targets generated from compositional bases. As noticed above, ANNE with CONCAT input has more shared neighbors between the target and the base (first two columns), while this is not the case for the ANNE with DIFF input (see heatmaps in (a) and (b) as example). This finding is further proof that a neural network that takes as input the concatenation of vectors for the base and the target argument attempts to generate an embedding as close as possible to the input relational embedding. In other words, this type of input could negatively impacts ANNE in learning the correct inference.

4.3 Architectures' comparison

Previous analyses reveal that some parameter configurations are better than others. ANNE models that take as input the SIMPLE concatenation of the RelEmb base and the word embedding generate vectors too similar to the base, while modifying the base with an operation similar to Mikolov's vector offset produces better results. Overall, it seems that ANNE trained with MULTIHINGE and MULTIMSE losses (with DIFF input) induce more consistent and explainable results, while MULTIAVG is suboptimal for its tendency to generate embeddings similar to the target's dependent.

5 General Discussion

An open issue in DSMs is how distributional representations can be projected from the lexical level to the sentence or even discourse level. Most previous approaches have tried to solve this issue by explicitly relying on the classic principle of compositionality. Given the Fregean assumption that phrase meaning is a function of the meanings of its constituents, different computational strategies have been proposed to derive vectors for phrases by taking word embeddings as inputs.

In this paper, we proposed a new methodology grounded on a usage-based perspective: we tried to generate new distributional representations by implementing an analogical function in the form of a neural network. Word analogies have been used as a standard intrinsic evaluation task for measuring the quality of word (Mikolov et al., 2013c; Levy and Goldberg, 2014; Linzen, 2016) and sentence embeddings (Zhu and de Melo, 2020; Wang et al., 2021; Ushio et al., 2021b). However, the task is usually defined as a candidate retrieval: given an analogical proportion, find the correct completion from a list of candidates to solve the analogy. On the contrary, our aim is to generate a completely new embedding, similarly to what is done in reasoning and computer vision (Reed et al., 2015; Sadeghi et al., 2015; Upchurch et al., 2016; Ichien et al., 2021): the task consists in training deep learning models to recognize a relationship among two images and generate a transformed query representation (in this case, an image) accordingly. We believe that future investigations in linguistic analogies should pick up from this literature, and ANNE is a first attempt along this direction.

Our ANNE approach is not without limitations. One controversial aspect of ANNE is the choice of building the target by simply changing the argument in the relation. While it is not too problematic for verbal phrases, it raises questions for adjective-noun phrases and noun compounds. Consider the expressions *blue car* and *fast car*. Many things can be blue and not be a car, but not everything can be fast (e.g., **fast carrot*) because *fast* constrains the possible realizations of its head. A similar observation could be shown for noun compounds: in some cases, their meaning is related to both components (e.g., *bank account*), but sometimes their meaning retains aspects of one component (e.g., *head teacher*). To take into account the specificities of each type of phrases, we could train different ANNE architectures for each type of phrases.

The main difficulty is to balance relational and attributional similarity. Indeed, the use of a new item in a construction requires a great deal of relational knowledge (Gentner and Markman, 1997); nonetheless, the importance of similarity or shared attributes to linguistic analogy is not less vital (Bybee, 2010). A qualitative evaluation of analogical inferred embeddings reveals that analogy is easier to compute if the similarity between the entities in the syntactic relations is high. For instance, most all architectures build a good representation of *science technology* generated from *earth science*, maybe because there are lots of "topic science" expressions (cf. Table 5). Conversely, if attribute similarity is lower (i.e., the words between the base and the target are somewhat dissimilar), the analogical model is challenged. The neighbors of *pedantic circle* (derived from *literary circle*, cf. Table 6) are odd and incoherent with the expected meaning, maybe because the adjective *literary* is usually associated with a work of literature (an inanimate

	concat	diff	concat	diff
SIMPLE	*earth science*	*area of technology*	*show (a) letter*	*guess* PERSON
	apply science	*apply technology*	*explain in letter*	*extol (the) virtue*
	marine science	*focus* ORGANIZ.	*(a) disciple* PERSON	*point_out* PERSON
	new science	*include technology*	*(a) letter address*	*complain about* PERSON
	area of technology	*area of engineering*	*refer in (the) letter*	*dismiss (an) idea*
MULTIHINGE	*earth science*	*focus* ORGANIZ.	LOCATION *scholar*	*state for example*
	new science	*area of technology*	*join on return*	*extol (the) virtue*
	apply science	*apply technology*	*accompany (an) expedition*	*join on return*
	relate to technology	*electronic technology*	*await (the) return*	*serve curacy*
	area of technology	*create technology*	*(a) letter address*	*say in july*
MULTIMSE	*earth science*	*area of technology*	*show letter*	*complain about* PERSON
	apply science	*include technology*	*explain in letter*	*guess* PERSON
	area of technology	*focus* ORGANIZ.	*letter address*	*extol (the) virtue*
	new science	*aspect of technology*	*enlist aid*	*point_out* PERSON
	area of engineering	*aspect of use*	(a) PERSON *demand*	*say according to* PERSON
MULTIAVG	*apply science*	*information technology*	*see before* PERSON	*see before* PERSON
	information technology	*apply technology*	*like (one's) style*	*feel like* PERSON
	development in science	*area of technology*	*tell (a) girl*	*tell (a) girl*
	role of technology	*apply science*	*tell about time*	*realize* PERSON
	area of technology	*new technology*	*everyone tell(s)*	*want (a) baby*

Table 5: 5-nearest neighbors of *technology science* (compound) generated *earth science*.

Table 6: 5-nearest neighbors of *pedantic circle* (amod) generated from *a literary circle*.

object), while *pedantic* collocates with a person. In these cases, different factors could contribute to the success or failure of the model, which should be further investigated.

The introduction of analogy as a strategy to derive meaning for novel expressions does not entail the entire suppression of compositional approaches. From a theoretical stance, not every expression can be built using analogical inference: if analogy fails, compositional operations switch over to guide interpretation. In this regard, the question should not be whether analogically-generated vectors are better than computationally-built ones, but when one mechanism is preferred to the other. Answering this question is challenging from both a psycholinguistic and computational stance. The issues related to computational models of analogy as a productive mechanism in language are theoretical before methodological. While it is true that the cognitive process of analogy represents a central mechanism in human cognition (Hofstadter, 2001), the problem in defining a linguistic theory that formalizes precisely what an analogy is and when it occurs is complex. In other words, it is hard to predict which analogies will actually be drawn and at what linguistic level (Behrens, 2017, p. 215). Ideally, future systems aiming at modeling language comprehension should be able to include this mechanism too. New benchmarks will have to be built with the aim of identifying analogical inferences. These datasets could also be valuable for behavioral analyses.

6 Conclusion and Future Works

In this paper, we presented a new approach that simulates the construction of phrasal meaning as an analogical process implemented with deep learning techniques. We proposed a distributional representation of constructional phrases and a model of generating new embeddings analogically rather than applying traditional compositional operations. We experimented with our analogical neural network to understand how it can generalize and be extendable to different scenarios. We argued that the proposed methodology could open the doors to new analyses in distributional semantics as well as in computational models of language processing.

The future research perspectives on ANNE are considerable. Firstly, we could build a more sophisticated phrasal representation using contextualized embeddings (Ethayarajh, 2019) based on Transformers (Vaswani et al., 2017; Devlin et al., 2019). Moreover, we should compare our Relembs with other phrasal representations representations (Shwartz, 2019; Alipoor and Schulte im Walde, 2020) and Relation Embeddings (Camacho-Collados et al., 2019; Ushio et al., 2021a). Moreover, while we performed analogy over preselected base-target pairs, we aim at investigating methods to automatically retrieve the best analogical candidate. Finally, we plan to evaluate ANNE's ability to model human behavior on more complex tasks regarding compositionality and language productivity.

References

Eneko Agirre, Enrique Alfonseca, Keith Hall, Jana Kravalova, Marius Pasca, and Aitor Soroa. 2009. A Study on Similarity and Relatedness Using Distributional and WordNet-based Approaches. In *Proceedings of NAACL-HLT*.

Pegah Alipoor and Sabine Schulte im Walde. 2020. Variants of vector space reductions for predicting the compositionality of English noun compounds. In *Proceedings of the Twelfth Language Resources and Evaluation Conference*, pages 4379–4387, Marseille, France. European Language Resources Association.

Ben Ambridge. 2020. Against Stored Abstractions: A Radical Exemplar Model of Language Acquisition. *First Language*, 40(5-6):509–559.

Marco Baroni, Raffaella Bernardi, and Roberto Zamparelli. 2014. Frege in Space: A Program of Compositional Distributional Semantics. *LiLT (Linguistic Issues in Language Technology)*, 9.

Marco Baroni and Roberto Zamparelli. 2010. Nouns Are Vectors, Adjectives Are Matrices: Representing Adjective-noun Constructions in Semantic Space. In *Proceedings of EMNLP*.

Heike Behrens. 2017. The Role of Analogy in Language Processing and Acquisition. *The Changing English Language: Psycholinguistic Perspectives*, pages 215–239.

Elia Bruni, Nam-Khanh Tran, and Marco Baroni. 2014. Multimodal Distributional Semantics. *Journal of Artificial Intelligence Research*, 49:1–47.

Joan L. Bybee. 2010. *Language, Usage and Cognition*. Cambridge University Press.

Jose Camacho-Collados, Luis Espinosa Anke, and Steven Schockaert. 2019. Relational word embeddings. In *Proceedings of the 57th Annual Meeting of the Association for Computational Linguistics*, pages 3286–3296, Florence, Italy. Association for Computational Linguistics.

Jianpeng Cheng and Dimitri Kartsaklis. 2015. Syntax-aware Multi-sense Word Embeddings for Deep Compositional Models of Meaning. In *Proceedings of EMNLP*.

Emmanuele Chersoni, Enrico Santus, Alessandro Lenci, Philippe Blache, and Chu-Ren Huang. 2021. Not All Arguments Are Processed Equally: A Distributional Model of Argument Complexity. *Language Resources and Evaluation*, 55(4):873–900.

Emmanuele Chersoni, Enrico Santus, Ludovica Pannitto, Alessandro Lenci, Philippe Blache, and C-R Huang. 2019. A Structured Distributional Model of Sentence Meaning and Processing. *Natural Language Engineering*, 25(4):483–502.

Bob Coecke, Mehrnoosh Sadrzadeh, and Stephen Clark. 2010. Mathematical Foundations for a Compositional Distributional Model of Meaning. *arXiv preprint arXiv:1003.4394*.

Silvio Cordeiro, Aline Villavicencio, Marco Idiart, and Carlos Ramisch. 2019. Unsupervised Compositionality Prediction of Nominal Compounds. *Computational Linguistics*, 45:1–57.

William Croft. 1991. *Syntactic Categories and Grammatical Relations: The Cognitive Organization of Information*. University of Chicago Press.

William Croft. 2001. *Radical Construction Grammar: Syntactic Theory in Typological Perspective*. Oxford University Press.

Matthew Crump, Randall Jamieson, Brendan T Johns, and Michael N Jones. 2020. Controlling the Retrieval of General vs Specific Semantic Knowledge in the Instance Theory of Semantic Memory. In *CogSci*.

Jacob Devlin, Ming-Wei Chang, Kenton Lee, and Kristina Toutanova. 2019. BERT: Pre-training of Deep Bidirectional Transformers for Language Understanding. In *Proceedings of NAACL*.

Kawin Ethayarajh. 2019. How Contextual Are Contextualized Word Representations? Comparing the Geometry of BERT, ELMo, and GPT-2 Embeddings. In *Proceedings of EMNLP*.

Stefan Evert and Gabriella Lapesa. 2021. FAST: A Carefully Sampled and Cognitively Motivated Dataset for Distributional Semantic Evaluation. In *Proceedings of CONLL*.

Lev Finkelstein, Evgeniy Gabrilovich, Yossi Matias, Ehud Rivlin, Zach Solan, Gadi Wolfman, and Eytan Ruppin. 2001. Placing Search in Context: The Concept Revisited. In *Proceedings of International Conference on World Wide Web*, pages 406–414.

Dedre Gentner and Arthur B Markman. 1997. Structure Mapping in Analogy and Similarity. *American Psychologist*, 52(1):45.

Talmy Givón. 1995. *Functionalism and Grammar*. John Benjamins Publishing.

Anna Gladkova, Aleksandr Drozd, and Satoshi Matsuoka. 2016. Analogy-based Detection of Morphological and Semantic Relations with Word Rmbeddings: What Works and What doesn't. In *Proceedings of the NAACL Student Research Workshop*.

Adele E. Goldberg. 2006. *Constructions at Work: The Nature of Generalization in Language*. Oxford University Press on Demand.

Thomas Hoffman and Graeme Trousdale, editors. 2013. *The Oxford Handbook of Construction Grammar*. Oxford University Press, Oxford.

Douglas R Hofstadter. 2001. Analogy as the Core of Cognition. *The Analogical Mind: Perspectives from Cognitive Science*, pages 499–538.

Paul Ibbotson. 2013. The Scope of Usage-based Theory. *Frontiers in Psychology*, 4:255.

Nicholas Ichien, Qing Liu, Shuhao Fu, Keith J Holyoak, Alan Yuille, and Hongjing Lu. 2021. Visual Analogy: Deep Learning versus Compositional Models. *arXiv preprint arXiv:2105.07065*.

Randall K Jamieson, Johnathan E Avery, Brendan T Johns, and Michael N Jones. 2018. An Instance Theory of Semantic Memory. *Computational Brain & Behavior*, 1(2):119–136.

Michael N Jones and Douglas JK Mewhort. 2007. Representing Word Meaning and Order Information in a Composite Holographic Lexicon. *Psychological Review*, 114(1):1.

Diederik P Kingma and Jimmy Ba. 2014. Adam: A Method for Stochastic Optimization. *arXiv preprint arXiv:1412.6980*.

Nikolaus Kriegeskorte and Rogier A Kievit. 2013. Representational Geometry: Integrating Cognition, Computation, and the Brain. *Trends in Cognitive Sciences*, 17(8):401–412.

Nikolaus Kriegeskorte, Marieke Mur, and Peter A Bandettini. 2008. Representational Similarity Analysis-connecting the Branches of Systems Neuroscience. *Frontiers in Systems Neuroscience*, page 4.

Ronald W Langacker. 1987. *Foundations of Cognitive Grammar: Theoretical Prerequisites*, volume 1. Stanford University Press.

Alessandro Lenci. 2018. Distributional Models of Word Meaning. *Annual Review of Linguistics*, 4(1):151–171.

Alessandro Lenci, Magnus Sahlgren, Patrick Jeuniaux, Amaru Cuba Gyllensten, and Martina Miliani. 2022. A Comprehensive Comparative Evaluation and Analysis of Distributional Semantic Models. *Language, Resources and Evaluation*.

Omer Levy and Yoav Goldberg. 2014. Dependency-based Word Embeddings. In *Proceedings of ACL*.

Maya R Libben and Debra A Titone. 2008. The Multi-determined Nature of Idiom Processing. *Memory & Cognition*, 36(6):1103–1121.

Tal Linzen. 2016. Issues in evaluating semantic spaces using word analogies. In *Proceedings of the 1st Workshop on Evaluating Vector-Space Representations for NLP*, pages 13–18.

Christopher D Manning, Mihai Surdeanu, John Bauer, Jenny Rose Finkel, Steven Bethard, and David McClosky. 2014. The Stanford CoreNLP Natural Language Processing Toolkit. In *Proceedings of ACL: System Demo*.

Tomas Mikolov, Ilya Sutskever, Kai Chen, Greg S Corrado, and Jeff Dean. 2013a. Distributed Representations of Words and Phrases and their Compositionality. *Advances in Neural Information Processing Systems*, 26.

Tomáš Mikolov, Wen-tau Yih, and Geoffrey Zweig. 2013b. Linguistic Regularities in Continuous Space Word Representations. In *Proceedings of NAACL-HLT*.

Tomas Mikolov, Wen-tau Yih, and Geoffrey Zweig. 2013c. Linguistic regularities in continuous space word representations. In *Proceedings of the 2013 conference of the north american chapter of the association for computational linguistics: Human language technologies*, pages 746–751.

Jeff Mitchell and Mirella Lapata. 2010. Composition in Distributional Models of Semantics. *Cognitive Science*, 34(8):1388–1429.

Jeff Mitchell, Mirella Lapata, Vera Demberg, and Frank Keller. 2010. Syntactic and Semantic Factors in Processing Difficulty: An Integrated Measure. In *Proceedings of ACL*.

Denis Paperno, Nghia The Pham, and Marco Baroni. 2014. A Practical and Linguistically-motivated Approach to Compositional Distributional Semantics. In *Proceedings of ACL*.

Barbara H. Partee. 2004. *Compositionality in Formal Semantics: Selected Papers*. Explorations in Semantics. Blackwell Publishing Ltd.

Adam Paszke, Sam Gross, Francisco Massa, Adam Lerer, James Bradbury, Gregory Chanan, Trevor Killeen, Zeming Lin, Natalia Gimelshein, Luca Antiga, et al. 2019. Pytorch: An Imperative Style, High-performance Deep Learning Library. *Advances in Neural Information Processing Systems*, 32.

Siva Reddy, Diana McCarthy, and Suresh Manandhar. 2011. An Empirical Study on Compositionality in Compound Nouns. In *Proceedings of IJCNLP*.

Scott E Reed, Yi Zhang, Yuting Zhang, and Honglak Lee. 2015. Deep Visual Analogy-making. *Advances in Neural Information Processing Systems*, 28.

Fereshteh Sadeghi, C Lawrence Zitnick, and Ali Farhadi. 2015. Visalogy: Answering Visual Analogy Questions. *Advances in Neural Information Processing Systems*, 28.

Vered Shwartz. 2019. A systematic comparison of English noun compound representations. In *Proceedings of the Joint Workshop on Multiword Expressions and WordNet (MWE-WN 2019)*, pages 92–103, Florence, Italy. Association for Computational Linguistics.

Richard Socher, Brody Huval, Christopher D Manning, and Andrew Y Ng. 2012. Semantic Compositionality through Recursive Matrix-vector Spaces. In *Proceedings of EMNLP-CONLL*.

Michael Tomasello. 2009. The Usage-based Theory of Language Acquisition. In *The Cambridge Handbook of Child Language*, pages 69–87. Cambridge University Press.

Peter D Turney. 2012. Domain and Function: A Dual-space Model of Semantic Relations and Compositions. *Journal of Artificial Intelligence Research*, 44:533–585.

Paul Upchurch, Noah Snavely, and Kavita Bala. 2016. From A to Z: Supervised Transfer of Style and Content Using Deep Neural Network Generators. *arXiv preprint arXiv:1603.02003*.

Asahi Ushio, Jose Camacho-Collados, and Steven Schockaert. 2021a. Distilling relation embeddings from pretrained language models. In *Proceedings of the 2021 Conference on Empirical Methods in Natural Language Processing*.

Asahi Ushio, Luis Espinosa Anke, Steven Schockaert, and Jose Camacho-Collados. 2021b. BERT is to NLP what AlexNet is to CV: Can pre-trained language models identify analogies? In *Proceedings of the 59th Annual Meeting of the Association for Computational Linguistics and the 11th International Joint Conference on Natural Language Processing (Volume 1: Long Papers)*, Online. Association for Computational Linguistics.

Ashish Vaswani, Noam Shazeer, Niki Parmar, Jakob Uszkoreit, Llion Jones, Aidan N Gomez, Łukasz Kaiser, and Illia Polosukhin. 2017. Attention Is All You Need. *Advances in Neural Information Processing Systems*, 30.

Yizhe Wang, Béatrice Daille, and Nabil Hathout. 2021. Caractérisation des relations sémantiques entre termes multi-mots fondée sur l'analogie (semantic relations recognition between multi-word terms by means of analogy). In *Actes de la 28e Conférence sur le Traitement Automatique des Langues Naturelles. Volume 1 : conférence principale*, pages 115–124. ATALA.

Xunjie Zhu and Gerard de Melo. 2020. Sentence analogies: Linguistic regularities in sentence embeddings. In *Proceedings of the 28th International Conference on Computational Linguistics*, pages 3389–3400.

A RelEmbs parameters

We use the skip-gram algorithm adopting the default configuration: no hierarchical softmax, 15 negative samples (how many negative contexts to sample for every correct one), and 300 as the vector dimension.

B ANNE losses

The basic architecture (SIMPLE) uses the cosine similarity between original and predicted vectors to make backpropagation. The CosineEmbeddingLoss[7] criterion from PyTorch library (Paszke et al., 2019) measures whether two inputs t and t' are similar or dissimilar using the cosine distance (cos):

$$\text{CEloss}(t, t', y) = \begin{cases} 1 - cos(t, t') & \text{if } y = 1 \\ max(0, cos(t, t')) & \text{if } y = -1 \end{cases} \quad (1)$$

The loss function takes as inputs t, t', and a label tensor y containing values (1 or -1). For our purposes, we set y=1, so the loss is *1 - cos(t, t')*: The closer the cosine value to 1, the more the two inputs are similar, and then the loss is closer to 0. The optimization strategy is to minimize the cost function, that is, obtaining a loss value near 0 for all items in the training set.

The MULTI-criterion loss function is defined by the general formula:

$$\begin{aligned} loss_{multi} = & \; CEloss(t, t') \\ & + g(CEloss(b, b_{head}), \\ & \quad CEloss(t', t_{head})) \\ & + g(CEloss(b, b_{dep}), \\ & \quad CEloss(t', t_{dep})) \end{aligned} \quad (2)$$

where t stands for the vector originally attested in RelEmbs space and t' corresponds to the output vector generated by the network; b represents the analogical base vector, $b_{head/dep}$ represents the vectors for the head and the dependent of the base (the same applies for $t_{head/dep}$). Finally, g(·) represents the function used to compare the phrase-argument similarity scores, which can be either the Mean Squared Error (equation 3), the mean of the scores difference (equation 4), or the hinge loss function (equation 5).

$$\text{MSE}(x, x') = (x - x')^2 \quad (3)$$

$$\text{AVG}(x, x') = mean(x - x') \quad (4)$$

$$\text{HINGE}(x, x') = max(0, x - x') \quad (5)$$

For each loss function, the cost derivative for the model's parameters (weight matrices W_1, bias vector b_1) is computed, and the appropriate parameters are updated through backpropagation.

[7]https://pytorch.org/docs/stable/generated/torch.nn.CosineEmbeddingLoss.html

C ANNE Test unseen preparation

We randomly selected 15 verbs, 15 nouns, and 15 adjectives attested in the RelEmbs vocabulary and we picked out from the original list all pairs in which one of these lemmas appeared. For instance, given the verb *study*, we saved in a separate file all pairs in which the verb occurs, such as <$study_V$, $aspect_N$, *dobj*> ("to study the aspect") → <$study_V$, $development_N$, *dobj*> ("to study the development").

D ANNE Training Setup

Given the possible combinations of input type (CONCAT and DIFF) and losses functions (SIMPLE, MULTIMSE, MULTIAVG, and MULTIHINGE), we trained eight different versions of ANNE. All models were trained using 5-cross validation for 10 epochs with the Adam (Kingma and Ba, 2014) gradient descent, using a batch size of 25. Hyperparameter values equal for all models. The training was performed on a TITAN Xp GPU (12gb).

E Task1-Correlation of the component similarities of the base and the generated target

In order to visualize how these measures differ among architectures, we plotted the similarity scores using boxplots (Figure 4). Each subfigure represents the similarities computed over embeddings generated from a specific model architecture. The plot on the left refers to the RelEmb-head similarities; the plot on the right illustrates the RelEmb-dependent similarities. In each plot, we grouped boxplots for the type of base (idiomatic or compositional) and the syntactic type of phrase (verbal —VN —or nominal —NC). Finally, similarities are computed for both the base embedding (blue) and target embedding (orange).

F Task 2-Intersection of neighbors

We propose here a visual aid to investigate ANNE behavior. Figure 5 groups a series of heatmaps. In each heatmap, rows correspond to a specific item from the dataset, while columns represent the intersection between the neighbors of:

- The base and the generated target (*NNbase_NNtarg*; $NNbase\_NNtarg_{re}$ considers only RelEmbs)
- The generated target and the respective head (*NNtarg_NNhead*) or dependent (*NNtarg_NNdep*) —for these, we consider only RelEmbs neighbors.

Numbers in the cells correspond to the number of neighbors retrieved. We present the results of analogical targets generated from a compositional (on the left) or idiomatic (on the right) base separately. Each subplot shows the results obtained for a specific model architecture.

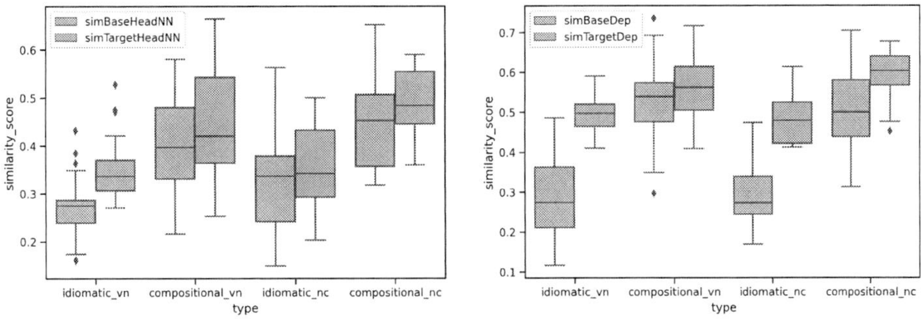

(a) SIMPLE with CONCAT input.

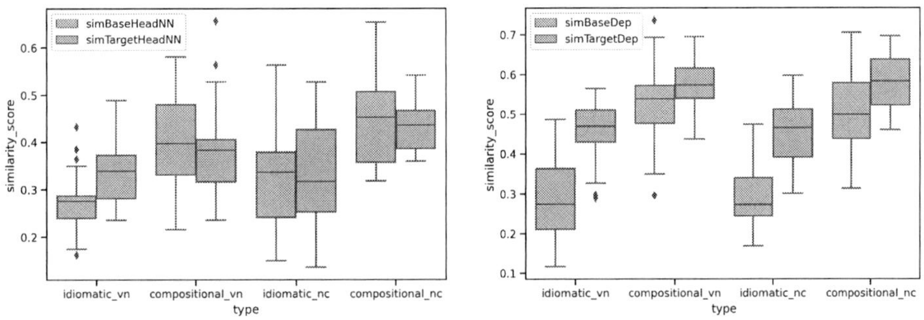

(b) SIMPLE with DIFF input

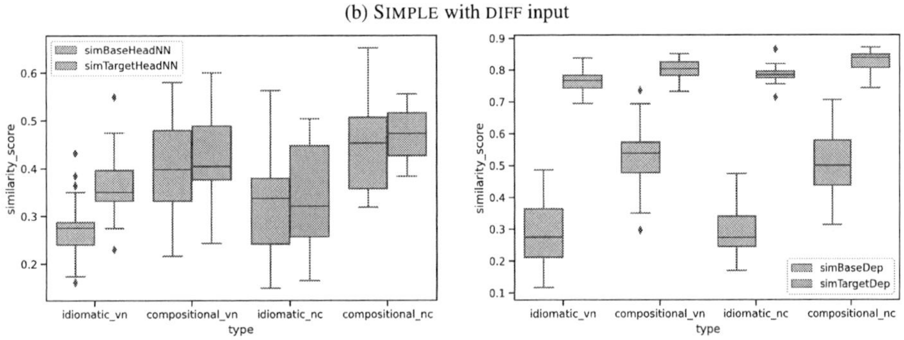

(c) MULTIAVG with CONCAT input

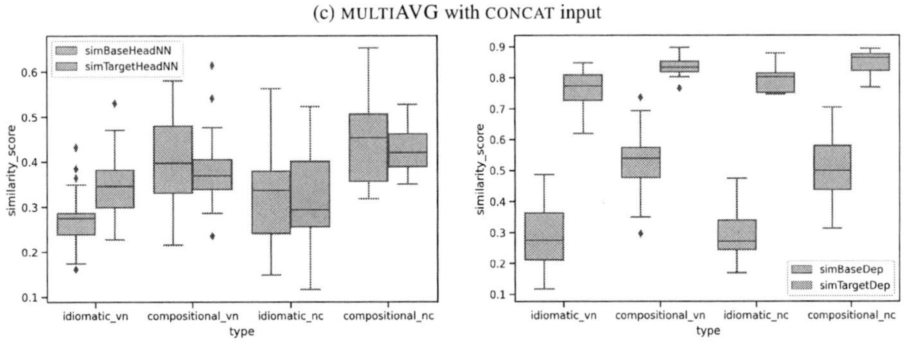

(d) MULTIAVG with DIFF input

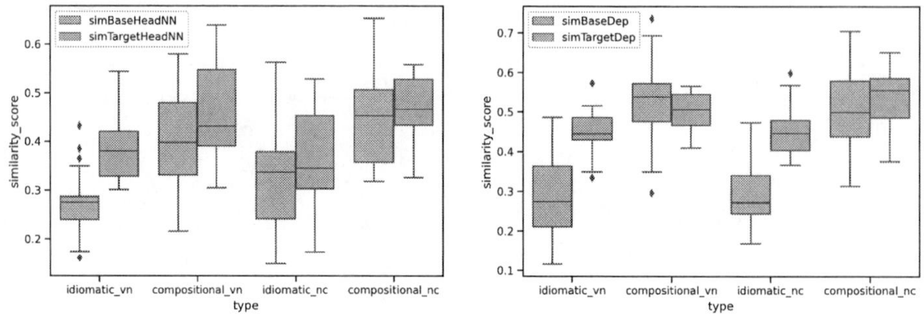

(e) MULTIMSE with CONCAT input

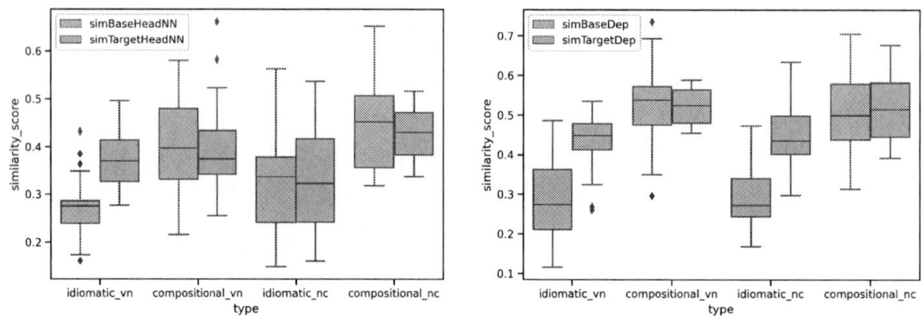

(f) MULTIMSE with DIFF input

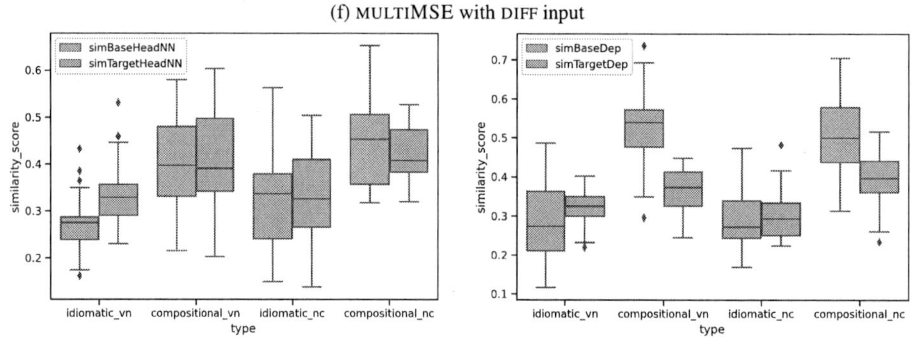

(g) HINGE with CONCAT input

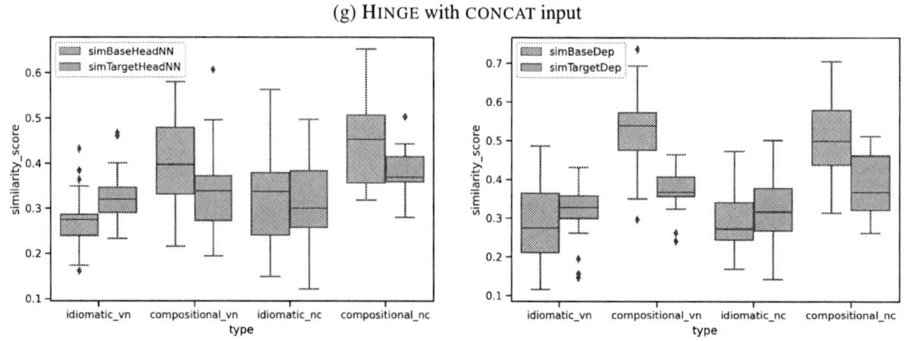

(h) HINGE with DIFF input

Figure 4: Distribution of the similarities between the RelEmb and its head (left), between the RelEmb and its argument (right). Data are grouped for syntactic type (nominal, NC, or verbal, VN) and if it is compositional (*compos*) or idiomatic (*idiom*). Similarities are computed for both the base embedding (blue) and target embedding (orange).

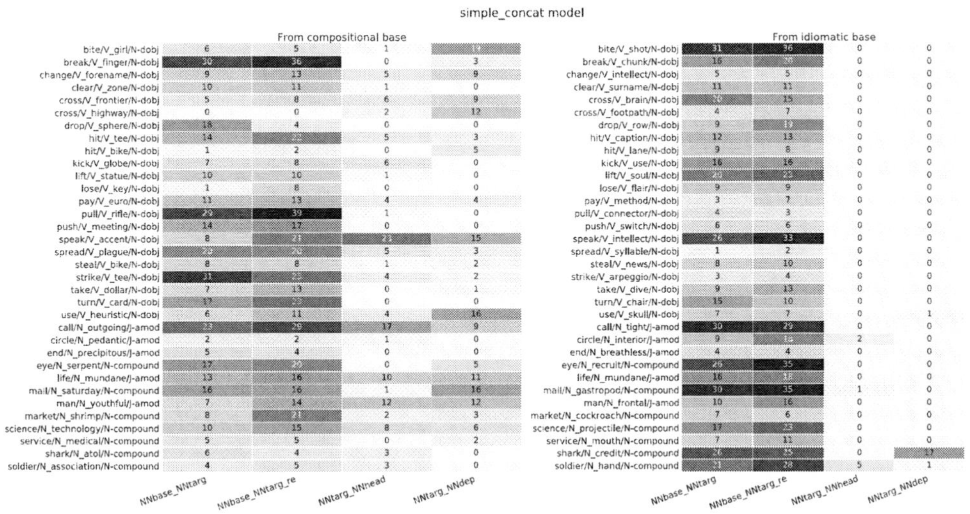
simple_concat model
From compositional base
From idiomatic base
bite/V_girl/N-dobj
break/V_finger/N-dobj
change/V_forename/N-dobj
clear/V_zone/N-dobj
cross/V_frontier/N-dobj
cross/V_highway/N-dobj
drop/V_sphere/N-dobj
hit/V_tee/N-dobj
hit/V_bike/N-dobj
kick/V_globe/N-dobj
lift/V_statue/N-dobj
lose/V_key/N-dobj
pay/V_euro/N-dobj
pull/V_rifle/N-dobj
push/V_meeting/N-dobj
speak/V_accent/N-dobj
spread/V_plague/N-dobj
steal/V_bike/N-dobj
strike/V_tee/N-dobj
take/V_dollar/N-dobj
turn/V_card/N-dobj
use/V_heuristic/N-dobj
call/N_outgoing/J-amod
circle/N_pedantic/J-amod
end/N_precipitous/J-amod
eye/N_serpent/N-compound
life/N_mundane/J-amod
mail/N_saturday/N-compound
man/N_youthful/J-amod
market/N_shrimp/N-compound
science/N_technology/N-compound
service/N_medical/N-compound
shark/N_atol/N-compound
soldier/N_association/N-compound
bite/V_shot/N-dobj
break/V_chunk/N-dobj
change/V_intellect/N-dobj
clear/V_surname/N-dobj
cross/V_brain/N-dobj
cross/V_footpath/N-dobj
drop/V_row/N-dobj
hit/V_caption/N-dobj
hit/V_lane/N-dobj
kick/V_use/N-dobj
lift/V_soul/N-dobj
lose/V_flair/N-dobj
pay/V_method/N-dobj
pull/V_connector/N-dobj
push/V_switch/N-dobj
speak/V_intellect/N-dobj
spread/V_syllable/N-dobj
steal/V_news/N-dobj
strike/V_arpeggio/N-dobj
take/V_dive/N-dobj
turn/V_chair/N-dobj
use/V_skull/N-dobj
call/N_tight/J-amod
circle/N_interior/J-amod
end/N_breathless/J-amod
eye/N_recruit/N-compound
life/N_mundane/J-amod
mail/N_gastropod/N-compound
man/N_frontal/J-amod
market/N_cockroach/N-compound
science/N_projectile/N-compound
service/N_mouth/N-compound
shark/N_credit/N-compound
soldier/N_hand/N-compound
NNbase_NNtarg
NNbase_NNtarg_re
NNtarg_NNhead
NNtarg_NNdep

(a)

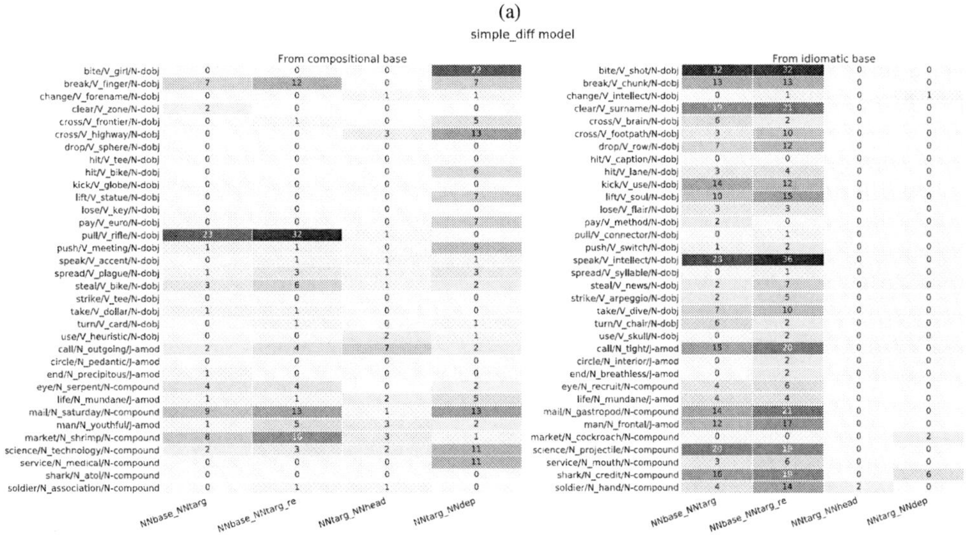
simple_diff model
From compositional base
From idiomatic base
NNbase_NNtarg
NNbase_NNtarg_re
NNtarg_NNhead
NNtarg_NNdep

(b)

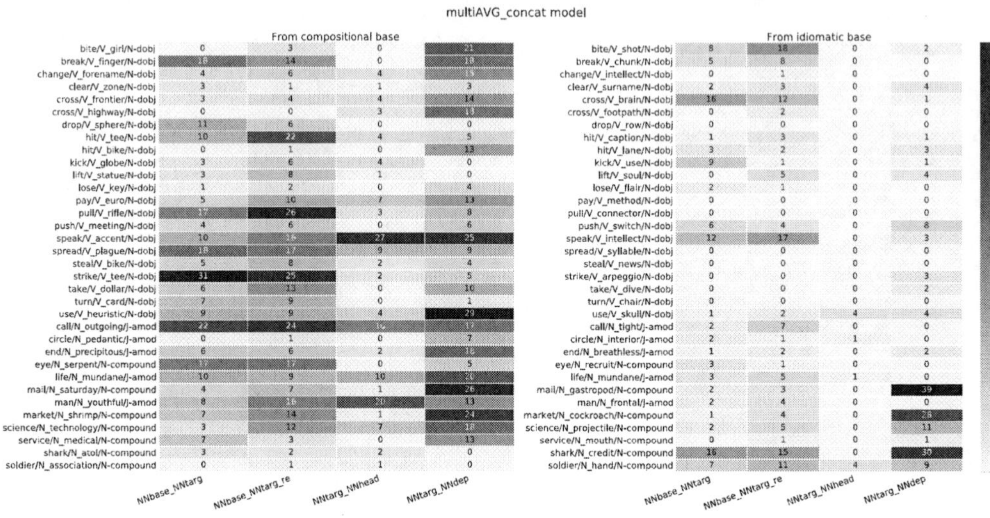
multiAVG_concat model
From compositional base
From idiomatic base
NNbase_NNtarg
NNbase_NNtarg_re
NNtarg_NNhead
NNtarg_NNdep

(c)

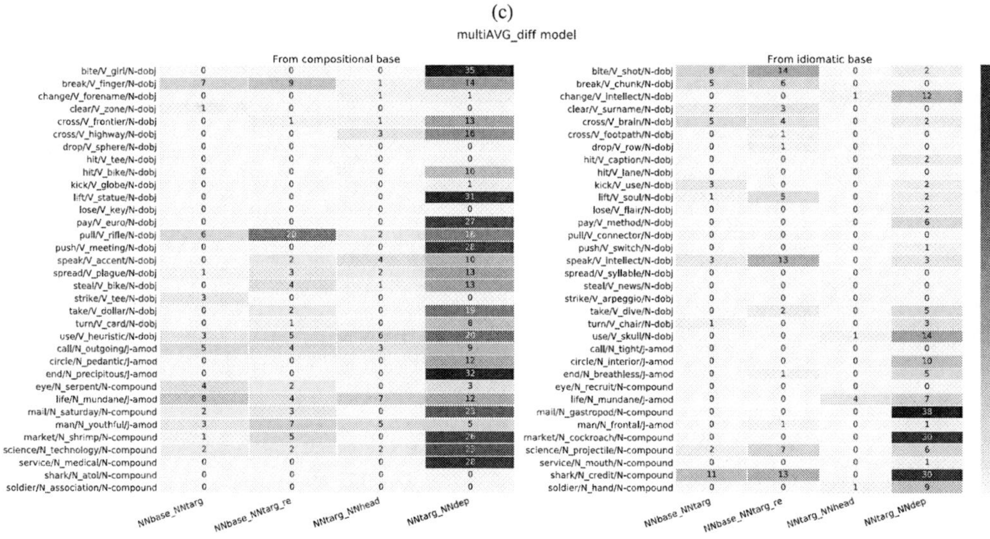
multiAVG_diff model
From compositional base
From idiomatic base
NNbase_NNtarg
NNbase_NNtarg_re
NNtarg_NNhead
NNtarg_NNdep

(d)

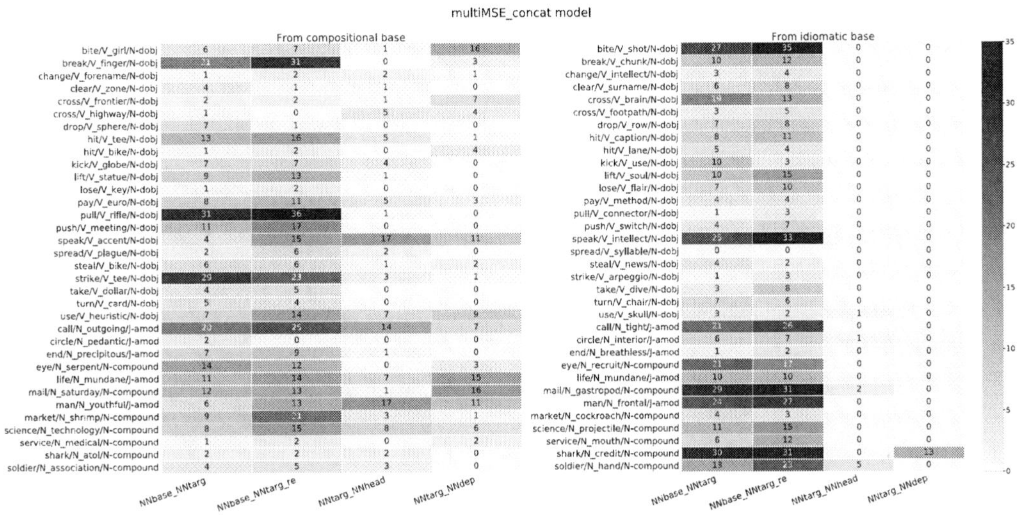
multiMSE_concat model
From compositional base
From idiomatic base
NNbase_NNtarg
NNbase_NNtarg_re
NNtarg_NNhead
NNtarg_NNdep

(e)

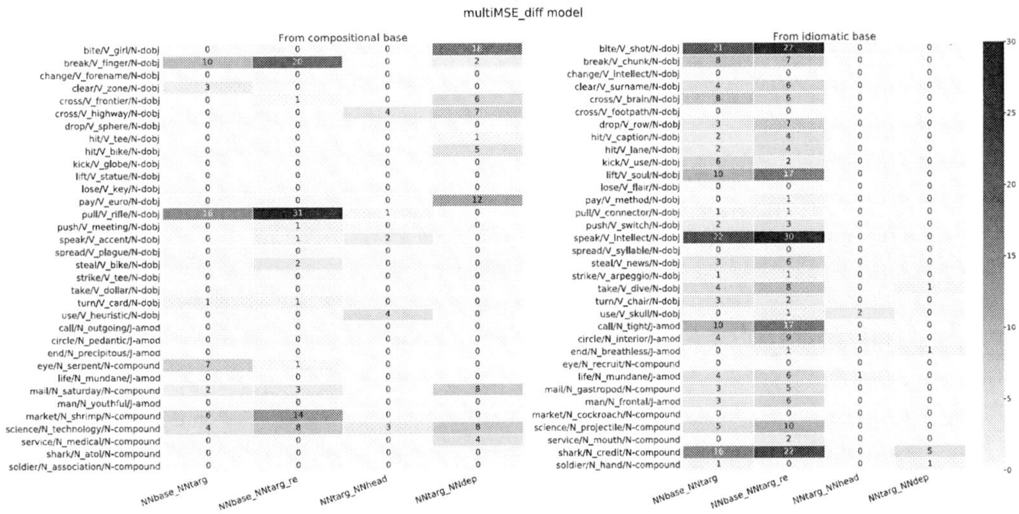
multiMSE_diff model
From compositional base
From idiomatic base
NNbase_NNtarg
NNbase_NNtarg_re
NNtarg_NNhead
NNtarg_NNdep

(f)

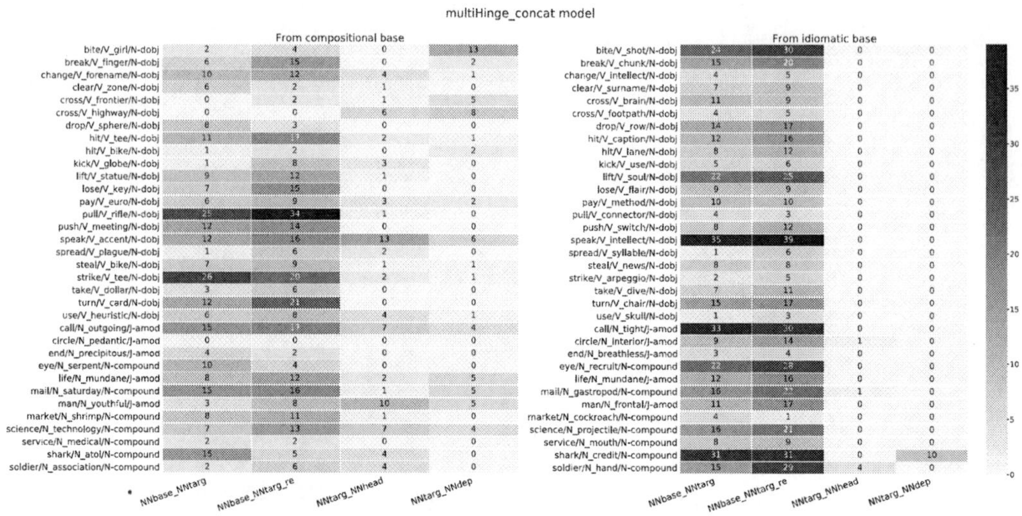

(g)

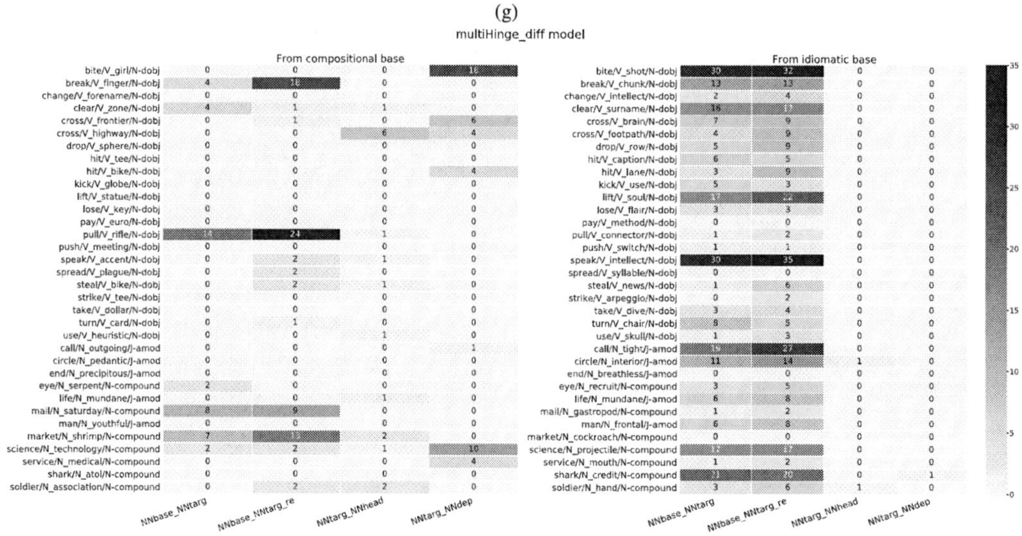

(h)

Figure 5: Heatmaps showing the intersection of common neighbors. Plot on the left refers to the target computed from a compositional base, plot on the right shows results for vectors generated from idiomatic base.

Author Index